D1134383

WITHDRAWN

The Innovation Wave
Meeting the Corporate Challenge

Bettina von Stamm

JOHN WILEY & SONS, LTD

S 658.4063 VON

Copyright © 2003 Bettina von Stamm
            Published by John Wiley & Sons Ltd, The Atrium, Southern Gate, Chichester,
            West Sussex PO19 8SQ, England

            Telephone   (+44) 1243 779777

Email (for orders and customer service enquiries): cs-books@wiley.co.uk
Visit our Home Page on www.wileyeurope.com or www.wiley.com

Bettina von Stamm has asserted her right under the Copyright, Design and Patents Act, 1988, to
be identified as the author of this Work.

All Rights Reserved. No part of this publication may be reproduced, stored in a retrieval system
or transmitted in any form or by any means, electronic, mechanical, photocopying, recording,
scanning or otherwise, except under the terms of the Copyright, Designs and Patents Act 1988 or
under the terms of a licence issued by the Copyright Licensing Agency Ltd, 90 Tottenham Court
Road, London W1T 4LP, UK, without the permission in writing of the Publisher. Requests to the
Publisher should be addressed to the Permissions Department, John Wiley & Sons Ltd, The
Atrium, Southern Gate, Chichester, West Sussex PO19 8SQ, England, or emailed to
permreq@wiley.co.uk, or faxed to (+44) 1243 770571.

This publication is designed to provide accurate and authoritative information in regard to the
subject matter covered. It is sold on the understanding that the Publisher is not engaged in
rendering professional services. If professional advice or other expert assistance is required, the
services of a competent professional should be sought.

Other Wiley Editorial Offices

John Wiley & Sons Inc., 111 River Street, Hoboken, NJ 07030, USA

Jossey-Bass, 989 Market Street, San Francisco, CA 94103-1741, USA

Wiley-VCH Verlag GmbH, Boschstr. 12, D-69469 Weinheim, Germany

John Wiley & Sons Australia Ltd, 33 Park Road, Milton, Queensland 4064, Australia

John Wiley & Sons (Asia) Pte Ltd, 2 Clementi Loop #02-01, Jin Xing Distripark, Singapore 129809

John Wiley & Sons Canada Ltd, 22 Worcester Road, Etobicoke, Ontario, Canada M9W 1L1

British Library Cataloguing in Publication Data

A catalogue record for this book is available from the British Library

ISBN 0-470-84742-5

Typeset in 11/15 pt Garamond by Footnote Graphics Ltd, Warminster, Wiltshire.
Printed and bound in Great Britain by T.J. International Ltd, Padstow, Cornwall.
This book is printed on acid-free paper responsibly manufactured from sustainable forestry
in which at least two trees are planted for each one used for paper production.

CONTENTS

ACKNOWLEDGEMENTS

The author would like to thank the following people whose cutting edge thinking has played an immense part both in shaping this book as well as the field of innovation in general:

Ben Bryant

Ben Bryant is a Fellow of the Centre for Management Development at London Business School and a researcher with the Innovation Exchange. Over the last two years he has developed a close working relationship with the Nutritionals Division of GlaxoSmithKline. His work has involved observing, researching and advising thefuturesgroup (an innovation team) and the senior management team. At LBS he is the Programme Director of the Global Business Consortium, (with Sumantra Ghoshal) and Programme Director of the Rubus Leadership Development Programme.

P-Y Gerbeau

Pierre-Yves Gerbeau is well-known for his role as Chief Executive Officer & Board Director, The New Millennium Experience Company Limited – the company responsible for the management of the Millennium Dome. Prior to the Dome project, P-Y was Vice President of Park Operations for Euro Disney, Europe's biggest visitor attraction, and a Management Consultant specialising in the transfer of top-level sport management and performance to the business world. P-Y has recently accepted a prestigious position of Executive-in-Residence at the London Business School, a role that involves developing MBA business cases and lecturing to MBA students.

Professor Gary Hamel

Gary Hamel is Visiting Professor of Strategic and International Management at the London Business School and Chairman of Strategos, an international consulting company.

Professor Hamel is the world's most sought-after speaker on strategy and innovation. He is a frequent speaker at the World Economic Forum in Davos, at the Fortune 500 CEO Roundtable and Bill Gates' CEO Summit.

Four of Professor Hamel's articles for *Harvard Business Review* have received the prestigious McKinsey Prize for excellence. His book, *Competing for the Future*, was *Business Week*'s management book of the year.

Professor Gareth Jones

Gareth's career has spanned both the academic and business worlds. He has held appointments at London Business School in Organizational Behaviour, as Senior Vice President for Polygram's global human resources and BT Professor of Organisational Development at Henley. His most recent business job was as Director of Human Resources and Internal Communications at the BBC. He is currently a visiting professor of Organisational Behaviour at INSEAD.

He has published several books, most recently 'The Character of a Corporation: How Your Culture Can Make or Break Your Business' (with R. Goffee). He has recently won the prestigious McKinsey award for the best article in HBR, entitled 'Why Should Anyone Be Led By You?' Gareth is a founding partner of Creative Management Associates (CMA), a consultancy focused on organisations where creativity is a source of competitive strength.

Dr. Jens R. Maier

Within Zurich Financial Services, Dr Jens Maier is responsible for the Leadership Development Process 'LEAD'. In that role, he supports the strategic agenda of an organisation operating in more than 60 countries with some 68 000 employees. Jens Maier serves on the Board of the European Foundation of Management Development (efmd), an organisation that acts as a common forum for the major Business Schools and leading blue-chip Companies.

Dr Jens Maier is a Fellow of the Centre for Management Development at London Business School and founder of the consulting group JAROX, supporting the accelerated transformation of large organisations.

Professor Costas Markides

Costas Markides is the Robert P. Bauman Chaired Professor in Strategic Leadership and Chairman of the Strategy Department at the London Business School.

Costas has taught on many in-company programmes for companies such as Unilever, British Aerospace, and Polygram. He is the Associate Editor of the *European Management Journal* and is on the Editorial Board of the *Strategic Management Journal*. He is a member of the Academy of Management, the Strategic Management Society and is a Fellow of the World Economic Forum in Davos, Switzerland. His most recent book is *Strategic Thinking for the Next Economy*.

Stephen Moon

Stephen Moon is Strategy Planning Director for Nutritional Healthcare, GlaxoSmithKline. This role encompasses strategy planning, business development, innovation, knowledge management and business reengineering. His interest in innovation led to the setting up of thefuturesgroup.

Stephen's key interest areas are entrepreneurialism and the innovation process in large organisations; and strategic alliances.

Dr Ian B. Owen

Ian Owen leads the Retail business for Zurich Financial Services in the UK. The Retail Financial Services business delivers a broad range of insurance and related financial and other services to over 2m consumers today. Ian also has wider responsibility for innovation and people development.

Ian has wide experience in finance, marketing and general management roles and was formerly Chief Executive of Eagle Star International Financial Services, Managing Director of Eagle Star Life and Managing Director of Eagle Star.

Sink or Swim – Introduction

Welcome to the Innovation Wave. Today there is generally little argument about the contribution innovation can make to a company's success and long-term survival. But leaders in many organisations struggle to translate this insight into action. As Rob Goffee, Professor of Organisational Behaviour at London Business School often puts it, 'They sometimes seem like rabbits in the headlights of a fast approaching car.' Or, to stay with the analogy of this book, they know a tidal wave is approaching and although they need to learn how to ride it, they are not quite sure where to start.

This book has been written to provide the reader with some practical and useful insights into how to infuse innovation into organisations, and how to manage and maintain the organisation's drive to improve its innovativeness. It will address both the input required to build an innovative organisation (vision and strategy, leadership, culture and work environment) and innovation outcomes (products, services and processes).

Innovation Exchange companies who have participated in the research	
Allied Domecq	GKN
AstraZeneca	GlaxoSmithKline
AxaSunLife	Integral
The Boots Company	LloydsTSB
British Airways	Marks & Spencer
BT	Mars Confectionery
Cadbury Schweppes	Pearl Assurance
Castle Cement Health	Roche Consumer
Centrica	Scottish Courage
Diageo	Unilever
The Post Office Research Group	

By combining insights gained from in-depth interviews within member companies of the Innovation Exchange, a networking initiative based at

London Business School, with best – and worst – practice found in the literature, this book fuses insight and wisdom from academia with the experience of practitioners. Not all best-practice insights are innovation-specific – they are part of general management best-practice – but they are found more often in innovative organisations, than non-innovative organisations, and hence form an important weapon in the armoury for creating a more innovative organisation.

When faced with the challenge of infusing innovation into an organisation or working on improving an organisation's innovativeness, company leaders generally face a series of challenges:

- how to convince others in the organisation that improving an organisation's innovativeness is not only important but increasingly urgent;
- where to focus the innovation effort;
- how to ride the innovation wave and where to find the people who are good at doing it;
- how to sustain the experience.

This book is structured to address each of these challenges and illustrate each step through stories told by the following experts:[1]

- Management guru and visiting professor at London Business School, Gary Hamel;
- P-Y. Gerbeau, who had been brought in to turn around the fortunes of London's Millennium Dome;
- Costas Markides, professor of international and strategic management at the London Business School;
- Gareth Jones, a wanderer between the worlds of academia (London Business School, Henley Management College) and commerce (EMI Records, the BBC);
- Stephen Moon of GlaxoSmithKline and Ben Bryant, Fellow of the Centre for Management Development at London Business School and a researcher with the Innovation Exchange;

---

[1]   The stories are based on presentations given at the 2001 Annual Innovation Exchange (http://iexchange.london.edu) Conference, held on 30 November 2001 at London Business School (www.london.edu).

- Jens Maier and Ian Owen from Zurich Financial Services.

Addressing the challenges associated with innovation necessitates a holistic approach that realises the importance of considering context and the need for aligning all aspects of an organisation to the innovation goal. The five key areas where innovative organisations do something differently from their less innovative counterparts are:

- strategy and vision
- leadership
- culture
- processes
- (physical) work environment (see Figure 1).

Quotes from the interviews are used throughout the book, in boxes and in the text, and anchor points, summaries of best – and sometimes worst – practice are offered at the end of each Chapter.

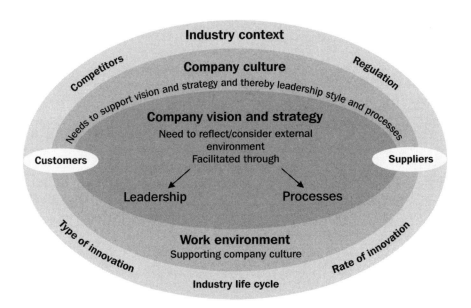

Figure 1: The innovation framework

Again, welcome. I hope that you will enjoy reading this book and, more importantly, it will provide you with useful insights that will help your organisation ride the tidal wave of innovation.

Gauging the sea – understanding where we are

CHAPTER 1

'We make it clear that innovation is not only about new product development.'

What do we mean by 'Innovation'?

At the DTI's first Innovation Lecture in 1992, Akio Morita, then Chairman of the Board of the Sony Corporation, felt it necessary to emphasise that innovation is more than technological advancement. In fact, his lecture was titled: $S \neq T$, $T \neq I$, meaning, Science alone is not Technology and Technology alone is not Innovation. He elaborated, 'Just having innovative technology is not enough to claim true innovation. I see true innovation to be made up of three key elements which I call "the three creatives". Creativity in technology, of course, plus creativity in product planning and marketing as well.' Since his lecture, this broader understanding of the term 'innovation' has spread and today more and more people understand innovation to be a mindset rather than a particular technological advancement. While this is certainly true for those who drive innovation in organisations, it is not necessarily true for the rest of the organisation.

This change in meaning has an important consequence for organisations that want to be innovative: in order to be innovative it is not enough to plough money into research and development (R&D): they need to consider all aspects of the organisation. They need to align

Important: you have to link it all together. Don't have separate initiatives, you have to integrate them. When a new initiative is introduced here the employees look at how it fits in with the existing initiatives; it has to be cohesive.

all systems and structures, culture and leadership styles, to support the goal of becoming more innovative.

The interconnectedness of key areas for innovation – leadership, culture, strategy and vision, and process – will be revisited throughout the book. Good leadership is a key ingredient but, without supporting processes and a clear strategy, it cannot achieve its full potential. The interconnectedness is something which Akio emphasised in his 1992 address:

> On a structural level, innovative management demands that all phases of the operation be seen as links in a single chain of innovation. Each link is allowed to pursue its own challenges – but is also aware of how it should integrate with the others. By links I am talking about applied research, development, design, production engineering, manufacturing, sales and service. Each link is vitally important – but equally so. It is important that the 'prestige level' of each link be similar in order to keep high achievers motivated in each group. And the creation and promotion of this approach is the responsibility of top management.
>
> The innovation process does not begin by bubbling up from the research and development laboratory, or from brainstorming sessions by the product planners. The innovation process begins with a mandate which must be set at the highest level of the corporation by identifying goals and priorities: and once identified, these must be communicated all the way down the line. The targets you set must be clear and challenging because you cannot wait for innovation to just show up at your company one day. But you need not, and should not, possess the entire solution to the challenge you set. You just have to be sure that the target you raise is realistic, though it might appear impossible.
>
> The innovative mandate, as determined by top management, can only succeed in an environment which nurtures it. That corporate environment must promote goal-sharing, unity of purpose, and the sense that everyone from the CEO to the factory operator are 'all in the same boat'. To sail, or sink, as one. Creating this environment is not an easy task, but without it innovation does not have much of a chance.

The importance of innovation

The importance of innovation as a key instrument for achieving competitive advantage was first emphasised by management gurus such as Tom Peters, Rosabeth Moss Kanter and Gary Hamel in the 1980s, then by governments. Now, there is hardly any manager who would deny the important contribution innovation makes to an organisation's success. This is reflected in the findings of a survey of 100 UK-based best-practice companies, conducted by the British Department for Trade and Industry (DTI) and the Confederation of British Industry (CBI) in 1995. This showed that things such as quality, reliability and low cost are merely qualifiers; they are the minimum requirements that have to be met. The prime drivers for differentiation and competitive advantage are innovation and customisation.

But there are other reasons why innovation has moved up companies' agendas. While the 1990s saw a great deal of growth through mergers and acquisitions, many companies now feel that they have grown as much as they can via this route. Any future growth will have to come from different avenues, primarily innovation and collaborative partnerships. A few interviewees from Innovation Exchange member companies, when asked what drives them to become more innovative, also mentioned external forces, such as the need to respond to competitive pressures and the fact that today good financial performance is no longer enough to satisfy financial markets. Organisations are increasingly interested in understanding what it means to be innovative, and are keen to gain insights into what innovative companies actually do.

The current status of innovation – a view from the Innovation Exchange

While few companies would publicly disagree with the statement that innovation is essential for future business success, the reality varies considerably, as the following quotes from Innovation Exchange member companies show:

- 'Innovation in this company is not really wanted.'
- 'Innovation and new product development are something we worry about if we do not have anything else do to; we don't have time for it otherwise.'
- 'Innovation does not get high priority from the board; they say it is important but not urgent.'

- 'Innovation is someone else's job.'
- 'The attitude towards innovation in our organisation is: good idea but …'
- 'At present innovation is done enthusiastically by amateurs.'
- 'Once every two months there is a session solely on innovation; this involves three to four senior trade people plus three to four board members. This sends a clear message about the high priority of innovation.'

Every organisation will be at a different point in its innovation journey, and every organisation is likely to have taken a different path. Becoming a (more) innovative organisation is a journey, and as with any journey, it is helpful to know where you have come from, how far you have travelled and, most importantly of all, where you want to go. As one innovation exchange member put it, 'In order to innovate, you need to put strategy, planning and vision in place first.'

Although each organisation needs to understand its specific context and constraints, some overriding trends among innovation leaders can be identified. The CBI conducts an annual survey on the innovation performance of companies based in the UK. Building on insights from the previous year, the 2001 report, sponsored by 3M and the British Design Council, focused on company culture and collaboration. It opened with the statement that, 'Some things have certainly improved, such as faster development and turnover of products and processes – increasing the rate of innovation. But other factors affecting innovation, for instance collaboration, training and capital expenditure, have had their ups and downs.'[1]

As the CBI survey identified, collaboration is an important contributor to innovation, and a willingness to collaborate is strongly influenced by culture, not only company culture but the professional cultures that exist within the organisation. An interviewee from a scientific organisation observed, 'Scientists understand the rationale for collaboration but in their hearts they don't buy into it. To them, collaboration is a sign of weakness.' This point highlights the importance of understanding an

---

[1]   Further insights on collaboration can be found in Chapter 5.

organisation's culture and context when choosing a path to innovation, as a good understanding of a company's culture and the underlying models of the world can help identify potential obstacles to change and innovation.

Other characteristics that are widely believed to support an innovation culture include:

- accepting failure as an intrinsic part of innovation;
- having an explicit strategy for the development of new products that is linked to the organisation's overall strategy;
- having a product portfolio – actual and under development – that balances risky and less risky products as well as short-term and long-term projects;
- the existence of a new product development process – though if followed slavishly it can become an iceberg that sinks great ideas rather than a gentle current that carries them along;
- the use of multifunctional teams;
- reward and remuneration systems that encourage entrepreneurial behaviour;
- ensuring top management understands and buys into the importance of innovation;
- monitoring and measuring innovation activities.

How did Innovation Exchange member companies do against these criteria? At first glance, quite well:

- Two-thirds indicated that they accept failure as an intrinsic part of innovation.
- All declared that they use multifunctional teams or are at least starting to do so.
- About half stated that they do use compensation incentives to stimulate an entrepreneurial environment.

Taking a closer look at the answers, however, shows a slightly different picture, which is indicative of where organisations are with respect to their own innovation journey.

Accepting failure

While two-thirds of participating companies had spontaneously declared failure to be accepted as an intrinsic part of innovation, closer questioning revealed a gap between rhetoric and reality. Even if a company states it has a blame-free environment, reality may look very different:

- 'Yes, but then we would kill it in a very slow way.'
- 'Yes, we are trying desperately not to have a blame culture – to a degree where people don't get blamed even when they deserve it.'
- 'We tend to ignore failure.'
- 'People would not necessarily be sacked but moved sideways.'
- 'No, we get twitchy when we fail, and want to find the person responsible for it.'

So rhetoric and reality vary considerably but it is not all bad news, as there were some positive answers, including the following:

- 'Yes, it is accepted as a part of the process in supporting high risk/high potential projects. We have found that failing fast can be very useful.'
- 'Innovation does not happen over night, the big bright ideas take time to develop. I strongly believe that behind big successes is the learning from two to three years of experimentation – probably called failure by some.'

And despite the widely acknowledged fact that failure is an intrinsic part of innovation, how many organisations make a conscious effort to carry out post-mortems to capture the learning? Besides the most obvious excuse, a lack of resources, the problem lies in the expectation that failure is a one-off affair. The other is that people move so fast within organisations that it is often difficult to analyse and document failure without pointing fingers. And even if a 'post-mortem' is undertaken, are the lessons learnt shared throughout the organisation, and are mechanisms in place to ensure that the same mistakes are not repeated?

New product development strategies

When asked about a specific new product development strategy, only a few companies declared not to have one at all, but about 25% were in what one might call a 'grey area'. For example one company declared, 'Sort of, we have a strategy – me too. And while we are trying to break out of it and things are beginning to happen, it is by accident rather than design.' Continuity after change in top management was seen to be a problem: 'We used to have a clear product strategy, but it all got stifled when the person at the top changed: most of our projects were cancelled and are only now starting to come on line again.' Unless the reasons behind such change are explained and communicated well to those concerned, a U-turn can lead to resentment and frustration on the parts of those involved in the planning and execution of the projects. Problems can also arise when those who do the product planning do not involve those who have to execute the plans, as illustrated by another quote: 'Yes, we do have a product strategy. It is developed by our headquarters – but then it is us who have to find ways to sell it to the customer.' Without some sort of process to achieve buy-in, projects are unlikely to receive the level of energy required to drive them through. It is always worth remembering that one of the critical success factors for innovative projects is the enthusiasm and determination of the individuals involved. Without that energy, many will just die a slow death.

Balanced product portfolios

Eighty per cent of the participating companies declare to balance short- and long-term projects through a balanced project portfolio. To quote, 'Absolutely, that's what we spend a lot of time on. We have a portfolio management group which meets three times a year. Their aim is to ensure that our product portfolio is balanced across a set of established criteria.' Best-in-class companies may look at as many as three or four different aspects:

We have three balances:

1. Between brands and product portfolios by making sure there is enough innovation in each area.

2. Between developed and non-developed markets, recognising that non-developed markets take longer for payback.
3. Across time horizons, which in our case equate to different levels of innovation.

Only one participant emphasised the importance of co-ordinating company strategy and innovation activities – coming back to the theme that the entire organisation needs to be aligned to innovation. For example, looking at individual innovation activities without considering the broader picture can lead to the rejection of ideas or developments that do not yield immediate financial returns.

But having a strong vision for innovation activities creates another challenge for companies. How do they deal with promising innovations that are only marginally relevant to the company's core business or which could potentially threaten it? (This is discussed later when we consider radical innovation.)

New product development processes

It is surprising to find that not all participating companies had a defined new product development process even though, as one interviewee put it, 'Having a systematic process does not necessary mean that it is good.' Another issue is that many organisations have introduced a process – but it only exists on paper: 'Yes, we have a process, but it does not work. It exists on paper only because people do not have any faith in it.' Probed further, it turned out that there had been no training when the process had been introduced, which could have improved its acceptance rate. Having an overly complicated process is also likely to lead to problems:

> Yes, we have a very systematic new product development process. We also have launch assessment forms, detailed descriptions of products, all sorts of tables and declarations to fill in, information about packaging, et cetera, et cetera. All this has to be presented at the outset. We introduced the system about three years ago and over time it got more and more complicated. At present it is much too formalised and, as a consequence, development time may have been shortened but the time before approval has increased; in fact, time for approval has increased to three months where it used to be a couple of weeks.

An overly complicated process that requires the endless filling in of forms and schedules is likely to stifle innovation. Best-in-class companies tend to have a different approach to process, 'Yes, we have a systematic new product development process, in fact, in a matter of weeks we will have a new one. Headquarters is feeding learning into the process and it is continuously changing. For example, we used to have a process with four gates; now we are down to two. It is important to keep revisiting it and keeping it simple.' The theme of evolving and experimenting is one that is characteristic of innovative organisations.

The use of multifunctional teams

We found that all companies were – or were about to start – using multifunctional teams. Best practice is probably best reflected in the following two comments: 'Yes, we have a strong commitment to teams and this year we are using extra facilitators to help teams work together. We are aware that teams don't just happen,' and 'Yes, whether people are dedicated full time to any one project depends on the project size, importance and workload. People here are primarily attached to a brand, not a function or project.' The second comment also indicates that the kind of approach to teams that works best will vary from company to company.

Incentivising entrepreneurship

As to incentivising entrepreneurship, most answers actually related the question to the existence or absence of suggestion schemes, which is not really what is at the heart of the question. Entrepreneurial behaviour refers to the willingness to take risks, to be highly self-motivated, and not to give up when facing the first obstacle. But in some companies, the reward structures were clearly counter-productive: 'Incentive schemes here are set up for people to eat each other,' or 'At present people don't know why they do or do not receive awards.' The issue of schemes and incentivation for innovation will be discussed in more detail in Chapter 4, so all that should be pointed out here is that we have become increasingly aware that financial incentives are not the best motivator for innovation.

When it comes to rewards and remunerations, multinational organisations face a particular challenge, namely to find approaches and systems that work across more than one national culture. For example, some cultures are more group-oriented, others more individualistic. Finding approaches that work for all cultures can be challenging. As one member commented, 'The challenge is to find something that works and is right for the Scandinavian, Calvinistic culture instilled in people right from the early days at school as well as the AngloSaxon culture. At present a bonus is based on 50% company performance and 50% team performance. Individual performance is built in as a multiplier.'

While designing reward structures that are appropriate across cultures may be particularly tricky for companies with a multinational workforce, there is also a more general issue around the need for a 'one-company-ness' as one interviewee put it. If, as the findings indicate, innovation is dealt with more and more at the company rather than the business unit or departmental level, people need to have a sense of belonging that is associated with the company in general rather than with the particular part they are working in. Asking the simple question, 'who are you working for?' might provide some interesting insights. Understanding where the divide between 'them' and 'us' lies is important, as ideas, projects and other initiatives coming from 'them' quite frequently encounter the not-invented-here syndrome. Creating a sense of oneness tends to require a strong culture that is communicated though clear and simple messages that every employee can identify with. It is important that every employee understands what the company goals are and how his or her work fits into the wider scheme of things.

Top management buy-in

Spreading the gospel about innovation among top managers seems to have been a priority for the past few years, and many interviewees report that today they have good top management support: 'Yes, we have worked very hard over the last three to four years. Today in our gate-keeping system the most senior person in the company is the gate-keeper. This was definitely not the case five to six years ago.' But here, too, there is often a discrepancy between what is said and what is done.

Typical comments on this topic included, 'Yes, but words, not actions,' 'We talk about the importance of innovation and creativity but when it comes to it, there is no person at the top level who would actually understand creativity,' or 'There is a lack of clear signs of real commitment.' But sometimes it is the top management who are fully behind the drive for innovation, and their challenge is how to spread the gospel to the lower management levels: 'Where it dries up is two levels down; it is seen to be too much trouble and there are no resources.'

Measuring innovation

While most organisations have some kind of measures in place to monitor innovation, about 25% of participating companies did not track their innovation efforts at all, which seems a large number given that innovation is often seen to be the lifeblood of an organisation. But even if innovation performance is measured in some way, it is only meaningful if the insights are fed back and quickly translated into action: 'Yes, we are very good at it, it is one of our key performance indicators; we are learning from the insights but just don't act on them quickly enough.'

An interesting comment was made by a participant from one company that is generally considered to be highly innovative: 'Interesting question. We used to look at the number of projects that drop out of the innovation funnel – but what is the point? Even if people are being told 'no' they continue with their project anyway; we have a handful of people who are always breaking the rules.' It seems that innovative organisations are 'just doing it' rather than talking about it or measuring it. More observations about measurement can be found in Chapter 3.

Change is the only constant

'We know that if we fail to change, in a few years time there will be no business left.'

Although best practice provides important guidance and insights, what works in practice will vary from organisation to organisation. It is therefore very important for an organisation to understand where it is coming from, where it wants to go and what its specific context and constraints are. Understanding what one could call the organisation's starting point is important for another reason. The degree to which people within an organisation are open to change will depend to a certain degree on the company's culture, but more often it is driven by the 'state of affairs'. People in an organisation in crisis mode will be more open to change than people in an organisation that does extremely well. In the latter scenario we are most likely to encounter the complacency syndrome: 'we are doing very well, thank you very much. Why should we change? Never change a winning team.'

Some interesting insights on the implementation of change stem from research undertaken by Johne and Davies (1999). Investigating what caused some organisations to be more innovative than others revealed that in those organisations that were more successful, the CEOs had:

> used an unconventional approach to shock staff into action. They ruthlessly opened minds to market threats and opportunities. After administering shock treatment, they carefully returned responsibility to first-line managers through a deliberate managerial shift. In contrast, chief executives of companies that were less successful at starting innovation encouraged debate on alternative strategies as a prelude to any action. This apparently more logical approach led to frequent disagreements that sapped employee motivation.

This is an interesting observation, particularly in light of the commonly held belief that direct involvement is critical.

The openness to change in general will have an impact on the possible speed with which steps toward becoming a more innovative organisation can be taken. To understand an organisation's starting point, questions to ask could include:

- What is our cultural heritage? What kind of people work for the organisation and what are their beliefs and values?
- What are the implications of past and present organisational structure? Where does the power lie within the organisation, and why?

- What constraints are imposed by the wider context? What are the industry standards; are there regulatory boundaries?
- How open is our organisation to change. Are we facing a threat everyone in the organisation is aware of and understands?

Being aware of context and constraints by no means implies that an organisation has to stay within its existing boundaries. But understanding the status quo will help to inform the choice of approach that is most likely to work for the organisation, as well as highlight areas in which additional expertise or skills are required. There is no one right approach.

When embarking on the innovation journey, it also helps to start with a few realisations:

- Becoming more innovative is all about change.
- It will [have to] affect all aspects of the organisation.
- Change does not happen overnight.
- The journey will never be complete.
- Preparing the ground for innovation will help.

Let us look at these realisations in turn. Becoming a more innovative organisation is all about change. And that change has to go right through all aspects of the organisation. For example, it is not sufficient to introduce a new product development process and expect innovative new products to follow. Success requires training and if different working practices are involved, such as teamwork, an adjustment in performance management systems is also necessary. Nor is it sufficient to establish a suggestion scheme – which in fact, when handled badly, can have a detrimental effect. To have a stimulating effect, suggestion schemes require, as a minimum, quick response times and clear and well communicated selection criteria. The least useful step is probably to announce that henceforth innovation will be one of the company's core values. Such statements offer no insight into what staff are expected to do, nor how they are to do it. An organisation is a system of interconnected parts. Changing one will inevitably affect the rest.

The two key aspects of the change required to become more innovative are, first, that it has to be all-embracing and, second, that it involves changes in behaviour. In other words, it takes time. As one member of an Innovation Exchange company recalls, 'It has taken us three years just to get innovation on to the agenda!' The thing about change is, people tend to resent it, unless they are given a good reason to buy into it – a crisis introduced by the top is one such reason. Innovation generally arouses an additional layer of resistance, as becoming more innovative is not only about doing things differently, it is about behaving and thinking differently. Can patterns of behaviour change overnight? Becoming more innovative does not happen on command. Innovation is a frame of mind, a habit of constantly questioning the status quo and not taking for granted approaches that have worked in the past. However, neither is innovation change for change's sake. To quote again a member of the Innovation Exchange, 'We have the habit of experimenting; we never do things the same way twice. We always look at how we did it last time but then say, what has worked, what has not, let's keep what has worked and find a different way of doing what did not go too well last time.'

Anyone who has made a New Year's resolution will appreciate how difficult it is to change. And in the case of a New Year's resolution the person generally wants to change. Two insights follow. First, how much more difficult is it to change the behaviour and ways of thinking of someone who might not be quite so convinced about the necessity to do so? People might change their behaviour if the rewards are aligned accordingly, but when do people really start to think differently? Innovation is one of those things that will not happen 'because I told you so', but because people understand and experience the benefits. Second, even if people are happy to embark on the journey, they will need time to modify their behaviour and to internalise the change.

While taking time to change is not exactly appreciated by the City, it does have some advantages. For example, if we do not expect things to change overnight we might be more open to experimentation along the way. As there is no one right approach to infusing innovation into an organisation, finding what works best often requires trying different concepts or approaches. It is also necessary to consider the speed at which the change will occur, as well as the ambitiousness of the plans. To quote from the Innovation Exchange interviews again, 'Rather than starting in a blaze of glory we started slowly, then gathered strength. We believe that how we do it has to fit in with the company's way. This may be too slow for some, but to make it stick you have to find a balance between speed and company style.'

What does the last bullet point, preparing the ground for innovation, mean? As one interviewee said, 'You can only achieve innovation in stages.' In their particular case, it was a three-step process:

> 'Innovation builds on learning and insight; it is important that people understand this road to innovation.'

1   Get organised and put processes and procedures in place that will support innovation, including those related to new product development, human resource (HR) policies, idea generation and so on.
2   Learn more. Learn about what is known and what the company's strategy is.
3   Generate ideas.

Without the first step, ideas might get lost or might not be brought to a successful conclusion. Without the second, mistakes from the past may be repeated but, more importantly, no one will know or understand the criteria used to choose ideas.

If becoming more innovative is all about change, then we need to understand what the critical success factors for implementing change are:

- Provide strong and empathic leadership.
- Select only the best people for the change team, ensure consistency among team members, and give them far-reaching autonomy.
- Provide training at the outset.
- There must be a clear direction.
- Ensure people down as well as up the chain of command are motivated.
- Track benefits of the change programme – have people sign up to targets.
- Keep people informed; find the best way of ensuring the information actually reaches the recipients.
- Change should be propelled forward by excitement and enthusiasm, rather than time pressure.

Drivers of change

We know that change lies at the heart of innovation, but what is at the heart of change. What is driving it, and what are the implications for innovation? There are five trends:

1   mergers and acquisitions,
2   a quest for radical innovation,
3   globalisation,
4   megabrands,
5   centralisation.

Mergers and acquisitions

> 'I think that in most companies there are probably not too many new product development activities during times of a merger; the most you are likely to find are tactical changes.'

Most companies participating in the Innovation Exchange research had undergone significant periods of change over the recent year, mainly induced by merger and acquisition (M&A) activities. The change often had important implications for innovation. As one interviewee pointed out, 'The tremendous work overload means that there is no energy left for creativity and innovation, only for consolidation.' Another interviewee saw similar consequences: 'At present there is really no appetite for innovation – and there are no financial resources available while the companies are being consolidated. I generally feel that during times of a merger there is probably not too much innovation going on, rather tactical changes.' But the aftermath of a merger or acquisition and the desire to improve innovativeness have one thing in common; they both require revisiting all aspects of an organisation, including a change of culture, alignment of systems, procedures and processes, new structures, and so on. And a merger or acquisition might represent the necessary shock to open up people's minds for change, which might as well be used to improve innovativeness.

> 'We have invested a lot on culture after the merger and it has been hugely successful, but of course there is still a long way to go.'

Another aspect that needs careful management after mergers and acquisitions can best be described as continuity in change. This can be a particularly important aspect in customer-facing operations, as the following quote illus-trates. 'Personal relationships that develop between sales personnel and customers as well as company and individual reputation

> 'There is great value in continuity. It all grinds to a halt if everything changes at once.'

are important in most industries, yet these tend to get diluted through mergers and acquisitions.'

A quest for radical innovation

'Expected growth means that we need radical rather than incremental innovation.'

Achieving ambitious growth targets requires radical, not incremental, innovation. As one interviewee put it, 'We are quite capable of incre-mental innovation on a decentralised basis. In fact, we are quite good at it but it is all within the existing business framework and our comfort zone. We are not so good at transformation and moving outside the box – but at least we are aware of this and have started to work at it.' The anticipated shift towards radical innovation is interesting for two reasons. First, will the commitment to radical innovation be sustained in times of economic downturn? Second, what about voices that state that

---

In their article 'Achieving new product success in highly innovative versus incremental new industrial services', Ulrike de Brentani and Elko Kleinschmidt suggest that depending on how innovative a new service is, a different set of project dimensions is required:

Incremental:
- close contact with and intimate knowledge of customer needs and operations;
- a seamless fit with the specialised experiences and resources of the service firm;
- using a systematic and planned approach.

Discontinuous:
- contact with the market;
- high degree of corporate synergy;
- fit with the company's overall problem-solving capabilities;
- the company's long-term reputation;
- internal innovation environment: visionary leadership and a culture that encourages creative ways of viewing the world.

the consumer is not too keen on too much radical innovation? In a Masterclass held at London Business School, Professor George Day of the Wharton and London Business Schools commented, 'The market seems to get tired of radically new products.' But it is not just that people get tired of radical innovation. The market for innovative products is usually quite small initially, since only a small percentage of a potential pool of customers will be willing to buy a new product straight away (the early adopters). The vast majority will wait and see before making a purchasing decision (the late adopters). The laggards want to be reassured that the product works and represents value for money.

If radical innovation is in the area of delivery or process, it tends to be less visible to the end user. Examples include the selling of computers online (Dell) and online banking (Egg). In such cases, the take-up seems to be quicker because the consumer does not have to make a decision about the innovation itself but rather the outcome – which tends to be cheaper and faster (more convenient). It is probably questionable whether people would be equally keen to take up the idea if it was more expensive. In the case of tangible products, the risk seems to lie with the consumer, whereas in the case of services, it tends to rest with the provider.

So what kind of innovations are companies generating today? A survey conducted by the US-based InnovationNetwork (www.thinksmart.com) among its members revealed that the majority (67%) of innovations were derivative ideas (an extension of an existing product, for example a 14-inch TV now made in 19-inch), 23% were breakthrough ideas (a known idea, but not in the market yet, for example a TV set that is High Definition) and only 10% of innovations were radical (brand new products, for example a TV in eyeglasses). However, this 10% generated 24% of profit whereas the other 90%, made up of incremental innovations, generated only 76% of the profit.

Of course, despite the obvious benefits of radical innovation, there is a need to balance radical and incremental projects. This poses a significant challenge. How can organisations ensure that resources are available for both growing the existing business and investing in new and potentially risky projects? Most organisations are still not very comfortable with high-risk projects, which makes this all the more difficult.

The balance in allocating resources can tip either way, as the following two quotes illustrate: 'We find it difficult to find the discipline to liberate resources without disrupting existing business' was one company's view whereas another stated, 'Through the drive for new ventures we have neglected our core business.' There is no easy answer.

Another issue with the pressure to innovate was described by another interviewee:

> We have to find a way of managing a contradiction: when there is pressure to perform no one wants to innovate because it feels too risky, no one wants to stick their neck out – but that is just when innovation is required most, when you have to get out of the ditch. At the same time resources are generally only available when things are going well. This means that you need to put things into place while things are good. One thing we have learned is, you cannot turn innovation on and off like that, you have to keep it going through the good and bad times.

There are three messages here:

1   Prepare for innovation when times are good.
2   Keep innovating during difficult times; innovation is what is most likely to help prepare you for the upturn.
3   Understand that it is not a matter of 'let's be innovative today' but it is a question of being innovative all the time. It is a frame of mind, not a task on the to-do list.

The same interviewee describes how to keep innovation constantly on the agenda.

> We don't have innovation budgets at the local level, it is held at the centre. This is one way of ensuring that innovation budgets are not the first to be cut when the going gets tough. It also ensures that the central team has access to the best work and the best people. We believe that it is very important to protect the innovation budget from business pressures. And it works – in the last recession we did not cut our innovation budget – because that's when it is needed most – and it has paid off when we came out the other end.

Globalisation

'Within 5 years there will be two kinds of managers – those who think in terms of a world economy, and those who are unemployed.'

Drucker (1999)

'Recent research suggests that globalisation is a myth'

Rugman and Hodgetts (2001)

A third widely noticeable change is the trend towards globalisation. There is some debate as to whether it is a fact or only a myth, but this seems to be driven mainly by different starting points. Some people talk about globalisation at the economic level, some at the organisational level, and some refer to globalisation at the product level.

Economic globalisation

Tom Friedman, author of *The Lexus and the Olive Tree* (2000), is referring to the economic level when he defines globalisation as, 'The inexorable integration of markets, nation states and technologies to a degree never witnessed before in a way that is enabling individuals, corporations and nation states to reach around the world farther, faster, deeper, and cheaper than ever before.' For example, between the developed world and emerging markets, the dollar trade volume went up from $802 billion in 1986 to $2 trillion in 1996. Although trade between countries has existed for thousand of years, what makes people sit back and think is globalisation's recent and unprecedented speed and scale.

Organisational globalisation

Second, when globalisation refers to the organisational level, it is about the increasing degree to which organisations engage in cross-boarder activities.[2] The degree of globalisation will vary between industries. For example, the degree of globalisation in petroleum, timber, aluminium and chemicals industries is higher than in shoes, luxury goods or legal services,

'New product development activities are coordinated on a global basis by HQ which means that resources are harnessed and centralised.'

---

[2]   See Uljin *et al.* in References.

and significantly higher than in funeral homes or large-scale production materials.[3]

Product globalisation

At the product level, discussion tends to occur at two levels:

* whether products are sold globally; and
* whether they are being developed by global teams.

Another way of viewing this is by product development stage (idea generation, product development, product testing, production and distribution, launch, marketing and advertising, and after-sales service), and the degree of globalisation for any one product may vary from stage to stage.

The major influences determining the level of globalisation at the product level are variations in consumer taste between different countries. While often underestimated in the past, this is why there are very few truly global products.

For example, car specifications are fine-tuned to address local preferences; food products appeal because of their local or regional association, and even what kind of deodorant one can buy varies from country to country (for example, one can only buy antiperspirant, not deodorant, in the UK). And one should not forget that even Coca-Cola, widely cited as a 'truly global product', started off as a product that was developed in response to a specific local need in a specific market. Marketing and its taste, which appealed to a wide audience, have made it one of the most widely available products around the globe today. Coca Cola has become global, but it was not developed with that intention in mind.

There are many reasons for wanting to globalise, including the desire to cut costs, to increase efficiencies, to create a greater visible presence in the world market and, not least, to keep up with the competition. Being able to sell a product on a global basis can mean fewer manufacturing plants, longer production runs, and therefore reduced change-

---

[3]   See Bryan *et al.* in References.

Collaboration across national boarders – the example of Eurostar

International collaboration can also add an interesting dimension to developing products 'across boundaries', particularly if each participating country expects to get its share of the development task according to its financial backing, rather than its expertise. The need to share the task can lead to interesting and costly logistical dynamics, as with the development of Eurostar, a high-speed train connecting the capitals of the UK, France and Belgium. All three countries were represented in the manufacturing consortium responsible for the design and development of the new train. As a consequence, each country expected to be given its fair share of the design and development work, whereby it was agreed to split the task according to each country's financial backing of the project, 40% UK, 40% France and 20% Belgium. The design task was split as follows: the front end of the train (driver's cabin) was given to a British design consultancy; a French design consultancy was put in charge of the interior and livery, as well as the overall coordination, and the Belgian design consultancy was given the luggage racks, seats and toilets to design. Integrating the separately designed aspects turned out to be an extremely challenging task which, in the view of many, did not lead to the most successful result.

In addition there was the need to consider the areas of expertise of each company forming the individual consortia – which all had been formed in the expectation that the bid would be given to one consortium, rather than split between three. As a consequence, the splitting up of the development and manufacturing became complex, resulting in some components being produced by two different companies in two different countries and being shipped between as many as seven different sites.

---

over times, fewer products to stock and the opportunity to focus resources. However, there are down-sides, one being that a focus on a small number of products or global brands requires deep pockets to launch, market and support the selected few.

As usual, the difference between success and failure lies in the 'how', not the 'what'. One company explained how they manage the risk and try to make it work:

> We have a very limited number of global projects – or rather projects with global potential. That everyone understands the difference is very important, otherwise expectations become unrealistic. At no time are such projects managed from the centre; the leadership is always with one of our local innovation centres. We also make sure that batch sizes would work in smaller plants, just in case we find that global acceptance cannot be achieved. But since the local centre does not always have the right skills and resources to execute the project, we will second people from the centre or give part of the project to the central research facility to support them, and to make sure global considerations are taken into account early on. The teams often work together virtually – but the leadership always stays local.

There are several important insights we can draw from the quote:

- Carefully control the number of projects with global potential.
- Start with the premise that a project has global *potential* rather than expecting that it *will be* global. A step-by-step introduction will allow careful cost management as well as potentially integrating early feedback.
- An important question companies considering global product development should ask themselves is: 'Who is running the project, the centre or the region?' Most companies are aware of the fact that, as interviewees pointed out, 'Lots of information is held by regions and difficult to access.' A company that has made the effort to ensure a balance between global and local commented, 'The matrix we are using to balance global and local requirements was time-consuming to start with. And it was frustrating to get consensus and consistency across the process but we have managed it now. How have we overcome the initial problems? Because of the commitment of the people and the clarity everyone shares about business direction.'
- It might be helpful to fund the project from the centre to make sure the product developed is best for the company, rather than one particular country. In Chapter 5 Jens Maier and Ian Owen, both from Zurich Financial Services, share their experiences on how an initiative designed and introduced at the centre has been rolled out and applied at a local level.

Megabrands

'If megabrands become the name of the game, the question is, how to motivate those who are not working on megabrands?'

Because of the increased number of mergers and acquisitions and the strong regional orientation of managers, many organisations now have to deal with a myriad of brands, often competing against each other. To reap the benefits of these mergers and acquisitions, companies are looking at their product portfolios to see where products can be consolidated or merged.

A member of the Innovation Exchange describes their approach to consolidating their product portfolio

'The regions used to be fairly independent, which meant that we ended up with lots and lots of brands – until recently we were not even sure how many. When we looked at our portfolio we realised that a good 10-20% of products overlapped. After cutting out duplication there were still too many individual brands left. We wanted to focus and reduce further, and set a target of getting numbers down to about one-sixth of the original portfolio – and we knew that eventually we would want to go down even further than that. There were different ways of achieving the reductions:

- merging brands: if we found that we had two different brands in different countries that were otherwise the same;
- merging local brands with similar big brands;
- migrating brands: trying to get brands that have similar positioning under one name.

At the same time we wanted to ensure that we still offered enough diversity that we could address our customers' needs.'

Out of this has emerged the megabrands trend.[4] Streamlining the product portfolio does not only happen in industries where individual brands play an important role, such as fast-moving consumer goods or pharmaceuticals; the trend is similarly visible in manufacturing and the service sector. A side-effect of establishing megabrands is that they provide a focus for innovation, as a member described: 'We are trying to build brands. When doing that it means that innovation has to take place within the brand. We have brand keys that describe what the brand stands for; they provide clear guidelines.' However, one big challenge for companies moving towards megabrands is how to motivate those staff who do not work on the megabrands.

Centralisation

'Intellectually, people are buying into things but there is always some hope that it might not apply to them.'

Hand in hand with increasing trends towards innovation, globalisation and megabrands is the move towards stronger centralisation – at least for new product development and innovation activities. There are several arguments put forward to support this:

---

[4]   One participant defined megabrands as brands that make one billion US dollars within two years of introduction.

- 'We have a lot of duplication and dilution of resources. Bringing new product development and innovation under central control has made this visible and allows us to act accordingly.'
- 'For innovation to work, you want critical mass. That's a powerful argument for centralising innovation resources: more people, more money, more brainpower; this way you get much higher-quality work.'
- 'One of the hardest decisions is which projects to launch. It is a trade-off between size of opportunity and possibility of success; we use these two criteria to manage our pipeline; we want some savings and quick wins but also some risky but potentially highly rewarding projects. The advantage of doing this out of the centre is the bird's-eye view; another is cross-funding over a longer time horizon.'[5]

In best-practice companies, centralisation is underpinned by efficient resource allocation and projects that are aligned to company strategy: 'The central innovation and development department will look at new ideas, assess whether they fit with the company's strategy and, with a recommendation, pass them on to the leadership council, which makes the final decision. If it is decided to go ahead, headquarters also decide where it is executed and what resources are allocated to it.'

Even though there is a shift towards stronger centralisation, most interviewees mentioned that the role of the centre was mainly to deliver services, not to control. As one interviewee put it, 'The role of the centre is to provide services, to provide a hassle-free environment for the business units so they can get on with their business.' However, if the centre takes on a more prominent role, communication about what is going on, and why, is essential.

A supportive and company-wide IT infrastructure can be an important factor in making a stronger central focus work. While today's IT systems are capable of providing the capacity and speed that is required, unsatisfactory past experience can be a barrier to people's motivation to use it. People need to be convinced that speedy access to (quality) information is actually the norm rather than the exception, and that the

---

[5] A major hurdle for projects in companies with a strong focus on globalisation and 'megabrands' tends to be their global relevance and availability or resources.

information they receive is meaningful and up-to-date. In order to get buy-in, it is important that the main reason for centralisation should not be the desire to cut costs but to increase benefits.

Other benefits of centralisation include:

- achieving general synergies, such as sharing support functions;
- HR management, including identifying and nurturing leadership talent and moving people between the different parts of the company;
- intellectual capital, covering such things as the transfer of ideas and sharing of knowledge.

There are also down-sides to centralisation. Increasing centralisation means that someone has to give up power, and that is likely to cause resentment. The centre is often perceived to be negative and blocking, creating additional demands for reports and forms to fill in. So if not approached considerately, centralisation can cause increased bureaucracy, as one interviewee describes: 'In the past, when we developed designs for packaging, we used to be able to just go across the road to sort it out. But now that we are much more globally focused and design is centralised, it takes so much longer and it has lost the personal touch. Instead there are issues caused by language barriers and long-distance communication. Face-to-face communication is so much more effective and less prone to misunderstandings.'

A final observation on centralisation made by one of the interviewees was, 'The times when the pendulum swings from local to centre or vice versa are the most difficult ones because that's when you're not sure where the power lies and as a consequence most waste appears.'

But, as one interviewee summed it up, 'There is always a local–central tension; this is an issue bigger than innovation. That's why it is important to establish a company-wide "we". We have managed to break the barriers down bit by bit; having the "central guys" sit locally has also helped.' So centralisation is another strong reason why a company should strive to achieve an oneness which does not end at the business unit boundaries but stretches across the entire organisation. The binding element could be a code of conduct, a shared set of values, a common goal – all aspects of a strong company culture. There are a number of innovation paradoxes, however such as the local–central tension, which will be explored in Chapter 6.

Anchor points

- Innovation is a necessity, not a nicety – but many companies still think of innovation as being important rather than urgent.
- Becoming more innovative is about change – treating it like a change programme might help.
- Innovation is a journey – it takes time.
- Innovation is a frame of mind, not a fashion to be worn today and forgotten tomorrow.
- Innovation requires different behaviours and new ways of thinking.
- Intrinsic motivation is more important than financial incentives – people can be told to change their behaviour but not to think differently: they have to want to do it.
- Innovation needs direction – unless people know what is to be achieved, innovation becomes a lottery.
- Innovation requires a holistic approach – understanding a company's starting point and context are essential.
- More radical innovation is needed – today there is less and less scope to achieve future growth through mergers and acquisitions.

Rising tides – establishing an urgency

We have just seen that many companies believe innovation is important but not urgent. The consequence of this is that good intentions are not translated into action. Invited to share his views on companies' future innovation challenges, Gary Hamel, Visiting Professor of Strategic and International Management at the London Business School and chairman of the international consulting company Strategos, paints an urgent picture for companies to move innovation up the agenda and embrace change.

The Rapids of Change

Gary Hamel, Strategos

Contemplating future innovation challenges, and provoked by recent events in America, it occurred to me that there may be interesting lessons business can learn from the resilience of political systems – or rather, democracies.

Political systems have weathered enormous changes over the centuries with very few internal upheavals. These systems have a track record of responding and dealing with change that is unmatched by any commercial organisation in the world. So what can people leading commercial organisations learn from political life and from civic organisations about this challenge of staying resilient and vital in the midst of very, very turbulent times? What makes democratic systems so resilient?

I believe that the answer lies in their capacity to manage paradox. If you think about great constitutional democracies, they are not one thing or another, they are many things at once. They are both coherent in the sense that there is a sense of being British, being American and so forth, but at the same time there is also enormous diversity. There is community and a sense of togetherness, but there is also a great respect for individuals, which means that people, by their own political courage, can take on those systems from within. There is great courage, but also prudence; there is great strength, but also compassion. There is a commercial instinct, a respect for material gain, but at the same time there are also spiritual values. I would argue that the resilience of democracies comes from the ability to manage these paradoxes. The unfortunate reality about companies is that they are filled with accountants and engineers who are generally not too comfortable with paradoxes. Why? They want to be clear – is it A or is it B, is it black or is it white?

Charles Simeon, a famous eighteenth–century British clergyman, put it this way. He said that truth is not in one extreme and truth is not in the middle. The truth is in both extremes. Translating this into the corporate sphere, the fundamental paradox is the tension between optimisation and innovation. Organisations from the age of industrialisation forward were built for the purpose of optimisation. The assumption was that a company would do one thing more or less forever and simply get better and better at doing it. Xerox would make photocopiers. General Motors would make automobiles. So the values that were instilled in these and the many other organisations like them were about scale and efficiency, diligence and replication, and hierarchy and control. The virtues that we inherited from the industrial age have created almost all of the material prosperity that we enjoy – the ability to buy things at an enormously advantageous price, to be able to have automobiles and clothes and cars and everything else comes from the fact that we master those virtues of optimisation!

Success is no longer based on optimisation

We no longer live in a world where a company can do the same thing forever. Success is becoming harder and harder to defend as the world becomes an increasingly discontinuous place. We need to blend all of the virtues of optimisation with a new set of virtues that encourage experimentation, imagination, diversity and creativity – and we cannot look at these sets of virtues as either or. In the debate about Old Economy versus New Economy most of us have subscribed to the belief that companies that were the product of the industrial age were very good at optimisation and all the small start-up companies would be good at innovation. If you want to succeed, it is not a question of either or; you have to be good at both. In the end, Old Economy organisations will have to master the new virtues and New Economy companies will need to embrace the virtues of the Old Economy. I would argue that what we are searching for today is a new synthesis – a synthesis that can lead us to a truly post-industrial enterprise that is a perfect amalgamation of old and new virtues.

I do not believe that such an organisation exists today. However, I believe that 10 or 15 years from now, people will be writing about a new class of company that has mastered this new set of virtues that will have been able to combine optimisation with innovation. In many ways, these companies will look as different from today's large-scale industrial companies as they did from the fragmented craft-based businesses that preceded them. This requires resilience and the capacity to manage paradox.

The three challenges and the two imperatives

The three fundamental things that have come together, making life very challenging for every company, are:

1. The hi-tech implosion. The dot.com crash was actually the least of our problems in terms of the hi-tech implosion. Much more critical has been what has happened in telecoms. One and a half trillion dollars of market value have been destroyed over the last year in telecoms. British Telecom (BT), for example, has lost 60% of its market value in the last 12 months. There was a lemming effect when companies rushed to pour billions of dollars of capital into Third Generation technology and fibre-optic networks. As a result, there is now an enormous overcapacity that will take years to balance out. To add to the problem, companies

are cutting back on their IT spending. In 1990 US companies – and this is a pattern matched around the world – spent 16% of their capital budgets on IT. In the run-up to the Millennium, companies spent not 16%, but 59%. So IT's share of capital budgets tripled over a decade but it's not going to triple again. Arithmetically, it just cannot. Looking at what lifted share prices higher over the last decade we find that a huge part of it was the so-called TMT sector – Telecommunications, Media and Technology – and we have just established that this sector has almost totally run out of its ability to drive economic growth.

2. Most of the other strands that companies used in the 1990s for driving profit and share prices have simply run out of steam too. Most companies have reached the limits of what they can do with mergers, acquisitions, consolidation and cost-cutting. For example, at 2000/2001's rate of merger and acquisition activity, we would have one company in Europe ten years from now and one company in the USA seven years from now. This is not going to happen. So the wave of merger and acquisition activity, all the re-engineering, downsizing, e-procurement, all the cost cutting things that propped up earnings and therefore share prices over the last decade – those things are gone. I would argue that over the last decade or so there was a rising tide that lifted a lot of boats, the rising tide of all those easy efficiency games, the rising tide of all the enthusiasm about the Web, the rising tide of all this merger and acquisition activity which propped up share prices – today there's no more rising tide. We're going to learn over the next decade which companies are truly resilient and which aren't.

3. Let me add the third element of this perfect storm, strategy life cycles are becoming shorter and shorter, not least because the underlying tastes are continuously changing. Almost anything we look at today is changing at a non-linear rate. This is partly because of frictionalist capitalism and the long-term impact of the Internet, which will begin to erode profit margins as it erodes the kinds of friction from which companies have gained competitive advantage in the past. Despite the dot.com crash, the reality is that in virtually every industry the new wealth over the

last decade has been created by newcomers. That tendency will remain. We also see consumers being more fickle than ever before. Consider the market for sports shoes. Over the past few years, market leadership has passed from Adidas to Nike to Vance to Sketchers. This is an indication that no one will be able to build a brand that is capable of surviving more than a few years.

I believe that the three fundamental and irrevocable changes create two imperatives that every organisation will have to obey.

The first is the imperative of industry – or strategy – revolution, however one wants to describe it. In an increasingly non-linear world, only non-linear ideas are going to create new wealth. Why would McDonalds otherwise have bought 30% of Pret à Manger? Why else would South-West Airlines have a market capitalisation that is larger than the next three American airlines combined – United, Delta and American? Why? Because they have come up with a fundamentally different business model. So one of the questions one has to ask is, 'How do we build, inside of even the oldest companies, this capacity for radical innovation?' The danger with the current economic uncertainty is that many organisations are looking to retrench. This may buy you time, but retrenchment doesn't buy growth. Retrenchment doesn't buy opportunity. Retrenchment doesn't buy a future. It is becoming increasingly difficult to grow incrementally. The only way to grow is to stimulate new demand with new products and new services, as Docomo has done in Japan with the world's first packet-switched mobile network, which allows kids to download cartoon characters, horoscopes and much more.

With most economies entering a timeframe where there are going to be powerful deflationary pressures, it will be extraordinarily difficult for any company in any industry to raise its prices. If we are looking at companies that succeed in today's difficult economic climate, it is companies such as South-West Airlines and Dell computers. These companies have brought fundamental innovation to the cost structure – not the odd percentage here and there, but 70 or 80%. So if we want to work on cost it is important to recognise that you cannot succeed if you do it incrementally. Cemex, a Mexican cement company, have found a novel way of tackling its costs. Cemex has managed this by borrowing ideas from biological swarming (such as bees do), and translating the insights into a reduction of the average time it takes for a cement truck to do a delivery to a contractor from three hours to 20 minutes. This is not incremental improvement. This is non-linear innovation on the cost side. The same applies to prices. If you want to escape relentless price pressure, you have got to be able to do something like Starbucks did. You have to be able to create powerful new sources of differen-tiation (such as new flavours or types of coffee) that in the case of Starbucks gets consumers to pay £2.50 for a coffee.

The second imperative is about how to change the nature and definition of the company itself. In a world of continuous change, every company is going to have to become as nimble as change itself. In the past you could assume a company may have to funda-mentally change once a generation. And most companies only ever made such monumental shifts in the midst of crisis – and it usually meant sacking the CEO. In 2000, 22% of the top 200 executives in the USA lost their jobs. It's unprecedented. Never before have we seen change like this. Even if managers don't like to admit it, the sad reality is that many companies are a lot like banana republics where the only way to change the regime is to dispose of the leader. It is sad that most companies feel that the only way they can change is by getting rid of the top guy when the problem is a deeply systemic issue that arises from the fact that in most of these companies radical innovation is not even close to where it ought to be. At best it is rhetoric or maybe it is something happening to a limited extent in R&D. One of the things I think that's very crucial is we are going to have to dramatically expand our definition of what innovation is.

How do you renew a company?

So how do you continue to renew a company's deepest sense of purpose? Some have already achieved it, for example the French-

Canadian company, Bombardier, which has gone from designing and manufacturing snow-mobiles to being not only one of the most aggressive new competitors in aerospace with its regional jets but also the world's largest provider of electronic transportation (electric trains and so on). Other examples are Avon, which after 100 years is now moving into new indirect distribution channels, and Microsoft, which is shifting from shrink-wrapped software to software services, innovating faster than ever before, despite the fact that they almost have a monopoly.

The issue of renewal is critical, and there are many different routes. The easiest is a simple change in portfolio. When Cable & Wireless decided that they did not want to be in the local telephone business any more but an Internet Service Provider (ISP), they had to sell off their phone exchanges – which took a lot of courage but was not very difficult to do. Sometimes this is all you have to do, and part of this kind of renewal means getting over nostalgia and getting over, 'This is our beloved core business. How can we possibly "sell the crown jewels"?'

Another way of renewal is to spin out. This is essentially what Virgin is doing, which describes itself as a brand of venture capitalist, continually spinning out new companies. Every new business they create has its own capital and management structures, it carries nothing more than some aspects of the Virgin brand. It is interesting to note that very few of these spin-outs have made any material difference to shareholders. The simple reason for this is that they did not touch the huge core business that has tied up all those thousands of people and capital. I sometimes liken these venture funds and incubators and spin offs to 'putting a belly-button ring on Granny' – it is an interesting ornament, but in most companies what Granny needs is not a belly-button ring, but a liver transplant, something that goes to the heart of the problem, not some innovation ghetto off on one side of the company.

The question, then, is how do you create, internally and organically, new businesses, businesses that sit between the uncharted waters of the existing organisational chart? Disney discovered one of these white spaces when it moved into the cruise ship business.

And how does one transform the core itself in the way that Microsoft and Avon are trying to do? Companies have been skating around this issue of renewal for years. They did not want to address the problem, which is why incubators and venture funds have been so popular. But most incubators and venture funds are on the periphery and have not made much of a difference. I believe that to tackle renewal head-on, one has to confront the four enemies of renewal, because any innovation that does not deal with these enemies is not going to succeed. The four enemies are:

1. Political oligarchy.
2. Embedded orthodoxies.
3. Inflexible resources.
4. Core incompetencies.

The first, political oligarchy, refers to a tight concentration of power at the top of an organisation in the hands of people who are not learning as fast as the world is changing. One of the reasons that the failure rate of businesses is going up and one of the reasons why it is becoming harder and harder to sustain success is that companies are not decentralising the responsibility for innovation and strategy as fast as the world is becoming more complex and more discontinuous. So the concentration of political power in the hands of individuals who are filled with nostalgia is one of the reasons why companies fail.

But it is not only about the concentration of power, but the beliefs and dogma that have built up over time. These have become embedded in our language, in our market segmentation criteria, in our processes, and those orthodoxies become marbled throughout our organisations, what I call the 'embedded orthodoxies'. It is these orthodoxies that make it difficult to see new possibilities.

The third enemy is inflexible resources. One of the problems is that over time, patterns of resource allocation become entrenched. Existing business overheads, existing product programmes, year after year get plus or minus 5 or 10% of the same funding they got the last year. This makes it difficult to reconfigure and reassemble resources quickly to attack new opportunities. For example, funding in multidivisional companies is often determined by their previous year's cashflow. So if a department made a lot of money last year, they get more money the following year, and so on. Although this seems logical, it is the principal mechanism for continuing to perpetuate the status quo and embed inflexibility.

Finally there is the enemy called 'core incompetencies' of a company. In general, there are huge skill gaps in most organisations. The problem is that going after new opportunities requires a company to build new skills. Unfortunately, the other three enemies reinforce the fourth. Political oligarchy ensures that the top management of the company are deaf to the voices of new possibilities. Embedded orthodoxies ensure they are blind as well. And inflexible resources ensure they cannot reconfigure. As a result, core incompetencies become just another way of describing something or someone that is inept.

Getting to the heart of the matter

So how can innovation be made a systemic capability? I believe that there is a parallel to the development of the quality movement. If we went back to 1960 and visited, let's say, the top management of British Leyland or General Motors or Peugeot, and we said to them, 'You need to improve your quality,' they would all have looked at us and said, 'Well, of course, it's important. We want to have good-quality cars.' And yet they wouldn't have known where to begin because at least as far as Europe and the USA were concerned, in 1960 no one had ever heard of quality circles, statistical process control and all the other things that came to mean Total Quality Management. That was just being invented in Japan, and it took the West some 20 years to come to grips with quality as a deeply embedded competitive advantage. For most Western companies, quality was a function of the inspector at the end of the production line if you were Volkswagen or Ford, or the artisan with the magical hand if you worked for Rolls-Royce. All too often we think of innovation in a similar same way. Innovation is either being an artisan or a specific organisational unit like R&D or product development. The great insight of the quality movement was that it had to be everyone's job.

So what happened as the Western car industry came to grips with that? They went to Japan to figure out what quality was, and initially had a very superficial view, thinking, 'Oh, it's pretty easy! It's these quality circles. People sit there every Friday afternoon. They talk for a couple of hours and quality goes up. It's quite magical!' So every company put quality circles in place and, as many will remember, all of them failed at first. So they went to Japan again. This time they looked a bit harder and found that the Japanese trained their people, they gave them new skills, and most import- antly they put thousands of their employees through this kind of training. So they began to do the same, and they said, 'Well, that kind of helps, but it is still not the whole story.' When they went back and looked again they found that the Japanese companies had a whole new set of methods that drove behaviours in these com- panies. So it took Ford and British Leyland and its successors over 20 years to slowly come to grips with quality.

When we look at annual reports and other corporate documents, we find that about 90% emphasise the need for innovation – but this has not translated into being a core competence, and not many people on the shop floor would know how to describe the corporate innovation system. To change this, as with the intro- duction of quality, a systemic approach is required in which every employee feels part of the responsibility for innovation.

What must change – changing the foundations of thinking

In a way organisations have to get back to basics – back to the most basic assumptions of what organisations are all about, and for who and how they operate. The reality is that baked into every company born before yesterday is a set of deep principles and beliefs that view organisations as machines, as things that are inflexible, that are built to optimise some particular function with an input, a process and an output. To be successful in the future, organisations will have to shift from a machine view to a biological view. After all, other than constitutional democracies, the only other things that have demonstrated resilience across not only decades, but centuries and aeons, are biological systems.

There are three fundamental metaphors, or paradigms, that are going to be important as a foundation for our thinking in the years ahead:

1. Complex adaptive systems.
2. Markets.
3. Biological evolution.

What is interesting about complex adaptive systems is that they have a lot of joint action, a lot of coordination among their members, without there being a chain of command. Hence one of the deep questions today is, how do we get coordination, or rather, how do we get cooperation without centralisation? We know that a chain of command fails when the environment is changing very quickly. We also know that standard operating procedures and operational rules fail when the environment is changing very unpredictably. Imagine a very successful organisation that is not formally organised in any way, where there are no operational manuals, no budgets, no chains of command and no divisional structure. And yet this organisation delivers a complex service to millions of people and it has thrived for more than 60 years. The organisation I am referring to is Alcoholics Anonymous, one of the most effective mechanisms that has ever been invented for changing deep-seated addictive behaviour. What makes it hang together and work despite the absence of any trappings of a traditional organisation? The three things that are common to all complex adaptive systems: simple common goals, very simple rules, and local autonomy. There's no reporting relationship, it is all self-contained.

The second metaphor is that of a market. Markets are places of exchange, and markets have been proven again and again to be superior to hierarchies in giving the right resource to the right opportunity, at the right time, at the right price. Markets do not have a mission or CEO allocating resources. So why can't we think of organisations more like markets and less like hierarchies? Imagine if any employee in an organisation could publish internally on a web site the project or initiative that they are interested in pursuing? Other employees could buy financial options in those ideas, using their time as currency. Let me explain what I mean. You would say, 'Susan, I really love this thing you're going to do, you know, this new product or this new distribution system you're going to create. I can see it's going to add real value to our company. It's a great thing for us to do. I am willing to give you my next ten Saturdays to help you do this.' Just like a consulting or accounting company would keep a time and expenses report on a project, the time you give Susan would go on to the timesheet for that project. When it succeeds, if it succeeds, you are rewarded. Imagine another way of thinking about this. 3M thinks it's perfectly natural, for example, to say to R&D people, 'You can take 15% of your time and work on any project that's interesting to you.' Now imagine that we go to every single individual in a large company that has any discretionary budget whatsoever and say to every one of those individuals, 'You can take 2, 5, or 10% of your budget and you can play angel investor to any project initiative you think is interesting in the company.' Hierarchy will still be there, but here it is supported by a process that allows resources to move around in much more fluid ways.

The third metaphor is biological evolution. Focus, efficiency and alignment are universal. But the more absolute these values are, the lower a company's survival chances in a very discontinuous world. In biological systems there is no forecasting. There is a lot of variety but not a lot of alignment; there is mutation and sexual recombination. The way nature deals with the inability to forecast is by creating a lot of different variations of that one product. Some of the variations will fail, but the ones that are attuned to the future and have the skills and the genetic attributes that help them cope will survive. So it might help managers to think about that simple dynamic of variety, selection and retention – the rhythm of life. It also has to be the rhythm of innovation. When companies get serious about innovation, too often they hope that they can find the one big idea that will create the next driver of market value. This is not how it works. Companies have to get better stage-gate processes,[1] better review criteria, and better mechanisms for deciding which ideas should be taken forward and which shouldn't. Organisations have to find ways of launching many, many more low-risk, low-cost experiments and then simply sitting back and seeing which ones succeed.

Conclusion – bring your passion to work

Where we are in business history is a very exciting place to be. For the first time in a hundred years we have the chance to truly reinvent what it means to be a large company. We have the chance to reunite individuals with their passions. We have a chance to in many senses get the dead hand of orthodoxy and hierarchy off people's backs. We have the chance to create organisations where people can use their imagination.

In the industrial age, wealth was a product of three things – how long you worked, how hard you worked, and how much knowledge you brought to the job – time multiplied by diligence multiplied by expertise. It is a fact that in today's world, wealth is still partly dependent on that, but now it is more and more dependent on three different things – creativity, the ability to re-conceive (be it a company, product, service or industry) and the willingness to start something new. The connections you have with other skills, with other people, with other ideas are essential because in the end innovation is like DNA. It is all about the ability to mix and match individual pieces, and from the common pieces create new combinations and new possibilities. The ability to do that is completely determined by the diversity of the network of connections one has with people and resources that are different from what is currently available – creativity multiplied by courage multiplied by connections.

---

[1] The stage-gate process goes back to the 1960s when NASA introduced a structured process for the development of new projects which was broken down into phases, each of which concluded with a 'gate' at which checks and controls would take place. The stage-gate process as known in innovation and new product development today was devised by Robert G. Cooper. To find out more, visit his web site www.stage-gate.com.

Henry Ford was once reputed to have said, 'Why is it that whenever I ask for a pair of hands, a brain comes attached?' Henry Ford wanted robots. That is the legacy of the industrial age. These days, people can bring their brains to work. But what do we ask them to do with their brains? We ask them to figure out how to take another 3% of the cost out of the cost centre! We should ask them to bring not only their brains, but their imaginations and their passions as well. Not because we are setting out to build organisations that are humane, but because we are setting out to build organisations that can thrive in a world that has never been more turbulent.

Anchor points

- Times are more turbulent and discontinuous than ever.
- Innovators need to learn how to become resilient.
- To be innovative is to manage paradoxes.
- The past has been about optimisation, the New Economy seems to have been about innovation, the future is about the ability to combine both.
- Future economic growth will no longer come from a booming IT industry nor from mergers and acquisitions.
- Strategy and planning cycles are becoming shorter and shorter, and consumers ever more fickle.
- Companies will have to renew themselves continually, even if it means selling off the crown jewels.
- Obstacles to renewal are political oligarchy, embedded orthodoxies, inflexible resources and core incompetencies.
- To make the innovative organisation a reality, a systemic approach is required.
- Metaphors that might help organisations understand and achieve innovation are complex adaptive systems, markets and biological evolution.
- In the past, wealth was a product of how long you worked, how hard you worked and how much knowledge you brought in to the job – time multiplied by diligence multiplied by expertise.

- In the future, wealth will be a product of the diversity of the network of connections one has with people and resources that are different from what is currently available – creativity multiplied by courage multiplied by connections.

Fishing where the fish are – the need to focus

'Innovation needs to be focused. If it is not, there is an innovation overload. You will get variability in the quality of work. There will be too many initiatives everywhere and no one has an overview. This can lead to confusion and dilution of brands.'

Realising the urgency to innovate is an essential first step, but in itself will not change anything. In order to change and become more innovative, people need a clear sense of where they are going. That is why a company's vision and strategy should be like a magnet, pulling employees' thoughts and actions in the desired direction.

Strategy and vision

If the existence of a clear vision and supporting strategy are cornerstones for any successful organisation, they are even more important for an organisation which is seeking to improve its innovation performance. Without clear direction about where to innovate, people may come up with all kinds of ideas and suggestions that make no contribution to the company's long-term ambitions. What is so bad about that, one might ask. Can't there be commercially interesting ideas that are not directly related to what a company is about? There certainly can, but with resources being a limiting factor to the number of projects a company can execute at any one time, making the best use of these resources is important. Companies such as 3M may give their technical staff 15% of their time to explore ideas of their own, but all employees are very clear on what the company is about, so their ideas tend to be closely aligned with 3M's core technologies. If a company wants to encourage and pursue ideas that are outside its current scope, it might be advisable to do so through a separate venture unit.

Most of the recent reports on innovation best practice have focused on cultural and leadership issues, both of which are seen to be key to creating an innovative organisation. It is about how to *establish an atmosphere* where innovation can flourish (preparing the ground), whereas issues related to strategy, vision and processes are more concerned with the *effective execution* of innovative projects within the organisation. While strategy and vision do not receive specific attention in the same way that culture or leadership do, understanding and applying insights from these areas are part of innovation best practice and there are two other areas where best practice insights can be found: first, what makes good strategy in general and second, what good strategy and vision means in the context of new product development and innovation. The following aspects are highlighted as best practice for vision and strategy:

> **Insights from the Innovation Exchange research**
>
> - Most participating organisations have gone through some major change over the past year.
> - Much of the change was induced by merger and acquisition activities.
> - Many companies anticipate a shift from growth through mergers and acquisition to more organic growth, mainly through innovation.

Vision

- **Clarity** of what the company stands for and what it aims to achieve.
- **Sharedness** of the vision throughout the entire organisation.
- **Attainability** – the vision should be ambitious but realistic (at organisational, team and individual levels).

Strategy

- Having an explicit **innovation strategy** which is closely linked to the organisation's business strategy.
- Awareness of company-specific **context** and **constraints.**

Clarity

'The fact that the CEO has pronounced innovation to be at the top of the agenda means that people go crazy with it. We have chaos at present because people do not have direction yet.'

'Our vision and strategy are very clear, everyone knows what it is. The good thing about everyone knowing the strategy is that if and when ideas are getting rejected it is not taken personally. It also means that people are questioning what they are asked to do if they can't see how it fits in. For example, someone asked me why they should do X; they felt it did not really fit with the strategy. I replied, "Nor can I". So they did not do it.'

In the context of strategy and vision the key points are, unless people are given a direction in which to innovate, and a reason why it is important, it becomes a wild goose chase that consumes resources without producing results. An approach of 'Let's just do loads of stuff and if we're lucky we will be successful' is not likely to work. You have to try and stack the luck in your favour, otherwise you might end up like one company which realised that it was working simultaneously on 2400 different projects – losing about £20 million in the process! Everyone was trying to innovate but without a focus or common purpose. Such a discovery might lead many a CEO to stop innovation altogether – but in this case he knew better. He knew that the problem was a lack of direction and coordination. His response was to charge a small team with designing a deliberate innovation strategy that would provide a clear focus for all future innovation activities across the organisation.

Creating a clear vision across an organisation, particularly a large one, is not easy. One interviewee explained, 'There are too many values from different levels in the organisation: company, parent company, balanced scorecard, job objectives and so on. All that's too much, it is over-complicated and leads to confusion, particularly as nothing seems to be in synch with anything else.' Another interviewee commented, 'There can be too much of a good thing: in addition to the company values (that everyone in this organisation knows by heart and lives by) the new management has introduced 12 styles – no

'Typically in large organisations the board thinks it provides a clear vision and strategy. Middle management think they can do better and modify it – and the people on the ground are thoroughly confused.'

NAPIER UNIVERSITY L.I.S.

one in the organisation could name them, and it just leads to confusion and the dilution of previously strong values.'

The following quotes show the cument variation in the degree to which visions are clear:

- 'There is no clear vision on where to innovate, therefore we see only incremental innovation.'
- 'People are clear about the vision but are not sure how it applies to their jobs.'
- 'Vision and strategy are clear at board level but not below, because of the current level of uncertainty (possible imminent large acquisition and anticipated change in top management).'
- 'In last year's survey people were very clear about both the business and centre's vision and strategy.'

Sharedness

'The problem is the company does not have a shared culture or vision. If you were to ask people what the company stands for and what its vision is you would get lots of different answers.'

'Good leaders know about the past and are clear about the future. The challenge for such leaders is to define the future, whereby true leaders project back from the future rather than forward from the present.'

Involving as many parts and levels of the organisation as possible within the innovation process is beneficial. While it might take more time to start with, it saves time later on as people will be aware of what is going on, and are likely to have good levels of buy-in. However, involving people does not mean that the result is a consensus decision. It means consulting and collecting insights from those who might know the business better than the people on the board. It also means gaining buy-in, but certainly not arriving at a compromise on the lowest common denominator. As a successful company describes, 'The management style is consultative and informative. Our managers are easy to work with and our culture is characterised by teamwork. However, objectives are established by and cascaded down from the CEO.' The decision of 'what' should be firmly in the hand of a company's leadership whereas the question of the 'how' might be addressed more effectively by people further down the hierarchy.

After a merger or acquisition, consultation can have the added benefit of helping the different companies to integrate and develop a sense of shared destiny. But careful attention has to be paid to even the smallest detail. The Innovation Exchange member of one British company, having recently been bought by a foreign entity, highlighted the effort that had gone into the development of a mission statement. Over 300 executives from the various parts of the organisation had been involved in it. But in the end the document did not create the feeling of belonging and togetherness that was intended, but created dissonance. While the business language within the group of which the British company had become a part was English, the document was written in the foreign parent's language (albeit a translation was offered) which alienated many of those who had been involved in the consultation process. In addition, only the top person from the foreign parent had signed the document, signalling to other members of the group that they were clearly not equals in what they had assumed was a partnership.

Another reason why a clear and shared vision may be worth pursuing is that it is indirectly related to improving an organisation's innovativeness.[1] If one accepts that in the future companies will rely more and more on knowledge workers, as is frequently emphasised, and that these knowledge workers play an important part in the innovation process, then anything that helps bind these workers to an organisation must be worth pursuing. As the report 'Tomorrow's Leaders' recommends, 'Make sure employees understand the company's strategy for the future. Employees want to work for a company that will be a leader in its industry and that will continue to provide interesting work.' A clear and inspiring strategy can be the key to creating new psychological contracts with an increasingly fickle workforce. Hence once an organisation has established a reputation for innovation, a virtuous circle is created which allows it to attract and retain the best talent.

---

[1]   'Tomorrow's Leaders Today: Career Aspirations and Motivations', a study carried out by Korn Ferry International in collaboration with London Business School.

Attainability

For vision and strategy to be motivating and spark people's imagination it has to be challenging yet at the same time it has to be attainable – 'Make it difficult but not impossible' is the motto of the CEO of a highly successful technology company. If the reaction is, 'Yes, of course we can do that,' the target is probably not challenging enough. If the reaction is, 'Not a chance in hell' it has probably overshot the goal. If it is, 'Can we do this? Well, perhaps we can . . .' it is probably about right.

In the assessment of what is attainable and what is not, the individual's attitude plays an important role. People who see the glass as half empty will be less optimistic than those who consider it to be half full – and research indicates that people's own self-belief has a strong influence on success and failure – the famous self-fulfilling prophecy. Carol Kinsey Gorman, author of numerous books on creativity and change,[2] points out, 'Organizations don't change, people do. It is critical to identify the change-adept people, those who are most capable of responding to and facilitating change throughout the rest of the organisation.' She identified five qualities that such people share:

- They are confident. Even in the face of change, these people feel they can adapt, learn new skills and find a way to thrive.
- They welcome challenge. They have optimism. They focus on the positive aspects of the change and allow the brightness of the future they envision to galvanise them.
- They have great coping skills. They are flexible and focus on what they can control. They use tools such as humour to get through tough times.
- They are creative. The change-adept tend to challenge the status quo, find new ways to solve old problems, and the best of them anticipate and capitalise on change.
- They counter-balance. Change-adept people take care of themselves physically, emotionally, spiritually and realistically. They have fulfilling outside interests so their total focus is not on their job/career.

---

[2]   Her publications include *Creativity in Business: A Practical Guide for Creative Thinking*, *Adapting to Change: Making It Work for You*, *Managing in a Global Organization*, and recently, *The Human Side of High Tech*.

People are also more likely to believe something is possible when they understand why the goal has been set in the first place – hence the importance of getting buy-in.

In the interviews, it was also mentioned that regulation can have a fundamental impact on what is perceived to be attainable, and hence on strategy development. It is an interesting question, though, whether constraints, such as regulation, should be seen as fixed boundaries or as things that should be challenged and overcome. It is noteworthy that never taking no for an answer is a key characteristic of innovators.

The story told by P-Y. Gerbeau illustrates the difficulties involved in managing a highly ambitious vision, the need to establish clear criteria for success or failure for a project, and the crucial role people play in making a vision happen.

Throwing a Brand a Lifeline

P-Y. Gerbeau, former CEO of the Millennium Dome in London

Mayday, mayday, mayday

Just imagine a multi-million-pound business that is to be developed and constructed, run, has to break even and be closed down within just three years. And you are actually brought in for the last year – which is the operating, running and closing-down year of the business. This was the task I was facing when I joined the Millennium Dome as CEO in 2000 – it is impossible to imagine any big corporation even attempting to do that.

Now imagine that you inherit a business that is (supposed to be) one hundred per cent service-oriented and you find that this company is not orientated towards the consumer, with none of the attractions you are supposed to be running working. But that is not enough, nor are any of the performance targets set by the 'inventors' of the Dome being met. In the case of the Millennium Dome, all this was an understatement. The biggest problem that I was facing was the massive gap between actual and predicted attendance. Enquiring how the expected visitor numbers had been arrived at, I found that the number of six million visitors to the 1951 British Exhibition had simply been doubled. So much for market research! To improve this, I had to breathe new life into what seemed to be a poor and failing brand.

Lifting the wreck

I felt that the approach taken in the turnaround of Eurodisney's fortunes might be appropriate for the Dome, so my ambition was to establish a service business organization with values, vision and management support. As a result, the commercial operation was cashflow positive on 14 April, but due to the investment cost of £800 million it still lost about £1 million a day – it would probably be quite hard to come up with a business idea that would amortise an investment of £800 million in one year! Although much of the Dome's financial problems stemmed from poor attendance, there were plenty of other issues that had to be dealt with, especially poor business planning. For example, the Dome had a business plan for food and beverages – one of the three revenue-generating streams, the other two being ticket revenue and merchandising. This had required an investment of £13.4 million. Unfortunately, even the most optimistic view of cash generated from this part of the business was £10 million. The numbers just did not stack up. Everywhere was looking the same. The answer was to cut back on spending in every department, which was a major achievement.

Despite the impossible financial situation, in terms of volume the Dome was the second most popular visitor attraction in Europe. Six and a half million people visited the Dome during its short life. And if we consider that the customer satisfaction rating rose from 54% in January 2000 to 88% in April 2000, after the relaunch of the show and attractions, this was no mean feat. Of course, it depends on what criteria are used for success and failure, but in my book, the Dome was a success.

How to keep a ship afloat

Experiences at Eurodisney and the Dome can be distilled into a small number of must-dos. While I am not a brand guru, the following tips might be useful, as they are based on real life experience.

1. Create a culture that is self-confident.
2. Make the customer happy, and then happier.
3. Ensure that you meet the expectations set by the brand by working hard to ensure that management and staff understand the brand promise – ultimately they are the keeper of your brand. At the end of the day, if your employees do not trust the organisation and do not use the brand, you are going to fail.
4. Management must walk the floors and demonstrate leadership.
5. Be communication rich, so that you know what's happening on the ground. This does not mean sending lots of e-mails, it means having the right mix with a particular emphasis on face-to-face communication.
6. Understand your markets.
7. Create a win–win with all your partners, based upon understanding each other's brand, and making sure these are consistent.

Also worth noting is that the nature of turning a brand around has changed significantly over the last 20 years. Twenty years ago, it was all about physical assets and how to cut them by selling them off. Today it's exactly the opposite. Particularly if you are in a service business, 90% of your assets are intangibles and your best asset leaves your company at 6 pm every night'. So if you try to sell off that specific knowledge, you are never going to turn a business around.

Jumping ship

Since leaving the Dome I have realised that while the Dome itself is a thing of the past, the original concept has still got some life in it. I am currently introducing an offspring of the Dome concept; the idea of bringing together mainstream and extreme sports, and combining this with an entertainment venue and a retail proposition – all under one roof. I believe that such a concept is a real innovation in the leisure sector, and the brand definition will be around entertainment, sports, retail brands and food and beverages. The goal of the company will be to deliver extreme fun. This is already reality in Milton Keynes and we plan to extend the concept across Europe. Since opening in 2001, the Milton Keynes centre has already attracted over five million visitors. What has caught the attention of City investors is the different business model, which is based on property – constructing buildings for investment. We place a strong emphasis on cash flow, and all attractions we build are based on a joint venture model.

To summarise, in managing or revitalising a brand, it is essential to understand the following:

1. It's all about people. Making a brand popular and financially successful depends on how you manage people.
2. Knowledge management. This is about sharing information and knowledge about what's happening in the organisation. It is about learning from mistakes and failure.
3. Get the relationship management right with your shareholders, your end customers and your employees.

Context and constraints

So clarity of vision alone is not enough, it has to be attainable, and strategies have to be in place to realise it. Furthermore, both should be echoed in a company-wide innovation strategy in which the plans for new product development and other innovation activities are outlined. The innovation strategy should reflect what kind of company the organisation aims to be (vision) and how it wants to achieve it (strategy). To ensure success, senior management might want to ask themselves the following questions:

- Are the company's innovation and product strategies compatible with its corporate objectives?
- Have the corporate objectives for innovation and development activities been properly defined and are they being periodically reviewed?

- Are the innovation objectives understood by all involved and do they inspire enthusiasm?
- Have sufficient resources been provided to realise the ambitions set out in the innovation strategy?
- Are processes and procedures in place that facilitate the free flow of communication between different parts of the organisation (functions and departments)?
- Are the organisational policies and procedures for managing the innovation and design and development processes appropriate?
- Is there a sincere and visible commitment to realising the innovation strategy?
- Are innovation activities monitored and evaluated?
- Is progress measured against the innovation ambition?

Innovation is about crossing boundaries, but for boundaries to be crossed there needs to be an awareness of their existence in the first place. This is why it is important for managers to understand their organisation's specific context, and the constraints that arise from it. The constraints can influence how a company responds to an innovation challenge; in fact, how it sets its innovation challenges in the first place (see Figure 3.1).

There are three levels of context that managers need to understand when setting the innovation agenda; company-specific context (which includes company history), industry context, and national or regional context. Before looking at each level in turn it should be made clear that the constraints do not define what a company can or cannot do. Most

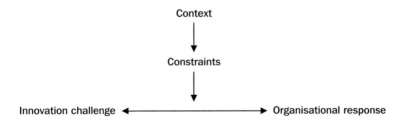

Figure 3.1: Innovation challenge and organisational response

constraints are negotiable – in fact, they tend to involve trade-offs that managers can control. And constraints can be associated both with the innovation challenge and the organisation's response. An example of the former might be the existence of a widely accepted industry standard. A company can decide to challenge such a standard, as Apple did.

Company context

The potential influence of a company's heritage has already been mentioned in Chapter 1. If the cultural implications are not understood and managed accordingly, they can become a major constraint to an organisation's ability to change and improve its innovativeness. Other aspects of context include:

- the company's strengths (core competencies) and potential weaknesses;
- the skills and technologies available;
- processes and IT landscape.

Industry Context

The second level is the industry context where norms and standards can create constraints. While industry standards may not be binding, adhering to them is often seen as a minimum requirement from the customer's point of view. Norms can be considered to be qualifiers which are the minimum set of requirements that have to be fulfilled in order for consumers to consider the product at all. This is supported by a London Business School survey[3] which identified the underlying reasons for introducing an industry standard such as ISO 9000 as company reputation and customer requirement – not to win more orders.

National context

The third level is the national – or sometimes the regional – context. Aspects of this wider context that can influence an organisation's approach and willingness to innovate include:

---

[3] Design and ISO 9000, preliminary report to the Design Council by Paul Temple and Bettina von Stamm, 1996.

- the overall economic conditions. For example, whether the economy is in a boom or bust, what tax and investment policies are in place and so on;
- legislation, including patenting laws, environmental as well as health and safety regulations, company law, and so on;
- attitude towards environmental issues. For example, what is acceptable in new products and what is not, what kind of materials are in fashion, etc.,
- national characteristics, preferences and values (culture); for example, focus on design and aesthetics in countries such as Italy, focus on engineering and quality in Germany, focus on natural materials in Scandinavian countries.

Another reason why managers should want to understand context, particularly company context, is that it will influence the speed at which change can be implemented, and to a certain degree also what level of innovation is appropriate. Different approaches to infusing innovation into organisations will be explored in Chapter 4.

Finally understanding context helps managers decide what kind and level of innovation is most appropriate for their organisation. Most organisations declare, 'We want to be more innovative.' But what exactly does that mean? Does it mean that everyone in the organisation innovates all the time or is it delegated to dedicated teams? What about the existing business that generates the cash to fund new initiatives? How can a healthy balance be struck between the need to create new things and the need to nurture existing products? And what about radical innovations that might undermine the company's core products? Some organisations may decide innovation, at least radical innovation, is not for them, as the following example illustrates.

Like in many other companies, managers in one large UK-based organisation, which I will call company A, decided that they had to become more innovative as an organisation. To facilitate this, they set up a high-level steering group at corporate level and appointed a well-respected person as an *innovation champion* who, unlike many other innovation champions, had strong and visible support from the top. A model with three planning horizons was adopted where horizon 1 referred to the extension of existing products, horizon 2 to existing products that were introduced into a new market or new products that were introduced into new markets, and horizon 3 was to be more experimental and did not necessarily have to fit into any of the existing categories.

The creation of the group and the introduction of the three product horizons came just in time for a revolutionary product that had been under development for several years but without getting anywhere, as it would not immediately hit existing sales requirements and was seen to be just outside the company's core product range. When the project champion presented his case to the steering group, he was given the go-ahead to pursue the project further. The steering group wanted to create a showcase that could be used as an illustration of what the company wanted to achieve and act as a model for future projects. As management felt it was too far removed from the core, it was agreed that the project champion should try to find external investors, with the parent company retaining a substantial equity stake. When the project champion had secured two potential investor groups, performance pressures hit and, to cut costs, top management decided to dissolve the steering group with the people involved either moving on or leaving the company. Perhaps alerted by the level of investor interest, management decided to reconsider the option of developing the product in-house after all and asked for negotiations with investors to be put on hold. However, changes in senior management and some restructuring led to the decision to sack all but two people associated with the project, including the project champion, and move the technology into their distribution division, probably with the intention to wind down the project quietly.

While the insights into this story are biased, as they came primarily from the project champion, it is clear that such a story can have far-reaching consequences for the organisation's culture. Should this story become known throughout the organisation, would anyone else be willing to promote radical innovation, something that is perceived to be risky or unusual? If the management of a company decides that innovation is not for them, which is fair enough, this change of heart has to be communicated carefully and clearly.

Best practice strategy and vision can be summarised as:

- having a clear and shared strategy and vision, developed from the future, not the past;
- linking company strategy and innovation strategy;
- being aware of the organisation's context and possible constraints.

The future challenges identified through the research for **Strategy and Vision** were all about change and balance:

- How to lead change effectively and still achieve output.
- How to ensure that employees are not only clear about the vision but also know how it applies to their job.
- How to define the role of the business unit and the centre.
- How to find the right balance between management and control.

But much of the above is primarily about how companies innovate within existing business boundaries. What Gary Hamel emphasised in his contribution in Chapter 2 is that this may no longer be enough. It is no longer about a radically new product or service, it is about how to revolutionise the business itself, and redefine what it is about. It is this kind of innovation Costas Markides, Professor of Strategic and International Management at London Business School, talks about, urging managers to find new ways to define their company's *what, who* and *how.* He also explores why, even though we know what we ought to do, we tend to be unable to translate that knowledge into action.

Walking on water – how to win by breaking the rules

Costas Markides, London Business School

Innovation in organizations – it doesn't just happen

Many managers complain that their organisations are not innovative enough. But is it a lack of ideas? A study by Mike Keens in the USA showed that about 85% of all the entrepreneurs in the research had their ideas while employed by a large and established company – one of those companies that claim to have problems with creativity and innovation. By the way, creativity and innovation, often used interchangeably, are entirely different things. Creativity is about coming up with an idea, while innovation is coming up with the idea and doing something about it. But when these entrepreneurs try to get management in these large established organisations to listen to their ideas and to do something about it they eventually get frustrated and leave to take the idea forward themselves. So it is not a question of how to get innovation and creativity in organisations but, rather, how to stop preventing it from happening.

And who is generally involved in the generation of business concepts and ideas? If you rely on the top 20 or even 50 people in your organisation you are not going to be as successful as when ideas can come from 10 000 or even 100 000 people. The chance that you will be creative increases the more people you get involved. This is what my colleague Gary Hamel calls 'making your strategy process democratic'. It basically says, 'Bring everybody inside and get them involved in giving you ideas.'

Strategic innovation – changing the rules of the game – is not something that established organisations are generally good at. It was not British Airways who introduced low-cost point to point flying in the airline business. It was somebody else, and British Airways had to respond. It was not Merrill Lynch who introduced online brokerage into the brokerage business. It was somebody else, and they had to respond. Most of the time you will see that established companies have to respond to strategic innovation, rather than being innovators themselves – but it is this kind of innovation that propels organisations forwards.

An interesting insight into strategic innovation is that even if one company has successfully innovated strategically, established competitors tend to take years and years to respond to it. But before illustrating through examples what I mean by strategic innovation, let me briefly explain what it is. It is not about introducing a new product or a new technology – though that can be part of it. Strategic innovation has to do with three things. First, the 'who' – discovering new customers, new, probably quite small segments that nobody pays attention to. Second, the 'what' – discovering new value propositions with your existing product. And third, the 'how' – discovering new ways of manufacturing and delivering the product.

Enterprise – Beating the competition by choosing a different game

Enterprise is the largest vehicle rental company in the world, but why? It's certainly not as well known as Avis or Hertz, but what did Enterprise do in 1957? When other car rental companies were focusing on business users, they targeted people who would need a replacement car while their own was being repaired, or when a second car was needed. This customer segment was considered to be insignificant; in fact it was only about 2% at the time. What is special about Enterprise is that their little niche grew to become a mass market in the period from 1960 to 2000. What Enterprise demon-strates is that one way to achieve strategic innovation is by identifying a new customer segment which today looks small but which grows into a huge market. The car replacement market might have looked tiny and insignificant at the time – and that is why nobody paid attention to it – but over time it grew. By targeting different customers, Enterprise was also able to start playing a different game. Below are some other aspects where Enterprise differs from the other players such as Hertz and Avis:

- *Location*: Hertz or Avis are primarily found at airports. You find Enterprise in towns.
- *Advertising*: Hertz and Avis use 'pull'. They're advertising their brand and try to pull you in. Enterprise use push.
- *Marketing*: travel agents push Hertz products while, mechanics and insurance companies push Enterprise products.
- *Product delivery*: when renting a car from Hertz or Avis you pick up and deliver back to the airport. Enterprise delivers the car either to the garage where your car is being repaired, or they come to your house.

What Enterprise is doing is very different from what Hertz does; they really are playing a different game. But they are not playing a different game for the sake of being different; they are playing a different game because they are serving a different type of customer.

But there is another important insight. If you went back to the 1950s when the car rental business first started and asked who were the customers that rented cars, the answer would have been, mainly business travellers. In fact, that segment would have been about 95% of the market. But there were also a couple of niches. First, there were the people who had just had accidents and were in need of a replacement car (the replacement niche). This represented about 2% of the market. Second, there were people who, for whatever reason, needed to rent a car for a short period (the discretionary niche). This represented another 2% of the market. And then there was a 1% niche that represented the others.

If you were Hertz looking at this market and you were trying to decide who to target, it would have been obvious to go for the traveller segment. But notice what happened. Once they made the choice to target travellers, where did they put their offices? At airports. Who was going to push their product? Travel agents. Where were you going to put the product? At the airport. Where were the customers going to get it? At the airport.

Avis was the next company to enter the rental car market. When they looked at the market segments, which market were they likely to target? Exactly the same one as Hertz. And by targeting the same market segment, they followed exactly the same strategy: airport, travel agents, and so on. The question then becomes, if you are doing the same things as Hertz, how are you going to make money? If this question had been put to Avis back in the 1950s, the answer would have been, 'We'll do it better.' The only strategy available to them at that time was to be better than Hertz.

According to strategist Michael Porter, there are two ways of becoming better. The first is lower cost which is reflected in lower prices, and the second is differentiation, meaning a better or higher-quality product. What I am now suggesting is that there is a third way; that of starting to play a different game.

The question is, how do you start playing a different game? Is it sheer luck? The person who started Enterprise originally owned a garage and when people brought in their cars for repair they commented on the problem of not having a second car to use while their primary car was in the garage. So he felt that there was a market niche, and he took the risk of exploiting it. He did no detailed market analysis, nor did he use any other business school techniques. How do companies get lucky? Simple: by experimenting and 'being there' when outside events create 'luck' for them. The message is, if you do not experiment, there is no chance of getting lucky.

Growing niche markets

Another example of a company that experimented and 'got lucky' is Honda. When Honda entered the motorcycle market back in the 1950s the market was dominated by big motorcycles made by companies such as Harley-Davidson and Triumph. Honda would not have been able to compete head-on so it started a niche, making small scooters. At the time it was a tiny niche but it started growing and growing and growing. Twenty years later it had secured 40% of the market. The same is true for Canon. When Canon entered the photocopier market they went for a niche called individuals. Would you have been able to imagine in 1960 that one day people would have photocopiers at home? Would you have been able to imagine this at a time when a photocopier was the size of a room? And yet Canon started out by saying, I will target individuals as customers and I will make small photocopiers for them.

Identifying a different customer segment

Consider IKEA, and compare it to traditional furniture stores. Comparing a traditional furniture store on the high street with IKEA stores, which are generally located outside a big city with excellent access to motorways, some immediate and obvious differences spring to mind:

- *Size*: High Street furniture shops are small, IKEA stores are huge.

- *Focus*: Displays in traditional shops are organised around product, for example beds, chairs, tables. In IKEA stores the furniture is organised by room.
- *Help*: The traditional shop swarms with staff eager to help you. In IKEA there is no one to help.
- *Assembly*: In the traditional shop the furniture is ready-made and delivered to your door in a couple of days or weeks. At IKEA, you have to build the furniture yourself and you also have to transport it from the shop.

IKEA has changed the game and is extremely successful as a result. The source of the difference is that, like Enterprise, they have a different customer in mind. They are not looking at me or you as their customers. They are looking at young, urban couples who've just finished university and they would like to set up their first home. They don't have enough money, but they still don't want to sacrifice style. So IKEA says, 'We're going to have good Scandinavian designs at affordable prices.' Therefore, to repeat my main message, one aspect of strategic innovation is the discovery of a customer segment that might look small today, but will soon grow into a mass market.

Matsushita – custom-made bicycles

Let me give you an example of the second course of strategic innovation: identifying a new value proposition for your products. If you were told that Matsushita were moving into bicycles and were asked, 'Would you expect them to succeed?', what would you say? Probably 'no'. But, strange as it may seem, not only did they succeed, Matsushita, through its subsidiary, the National Bicycle Industry Co., became the market leader in mountain bicycles in California. How did they do it? By changing the value proposition of a bicycle.

If you go into a National shop there are no products at all. There is just a salesman and a catalogue. When you walk in, he says, 'Right, so you would like to buy a bicycle? Very good. Let me measure the length of your legs because based on this, we have a variety of bicycle frames which you can choose from. Then let me measure your upper body because this will determine the different handles you can put on the bicycle.' And the salesman will continue to measure a few more things and after the right frame has been chosen you can also choose the bicycle's colour, and put your name on it (and they even give you the choice of three different characters, English, Mandarin or Japanese). On top of that there are many optional parts you can put on your bicycle. And instead of having to wait for weeks or months for the delivery, you can take the bike home at the end of the day. So what National offers is custom-made bicycles. But the innovation is not just the offering of custom-made bicycles – custom-made is nothing new. What is innovative is that they can deliver a custom-made bicycle to your door anywhere in the world within 24 hours, for the same price as a mass-produced one. National has radically changed the value proposition of the product, but they have not changed the product; it's still a bicycle.

Swatch – more than a watch

Swatch has changed the value proposition in a different way. They have been successful at changing customers' perception of the benefits they are getting from their product. They changed what you thought was a watch. How did they do it?

In 1960, the Swiss had 80% of the watch market. The value proposition at the time was, 'Buy my watches because they are the best quality you can get. We have been making watches here in Switzerland since 1200.' Swiss craftsmanship was the dominant factor and this was reflected in the quality of the product, and most importantly, the accuracy of the movement. However, by 1980 the Swiss had only 20% of the market. From 1200 to 1960 they had 80% of the market and in just 20 years they had lost nearly all of it. What happened? Who came in and stole the market share? The Japanese. What did they do? Did they produce a better watch? A more accurate one? No. The Japanese did something else. They made watches cheap and modern, and added features and new function-ality. They were saying, 'Buy my watch because not only will it tell you the time accurately, but it will allow you to do a million other things. When you dive in the ocean, the watch can tell you the pressure of the water. When you go hiking in the Himalayas, it can tell you the oxygen level. When you wake up in the middle of the night and you don't know what time it is, you can light it up and see what time it is.'

By 1995 the Swiss were back up to 40% of the market. What happened? Swatch, once again, changed the value proposition of the watch. They said, 'Look, you don't buy a watch to tell you the time and how much oxygen there is in the room. You buy it because it's fashionable, it looks good on you – and, by the way, you need a different one for every occasion.' From being an instrument to measure time, watches had become a fashion accessory and a collector's item.

So, every product has many attributes and characteristics and one way to innovate strategically is to find a new dimension that will excite the customer. We do not buy a product for one reason only. For example, think about buying a suit. What do you look for? It might be the cut, the fit, the quality of the fabric, the name and maybe the price. And there are many more things that you may look for as a customer. The same is true with companies. The key to standing out relies on discovering a new dimension that nobody is focusing on.

But you may not only want to look at what everyone has over-looked in the product proposition; you may also find a gap in how products are made or brought to the customer, as the following story shows.

Seriously – incentivising barmen

The fastest-growing vodka company in Europe is a company called Seriously from Sweden. Rather than running their company like any other drinks company would, they decided to conduct some market research to understand how and where their product would be bought and consumed. And, perhaps not surprisingly, most vodka was consumed in bars, rather than at home or in restaurants. Now think of how you purchase your vodka in a bar. You go to the barman and what do you say? 'Can I please have a vodka, or vodka tonic or vodka with orange juice?' Do you specify the brand? Do you ever say, 'I want Absolute vodka?' And even if the bar tender gave you a different brand, could you tell? Probably not. What does that mean? Who is the decision maker as to what Vodka goes in your glass? Not you, the consumer, but the barman; he is the decision maker. So what Seriously has done is to approach all barmen in Sweden and to give them incentives to push their product: they have given them stock options in the company. Thus, whereas all other companies in the industry focus on a pull marketing strategy, Seriously go for a push strategy. They have radically redefined one of the 'how's' in this business – in this case the marketing strategy.

Therefore, to summarise, strategic innovation is the discovery of a new who, a new what or a new how in your industry. The next question is, how do we do it?

Sacred cows

One important step to achieve strategic innovation is to challenge sacred cows; that is, beliefs and values that are held dear by the organisation. Many people know this, but why is it so difficult to do? Let me tell you a story that may help you to understand why.

Imagine a cage containing five monkeys, a banana hanging from the ceiling of the cage, and a set of stairs underneath the banana. What do you think will happen? Of course, all the monkeys will run towards the banana. The moment they do that, they are sprayed with very cold water until they retreat. After a while they warm up again and one of them will gather enough courage to run towards the stairs again. The moment he or she does it, that monkey is sprayed with very cold water again – as well as the other four who are just sitting there. The monkeys are sprayed with cold water until they learn that it is not a good idea to try to get the banana. Once they have learned this, they just sit there and let the banana hang from the ceiling. Now one of the monkeys is taken out and replaced by a new one. The new monkey will walk in, look at the banana, look at the four other monkeys just sitting there, not understand why they are not running to the banana, and he will run towards the banana. What do you think will happen? Of course the others will jump all over him and beat him up, trying to prevent him from going to the banana because they do not want to be soaked with cold water! So he too will learn that it is not a good idea to try to get the banana. Then another one of the original monkeys is taken out and another newcomer put in. Again the newcomer will walk in, look at the banana, look at these four monkeys just sitting there, will not understand why they are not exploiting such an obvious food opportunity, and will run to get the banana. Again the other four will jump on him and they will beat him up, trying to prevent him from going to the banana. The interesting part of this is that the previous newcomer, the monkey who got beaten up just a few minutes ago, will take part in the punishment without even knowing why! He does not understand why they are beating up the newcomer, but he is joining in. Anyway, the experiment is repeated until all five original monkeys have been replaced. In the end, none of them goes for the banana. If you were to ask them why, they would say, 'We get beaten up!' which is a very valid reason for not going for the banana. And if you were to ask them, why do you get beaten up, what would they say? They do not know why, as they have never been soaked with water. But, thinking about human beings, they are not very good at saying, 'I don't know.' So what would they say instead? 'You just have to accept it. It's company policy, okay?' That is how they will justify their behaviour.

So that is what sacred cows are; company policies that no one knows why they are there and why they are still being followed – 'We have always done things this way'. Of course, not all of these rules and policies are wrong; they just go unquestioned. And when do we normally start asking questions and challenging the way we do things? When we are in crisis mode, hardly ever before. Who would not agree that it is a good idea to visit a doctor on a regular basis to identify any serious illness before it takes a hold? But how many of us actually do it?

Critical success factors

So this story has given you some idea of what strategic innovation actually is, and why, despite everyone agreeing that it is a good thing, it is difficult to actually make it happen. Your organisation is most likely to be open to innovation if you can achieve the following:

- Create a culture that allows people to experiment. Innovation requires that you take away the fear of failure. Employees must know that it is possible to fail without being punished. Once this happens people will reach out and try to maximise their creativity. If you want innovation, you are not going to get it simply because you ask people to innovate. You must create the right environment for them to innovate.
- Incentivise entrepreneurs. A thousand entrepreneurs try to start a company. Only 10 of them succeed, 990 fail. If the odds of success are so low, why would anybody try? Most of them do it to get rich! But it is also about ownership. Ask yourself how many millionaires do you have in your company? Staff are not going to experiment because they love experimenting. Maybe some will, but the majority will not. You have to give them an incentive to experiment and innovate. Make them millionaires. If they produce £100 million through one idea for you, give them £1 million.
- Allow ideas to be offered more than once or twice. The entrepreneur who thought of starting Cisco had to go to 76 venture capitalists before he got funds to start the company. In your company, how many opportunities does an entrepreneur have to pitch for his or her idea? The majority give their people, one, two, maybe three chances to sell their idea and get some financing, which of course means that most ideas never get off the ground.
- In order to help people in your organisation to challenge convention, the status quo and your sacred cows, try to create a sense of urgency or a positive crisis that helps to open people up towards change.

The role of communication

'We always have teams working on how to make communication work better.'

Costas has introduced some starting points from which leaders can begin to think about how to create a radical shift in the positioning of their organisation. He has also emphasised the difficulty we face when trying to implement change. The flow of information within an organisation and how communication is managed can be a major contributor to the successful implementation of change.

In fact, much of the management literature, be it on the management of change, innovation, or success and failure in new product development, highlights communication as one of the key ingredients for success. Communication enables people to understand that they have to change, why they are asked to do certain things, how they are to do them, and how what they do fits in with the bigger picture. Generally, if people are not given the option to understand why they are asked to do certain things, they tend to become resentful, are not likely to emotionally buy into decisions and will end up 'just doing their job'. For example, one interviewee commented, 'Scientists here are quite upset when their ideas are rejected; they just don't understand why.'

Alongside communication should go the provision of training, which helps employees to understand the change and enable them to behave in a different way. Ideally, such training should be given before employees are expected to use different approaches and display different behaviours. This can not only reassure them and improve acceptance, it is also a clear signal that change really is required and that management appreciates that this requires effort and is doing what it can to support employees in their efforts to change.

There is another reason why management should pay increased attention to communication during times of change, and this is that people may be uncertain and nervous about what is going to happen. In the absence of information, people will invent their own truth, and rumours will start.[4]

---

[4] *Company Image and Reality* by David Bernstein, first published in 1984, paints a convincing picture of why companies ought to take the initiative on communication. The 1986 edition was published by Rinehart and Winston, Eastbourne, UK.

Depending on the nature of the rumours, they might entice people into certain actions and behaviours that are not in the best interests of the company. For example, one interviewee pointed out, 'At the first sign of rumours, people start to leave.' But who are these people? Most likely not the ones the company might want to lose but those who can easily find a job elsewhere – the best. Only open, honest and timely communication can help to prevent the best people from leaving.

There can, of course, be one difficulty. In times of uncertainty, senior managers may not be quite sure themselves about the direction the company will follow. As experienced by one interviewee, 'Vision and strategy are clear at board level but not below because of the current level of uncertainty – there is the possibility of a big acquisition on the horizon as well as impending changes in management, which makes our board hesitant to communicate what is happening.' But even admitting that some major changes are imminent may be better than allowing rumours to spread. However, if a lack of communication is detrimental to innovation success, so too are frequent changes in the company's overall direction. 'If radical changes in direction are too frequent, changing what was an important project today into one that is irrelevant tomorrow, people will become cynical and reluctant to keep changing – a new set of rules and orders might be just around the corner, so why waste energy on trying to adapt to the most recent set?'

Good communication is also a key building block for developing a strong company culture. Stories and insights that are passed between members of an organisation help develop a mutually shared language and heritage. On how to aid the spreading of stories and creating a shared understanding, one interviewee commented, 'To help communication and team building we have introduced shadowing projects.' (A shadowing project involves people from one department observing people from another department in their daily routine to get a better understanding of the work and issues they are dealing with.)

Another issue that has become increasingly important, particularly since the emergence of e-mail and intranets, is the choice of medium for communicating. There is hardly anyone who is not complaining about being inundated with e-mails. Information overload becomes increasingly frustrating and often leads people to ignore e-mails altogether.

'We do a lot of communicating. For example, we have business TV sessions across the whole organisation. If the topic is quite specific and therefore only relevant to a limited audience, we use written documentation. Presentations are arranged on broader topics. And we also use circulars. Often initiatives are supported by a helpdesk or phone line. We also use conferences a lot. E-mail? There is such an overload that it is better to go back to the telephone and one-to-one communication. All this is coordinated by a central team that looks at all internal communications and PR. Customer communications are dealt with from within the marketing department but from one area to ensure consistency.'

When it comes to important information, people prefer face-to-face communication. Acknowledging this, one company banned internal e-mail, instead requiring their staff to seek face-to-face communication with their colleagues. It is here that the physical work environment can play a facilitating role. The deliberate design of meeting spaces around coffee machines can provide a focal point for informal and spontaneous meetings and exchange of information. Of course the appropriateness of 'no internal e-mail' will depend entirely on the size of the organisation, or rather, the part of the organisation in which the use of e-mail is restricted.

The findings on best practice companies presented in the DTI/CBI's 1995 report, 'Winning', are still valid today: 'Communication takes place in many directions throughout the organisation, and is always a two-way process. Senior management frequently gets out to meet employees by walking around the organisation and talking with individuals, encouraging the team concept of "us" rather than the divisive "them" and "us".' What is also worth noting is that best-practice companies do not tend to rely on one or two media for communicating. They tend to choose a whole range of different approaches to ensure that they reach each audience in the most appropriate way (see also box below).

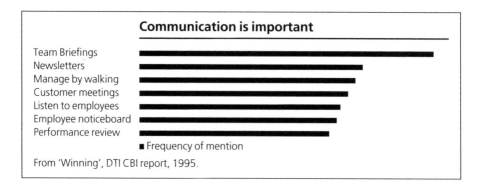

Communication is important

	Frequency of mention
Team Briefings	
Newsletters	
Manage by walking	
Customer meetings	
Listen to employees	
Employee noticeboard	
Performance review	

From 'Winning', DTI CBI report, 1995.

The best channels for communicating will, of course, also depend on the company context. One company with a strong marketing focus, for example, commented, 'We capture best practice on video – this is very powerful and the rule is, no video is allowed to be longer than seven minutes. A lot of our people have to watch videos anyway so it has become the most important medium for sharing best practice. We release about two per month.'

Not communicating, communicating late or with ambiguous content represents the worst practice in communication. If someone states, 'There is not too much clarity about who has the right to make what decision', there is clearly a problem.

While no future challenge with regard to communication was mentioned explicitly, the biggest future challenge in the area of communication is probably how to identify the best means for communicating and how to ensure that important information reaches people rather than getting lost in the jungle of information overload.

Best-practice communication includes:

- communication takes place in many directions throughout the organisation;
- communication is always a two-way process;
- senior management frequently walk around the organisation to talk with individuals;
- senior management create an inclusive atmosphere;
- use a variety of media for communicating.

The issue of measurement

'If it [innovation] can be measured, people will take it seriously.'

The question of how to measure innovation has been raised by many interviewees – but only a few were beginning to see some answers emerging. As there was little insight from the interviews that would help the reader address the question, this section will draw on a recently published book by Tim Ambler, *Marketing and the Bottom Line – The New Metrics of Corporate Wealth*, which devotes an entire chapter to *innovation metrics*.

Ambler starts the chapter by stating that the most difficult area for measurement is innovation. Nearly all respondents to a survey he conducted rated innovation as a top priority but also one which their assessment systems did not really address. But he also points out that, 'The concern with monitoring innovation health is not universal. Among those we talked to, the outstanding innovators do it so naturally that they were amazed by our questions. To them, innovation health is the oxygen in the air: you breathe it, not measure it. At the other extreme, the stick-in-the-muds, sometimes those who now hold the power, see change as a threat. They will not consider innovation, still less measure it.' I believe that measuring is important if one wants to track change, when one is learning and wants to keep track of progress.

One problem with innovation metrics highlighted by Ambler is, 'Too many indicators are chosen because they are easy to measure rather than because they give vital signs of innovation health.' In addition, companies tend to add to their existing set of metrics rather than starting afresh, selecting a few, meaningful ones. Again, Ambler points out that 'Counting innovations is less useful than measuring the strategic, cultural and process indicators of a firm's innovation health.' Given his criticism of existing practice, his list of recommended innovation metrics is short, as shown in Table 3.1.

He continues, 'Awareness of and commitment to innovation goals can be measured directly from staff surveys, as can the general question "are the resources adequate for these goals?" On the other hand, they can also be seen as summary or index metrics built up from a greater number of more detailed questions, such as the adequacy of finances for particular innovations.'

Table 3.1: Tim Ambler's innovation metrics shortlist

Strategy	Awareness of goals (vision)
	Commitment to goals (vision)
	Active innovation support
	Resource adequacy
Culture	Appetite for learning
	Freedom to fail
Outcomes	Number of initiatives in process
	Number of innovations launched
	% revenue due to launches during last three years

Table 3.2: Innovation metrics by Collins and Smith (1999)

	Lagging	Real Time	Leading	Learning
Stakeholder strategies	Gross contribution of new products	Net present value (NPV) of idea portfolio		
Processes		Milestones completed on time		Take-up rate of new processes
Resources			External alliances being pursued	
Culture/ organisation	Staff turnover rate		Innovation climate	Level of enquiry

Another metric companies would like to see is one on creativity. Ambler comments, 'If we had a satisfactory metric for creativity *per se*, it would have been included.' However, there are a few tests available that might be helpful. One is the *innovation potential indicator* developed by Fiona Patterson, and another is the test on styles of creativity, based on the earlier work of Kirton.[5,6]

A further framework on innovation metrics has been developed by Collins and Smith (1999) and is presented in Table 3.2.

Finally, the last set of possible innovation measures stems from the 1993 DTI/CBI report '*Innovation – the best practice*' (see Table 3.3).

As ever, there is no hard and fast rule for fixing the problem, and obviously the best treatment to use depends on the firm's symptoms, but Ambler provides a list of options of how to start, (see box on p. 81).

Best practice in innovation measurement can be summarised as:

- Select a short list of metrics meaningful to innovation, for example, related to strategy, culture and outcome.
- Choose innovation measures that are tailored to the organisation's needs. For example, 'Transplanting 3M's metrics into a firm without a similar strategy, culture and processes will be a waste of time.'

---

5   The *innovation potential indicator (IPI)* was developed by Dr Fiona Patterson, and is available through Oxford Psychologists Press.

6   E.g. *The way People Approach Problems*, by M. J. Kirton (1980), *Planned Innovation*, **3**, 51–54.

Table 3.3: The DTI's innovation metrics

Product innovation (absolute, trend, versus competitors)	- Number of new product ideas, product enhancement ideas evaluated last year - Percentage sales/profit from product introduced in the last 3 (5) years - Percentage sales/profit from products with significant enhancements in the last 3 (5) years - Product planning horizon – years, number of product generations - Market share – global, EC, UK
Product development (versus plan, versus existing products, absolute trends, versus competition)	- Time to market – average concept to launch time; time for each phase, for example concept, design, initial product launch; average overrun; percentage of product overrunning planned finish date; average time between product enhancements, redesign - Product performance – product cost; technical performance; quality; return on sales; market share - Design performance – manufacturing cost; manufacturability; testability
Process innovation (versus plan, absolute, trend versus competition)	- Process parameters, cost, quality, work in progress (WIP) levels, lead time and so on. Performance versus competitors; percentage improvement over 1, 3 years - Installation lead times – start to trouble-free working; percentage of new processes/process innovations considered successful - Number of new processes, significant process enhancements in year - Continuous improvement – number of improvement suggestions per employee; percentage implemented; average annual improvement in process parameters (quality, cost, lead time, WIP, reliability, downtime, capability) - Progress to lean production WIP, lead time, quality
Technology acquisition (versus plan, absolute, trend, versus competition)	- Number of licences in/out over last three years - Percentage of R&D projects that lead to successful new or enhanced products or processes, licences (percentage of R&D spend and percentage of number projects that have been successful) - R&D/ technology acquisition cost per new product - Failed projects – percentage number of projects - Percentage of projects killed off too late (after substantial expenditure) - Number of patents over last three years
Leadership (absolute, trend, versus competition)	- Number/percentage of members from product development/technical function – on main board; on subsidiary/divisional board - Percentage of employees aware of, sharing, company, innovation policies and values (from employee attitude survey) - Number of pages in annual report devoted to innovation/technology
Resourcing innovation (absolute, trend, versus competition)	- Percentage of – projects delayed/cancelled because of lack of human resources; personnel in product development who have worked in more than one or two functions; project delayed/cancelled due to lack of funding - Systems and tools - Percentage of designers/engineers with access to CAD screens; products of CAD database; products produced on processes with SPC; teams using specific techniques (for example, experimental design methods, failure mode and effect analysis); projects where specific tools are applied; (R&D) team leaders trained in design for manufacture; development projects using BS 5750 (now superseded by ISO 9000) certified processes

- Major audit. If the status quo is a long way from the desired state, a full-scale investigation of strategy, culture and process issues may be needed, involving the sampling of a broad range of measures.
- Removing obvious disablers. Taking positive action to improve innovation is much more difficult than finding and removing the most visible obstructions. Junior managers will know what they are – probably process.
- Creating or revising the corporate goals and, within those, the specific goals for innovation. At the least, they must show whether the intention is more and better of the same and/or radical change, and, if so, in what direction? The board needs to review the current level of innovation and take a view on quantity and quality.
- What will success look like? Setting benchmarks against which performance will be measured.
- Major internal communication programme to achieve awareness and commitment to goals and benchmarks.

Choosing metrics because they are easy to measure rather than because they give meaningful results and piling new metrics on top of existing ones is certainly the wrong thing to do.

Anchor points

- Provide a clear vision and strategy for innovation that is known and understood throughout the organisation.
- Ensure that the vision provides stretch – but is also attainable.
- Identify innovation threads that build on the areas the company wants to focus on, and ensure that every single project you undertake addresses these.
- Start to fish where the fish are. In other words, know that you are likely to get some benefits from your innovation before you invest in it.
- It is important to recognise company-specific constraints when designing the innovation strategy – not as a limiting factor but to understand which actions are necessary to achieve the goal.
- Make a conscious decision about the level of innovation the company is aspiring to and ensure that the appropriate systems and procedures are in place to support it.
- If you want to innovate at the strategic level, think about the 'who', 'what' and 'how' of your business.
- Clear and frequent communication and engagement of staff are key to achieving success.

- The desire to measure innovation has to be treated carefully, and managers should ensure that measures of innovation performance are appropriate for what the company wants to achieve. Just adding to an existing set of metrics is the worst possible solution – and also remember, what gets measured gets fiddled!

Riding the wave – how to make it happen

Once the vision and strategy are in place, systems, processes and procedures must be developed to deliver them. This chapter will take a closer look at how to manage ideas and their creators, and processes and new product development in particular. It will then explore different approaches for infusing innovation into organisations.

Where ideas come from

Messages from companies on idea generation seem to be conflicting. Some say they have more ideas than they can cope with, while others are still trying to find systems that will allow them to collect ideas more systematically. But perhaps it is not that much of a contradiction. A common thread seems to be a struggle with how to identify the right ideas. Chapter 3 suggested that it helps to have a clear innovation strategy which ensures idea generation activities have a focus. There are many different ways to approach idea generation, and these range from the random (through suggestion schemes), to the specific (brainstorming around a particular topic). It is worth reiterating that the method chosen should be aligned with the objective to be achieved.

For a taster of what innovative companies actually do, here are some findings from a study among members of the US-based Innovation-Network (www.thinksmart.com).[1] The questionnaire-based study was conducted in 1997/8, to address the following questions:

---

[1] Note that the sample is self-selecting; for example, one can assume that companies joining an innovation network already have a strong awareness of interest in innovation and could therefore be considered a best-practice sample.

- What methods do innovative companies use to generate new ideas?
- How do these companies encourage and reward innovation?
- How many new products and processes have these companies implemented?

The most relevant findings are shown in the box below.

- 33% of respondents reported that they use a formal process to collect ideas. A similar number reported that they have an ideation or innovation committee for promoting, collecting and screening ideas and improvements.
- It seems that most ideas are generated through customer analysis and brainstorming; for process-related ideas benchmarking was frequently used.
- Most ideas were generated internally by senior management, followed by research and development and sales/marketing; ideas for processes were mainly generated by people within R&D.
- While only 33% stated that they have formal processes to collect ideas, about 75% said that they use creativity sessions.
- Most frequently stated methods for encouraging and supporting innovation were: widespread commitment to creating customer value; small, autonomous project teams on a mission and an environment of mutual trust and respect.
- Informal praise by senior management followed by moderate compensation were most frequently mentioned methods of reward.

The use of idea generation or suggestion schemes seems to be a source of frustration for many companies. Many reported that they tend to get a large quantity of suggestions but that they are dissatisfied with the quality of these ideas. In one company it was suggested that the lack of ideas was due to the fact that no financial rewards were given. However, there is some controversy about the effectiveness of financial rewards in eliciting innovative ideas. In their book *Corporate Creativity: How Innovation and Improvement Actually Happen*, (1997) Alan G. Robinson and Sam Stern advocate the view that financial rewards are actually counter-productive – and there is increasing evidence to support this. An example of an idea generation scheme that seems to work is shown opposite.

Time is frequently mentioned as a barrier to innovation and concept generation, but one interviewee commented: 'People complain that there is no formal time to do things. People say, if only I had time – but I don't believe that. I believe people with the right attitude are not stopped by that and, at least initially, do it in their own time.' While this is true in many cases, relying on this approach will mean that many good ideas will fall by the wayside. How many good ideas for incremental and

Idea generation that works – the Innovation Fund

The underlying principle is, 'no risk, no money'. A company representative commented, 'This is a significant change in our culture and in the first year, about 30% of applications emphasised the low or no risk factor of the idea – we rejected them for that reason. We wanted to make sure people understood that we were truly looking for different, more risky projects.' The fund is non-bureaucratic. Initially all that is required is a two-page form, available either as hard copy or on the intranet, which will be turned around in two days. There are a number of set criteria – known by everyone – against which the suggestions are evaluated.

- Business and strategic fit.
- Substantial potential benefit to business – it has to be big.
- Not business as usual, think high risk.
- Needs to have a senior business sponsor.
- Potential substantial technology capability acquisition.

Other elements taken into consideration are:

- commitment, enthusiasm, vision (use virtual groups, wide range of backgrounds and so on);
- client/customer involvement (think early about realisation and implementation);
- supplier support/participation.

The funding process involves four stages:

1. Enrolment (that's when a senior business person's support is required).
2. Concept – developing the idea (what support would be needed to get to market).
3. Demonstration.
4. Pilot.

From the fourth stage, 50% of costs are to be carried by a business unit – for example, there is tapered funding – but these rules are not written in stone; people can jump to any stage. All suggestions are stored electronically and projects that have won awards are placed on the company web site.

radical improvements have you had, and how often have you managed to realise them? If there is no system for collecting ideas and no one dedicated to assessing and evaluating them, there is not much chance of getting that one big idea that really makes a difference.

Although idea generation is seen to be relatively straightforward, the real issue lies with managing the volume of ideas generated and trying to spot the good ones. The CBI Innovation Trend survey, published in February 2001, came to the same conclusion: 'Idea generation may not be a problem for most, but how effective are companies in picking up these ideas, recognising their worth and turning them into innovations?' Our survey and innovation seminars suggested that there might be more of a problem here, so we asked a number of questions to address this. Fewer than 40% of companies said that they had a formal process for monitoring and evaluating innovation and only 56% said that they reviewed past ideas regularly to spot new opportunities. Companies using IT systems to help keep track of ideas were even less common – just 15%.

Too many ideas generally lead to problems with managing resources. 'We are not selective enough about the number of projects we take forward. There are lots of good ideas from all our operating companies but there is not really a process for resource management. We start a lot of projects because the early stages are generally not very resource-intensive, and this gives a false sense of security. But the problem starts when resourcing levels go up; this is why we need ruthless gatekeepers.' This is why it is so important to have a clear innovation strategy, as this will help to select those projects that are likely to yield the best results. And when managing resources it makes sense to manage them across the entire portfolio. Resource constraints make the ability to terminate projects particularly important. One interviewee commented: 'We tend to let projects drag on even though it is quite clear that they are not going anywhere.' It is also very important to keep looking and checking after the launch.

When terminating projects it is important not to forget the human dimension. For those involved, it may mean giving up their ideas or dreams. To minimise the trauma, it is necessary for them to understand why this is the case. This is another important reason why companies should spend time and effort in making their product and innovation strategy explicit and known to everyone. If people know and understand why some projects are chosen above others they are more likely to accept it and tend not to take it personally. Also, any project termination should be viewed as a learning experience and this is something that should be embedded in the organisation's culture.

'You have to ensure that there is no witch-hunt in the case of failure.'

What people believed worked well was experimentation with selected ideas instead of lots of ideas. For successful idea generation, the willingness to experiment was seen to be much more important than the generation of vast quantities of ideas. One person commented, 'What I observe in innovative organisations is a willingness to consider alternatives. You will not find a single-line projection; the development of alternative ideas is actively encouraged and supported.' This is something that the traditional innovation funnel does not address. The traditional funnel recommends generating as many ideas as possible and then narrowing them down to a manageable level. Experimentation involves generating ideas, selecting one or two and then exploring how these can be optimised.

Experimentation is not only good at the idea generation stage. Later in the project, too, a taste for experimentation is usually beneficial, as one interview pointed out: 'We work on the 100% right theory. We just do not have an attitude of experimentation. People who do are able to bring products to market much faster.' However, the degree to which experimentation in the marketplace is feasible will depend on the specific context. If there are any health or safety implications, or if an imperfect product would result in a loss of reputation, using the marketplace as a test bed may not be a good idea.

Taking ideas and moving them forward can be a problem. Companies seem to go through spurts of idea generation with no real follow-up. One company reported, 'We had a series of brainstorming sessions to instil creativity into the company about three or four years ago. Within a cross-functional team we developed about 400 ideas, which in the end we brought down to 10 key ideas. But we did not prioritise them – and nothing has happened since.' Other interviewees commented along similar lines:

- 'We are good with coming up with ideas but not at narrowing them down and following through.'
- 'The company is good at generating ideas and bringing them to market, though often over-engineered and late.'
- 'To scientists, things are either black or white, which can be a problem in new product development and getting products out; they want to get things 100% right first.'
- 'We are not completer-finishers, it is all excitement at the front end.'

This confirms that innovation cannot work when it is just a task 'we do on Monday mornings'. It has to become second nature, a natural habit like driving a car where we no longer have to think about the actions we are taking, we are just doing it.

Another problem that can occur, particularly in engineering-driven organisations, is that projects become driven by technical possibilities rather than consumer needs. To quote one of the interviewees, 'We can lose focus on what the customer wants. The problem itself becomes the interesting thing. People think, fantastic, we can do that, so let's!'

Another question that often comes up when idea generation is discussed is, do we have the right people? Many managers call for more creative people, though they seem to dread them at the same time, considering them to be difficult to manage. And one interviewee recalls, 'We are very keen to bring in more creative people – but once we have got them on board we are not quite sure what to do with them!'

> 'Creative people are awkward to manage. In the 1980s Ben & Jerry ran their business hands on. People say it was the most exciting time, but also a real nightmare as it had no focus. Large organisations need a ruthless person behind the creative.'

Then there is the other school of thought which says that everyone is creative, it's just the degree to which we are creative that varies. It is undeniably true that there are some people who seem to have more creative energy than others, who seem to be bursting with ideas and suggestions all the time, and who are never satisfied with the status quo. It is the latter category Gareth Jones, formerly Head of Human Resources at the BBC, refers to in the following vignette.

Freak Waves – make the most of them

Gareth Jones, formerly Head of Human Resources at the BBC

In their drive for innovation, organisations today declare, we need more creative people – or 'krazies' as I sometimes call them. The problem is that once they have got them, then more often than not they will not know what to do with them because they are often difficult, unruly and very tense individuals. This places them firmly in the management problem box, which leads many organisations to leave them alone, or encourage them to leave. But to get the most from your krazies, you need to manage them. How should you go about it? Let us start by looking in turn at what we know about innovative individuals, innovative teams, and innovative cultures and processes.

Spotting the krazies

What sets the krazies aside from the rest of your staff? Four things:

1. They tend to demand high levels of autonomy. Creative people like to be left alone, unfettered by the mainstream organisational processes that bind everyone else. So they probably do not need a handbook that describes the company's innovation processes and they certainly do not want to receive vast tomes on 'Innovating the Corporation X Way'.

2. They have low structure needs; they do not need to have everything spelled out explicitly. They rather welcome uncertainty and ambiguity, and they thrive on it. People with high structure needs will think they are disorganised and behave in a chaotic and anarchic way but they just have a different way of dealing with things. These differences in level of structure needs may be a major source of organisational tension. They need to be openly acknowledged and discussed.

3. They are likely to flip between obsession and indifference – which tends to make them not exactly brilliant team players. They prefer to be on the edge of the team providing insights when you least expect it. So just as the team is about to reach a decision, they will say, 'James, why are we in the food business?' If the team responds to their ideas they become wildly engaged. If not, they may sulk. So they flip-flop between indifference and obsession. And by the way, not all the ideas they have are good ones. They may be creative ideas, but they're not always good. These are the people who dreamt of mountaineering holidays – in the Netherlands. This obsession drives the krazies to not only work long hours but also continue with their ideas outside of the working day – work is the only thing you will ever find them talk about. To give you an example, I did a lot of work with Glaxo, which I would consider to be an organisation full of obsessive people, working very long hours. When you go out with them at the end of a long day you would think they would sit down to dinner and talk about their families or holidays or football. Wrong. Instead, they talk about their work, their latest insights,

and how important it all is. Such obsessive behaviour may appear strange, but it can result in amazing innovations. For example, one guy's research into vomit centres allowed Glaxo to develop a drug called Zofran. This drug has revolutionised the treatment of some forms of breast cancer because it enables women to have much larger doses of chemotherapy without it killing them. And these people generally do not care much about for which organisation they are working – they are interested in their work, full stop. The organisation, from their perspective, exists to fund their obsessions. This leads to the last point.

4. They do not like the idea of either being managed or becoming managers themselves.

This last point is worth investigating further, as understanding what to do with your krazies is critical in determining whether you reap or destroy the value that their creativity could bring to your organisation.

Kultivating the krazies

Conventional wisdom suggests that krazies are a problem. But they are not. They are where you get much of your innovation from. The problem is that if they do not want to be managed and certainly do not want to be managers, what do you do with them? Let us look at possible scenarios.

1. The worst possible approach is to take the best R&D scientist, for example our vomit centre man referred to earlier, and make him the manager. Organisations do this all the time, and they lose twice: they lose their most innovative scientist and they get a lousy manager. They take the best salesperson and make them sales manager. Again, everyone loses.

2. A better way is to bring in a great manager from somewhere else. Imagine now that you are the top research scientist at Glaxo-SmithKline and we need someone to run your centre. It is decided to bring in a great manager from Tesco. The questions the scientists will fire at the new manager are likely to include:

'Where did you get your PhD from?' 'When did you last publish in the *Journal of Pharmacology*?' It is very unlikely that the guy from Tesco would be able to answer these questions in the affirmative, so they have a serious credibility problem before they have even started. But there is a way this approach might work. If the new manager starts the relationship by saying, 'Listen, I am aware that I do not understand your business. I am just going to keep the suits off your back so you can get on with you work,' they might just get away with it.

3. The best one is the most difficult because it requires long-term planning. Within your R&D personnel there will be some people who are great scientists as well as having some leadership and management potential. Identifying them early and giving them highly sensitive and focused development experiences is the best way to allow them to shine, while retaining their passions. But identifying them early on is key. Let us suppose we have got 600 people in our R&D function. If we end up with 10 great executives, we can beat the competition. This solution is definitely the one that promises the best results. Spot the great person in your music company who could one day run a record label, and you have a winner.

Krazies alone are not enough

Cultivation of your krazies is of course not enough. Innovation is nearly always a collective process and it only happens in a supportive environment.

The first thing to realise is that a creative idea does not come out of a vacuum. Take Darwin, for example. We often think of Darwin as a genius who saw things that no one else saw. Careful inspection of Darwin's correspondence shows that there were lots of other people around at the same time who were struggling with the theory of evolution. The same is true of Chomsky's breakthrough in transformational grammar and linguistics. So when we actually look inside organisations it is usually groups of people who bounce ideas off each other, cover each other's weaknesses, and by building on and developing an idea drive through innovation. What is interesting about this is that the teams are largely self-selecting. The truth is, we work best with people that we enjoy working with. It would be really nice if we could just throw very talented people together and say, 'Fine! Go on! You will be a great team!' The reality is very different.

So what does an innovative organisation look like?

First, they promote diversity. Creative and innovative teams are characterised by diverse people with different strengths and weaknesses, different backgrounds, different experiences. Creativity increases with the diversity of teams and declines with sameness. Diversity also means that highly innovative organisations can be rather edgy because creative people are pretty passionate about what they are doing. Diversity and passion stimulate debate and ensure questioning, which helps innovation. But are organisations good about recruiting for diversity? Most of them choose the same kind of person again and again, leading to a uniform workforce. What they should do is bring in a few people that are decidedly different, people that are like the grit in an oyster. One reason why companies go for sameness is that people enjoy the company of people who are like themselves; another is that managing diversity is much more difficult than managing homogeneity.

Second, they accept volatility and embrace failure. If you were a great car manufacturer trying to launch a new, highly innovative sports car, you would not have just one design team working on it. You would want to have as wide a span of innovation as possible to allow you to generate a number of alternative designs. Some will inevitably fail, but this is why creative organisations encourage failure. If you do not have failures, you cannot possibly have successes. This is true of any innovative organisation. Wouldn't it be great if the pharmaceutical industry only ever developed blockbuster drugs? Not possible. Wouldn't life in the music industry be easy if all the singles ever released became hit records? Again impossible. If a big music company launching 12 000 new products a year has 500 big successes, it would be doing really well. But it means that it has 11 500 failures! That is what you have to embrace and accept. And this is where most companies are inconsistent; they want innovation that makes a difference and yet what do they tell people? 'Jones! I want you to be as innovative as you can to launch this new product. Are you clear about that? Are you up to it? Good! But one thing, whatever you do, do not fail!' Utterly contradictory! If you want people who are innovative and entrepreneurial, they will sometimes fail, as sure as night follows day.

Third, there is much talk about an innovation culture, which is surely true, but let me make two points. First, it is more about removing obstacles to innovation than it is about encouraging innovation. Obstacles include

- too much control;
- segmentation – a lack of collaboration and cooperation between departments and functions;
- high levels of negative uncertainty – particularly when people are worried about their jobs;
- secrecy – no one knows about the strategy or important projects that are going on;
- short-termism;
- the reluctance to embrace innovation because it is difficult to manage.

On the other hand, things that keep innovation going include

- a shared long-term vision;
- a commitment to common goals;
- leadership at many levels – and note that there is an important difference between leadership and management (the former is about inspiration, the latter about efficiency);
- effective teamwork;
- lots of communication across functions and levels of hierarchy;
- restlessness;
- high standards which ensures people keep looking for new and better ways of doing things

- cognitive conflict – the sort of conflict where no one feels personally rejected
- fun – who does not achieve better results when having fun?
- finally, market pressure. There is nothing like a proper threat to the organisation to galvanise people into action.

Second, there is not just one innovation culture; there are lots of different types of culture that can inspire and support innovation. Many managers are looking for the one right answer – but culture is more complicated than that. A model of culture that my friend and colleague Rob Goffee, who is Professor of Organisational Behaviour at the London Business School and I, have developed (see box) might help you navigate through your culture and use it to manage innovation.[2]

Culture

The model of culture has two basic ingredients, sociability and solidarity. Sociability is, in essence, friendliness. This suggests that people enjoy working together, they tend to have fun and they are generally more creative. It works because friendships are not based upon careful calculations of who has done what for who. Solidarity is a measure of how you get things done. So, comments like 'I don't like Peter, but he is the best store manager in Dixons' would be typical in an organisation with high solidarity. Such organisations have a real shared interest in what has to be done – focus and efficiency. Combining these two dimensions leads to four possible cultures:

- *Networked cultures (high sociability, low solidarity) – Unilever. Unashamedly marvellously friendly. Go to the Unilever Training Centre at Kingston. It has a 24-hour free bar. What do people do there? Drink? No, they talk. They drink a little, but mainly they talk.*
- *Fragmented cultures (low sociability, low solidarity) – Harvard. The guy who runs Harvard says it's like herding cats. It's got 60 great professors, who'd rather not talk to each other!*
- *Mercenary cultures (high solidarity, low sociability) – Mars. A Mars executive used to say, 'We were all working very well together and then all of a sudden one of us just disappears!' Gone! They missed their quarterly targets.*
- *Communal cultures (high sociability, high solidarity) – Hewlett-Packard, Johnson & Johnson. Live the vision.*

Innovation is kick started by different things in each of the four cultures. In the communal culture it is triggered by teamwork and participation, in the fragmented culture it is triggered by cognitive conflict, in the mercenary culture it is triggered by market pressure, and in the networked organisation it is triggered by informality and

---

[2]   Goffee, R. and Jones, G. (1998) *The Character of a Corporation: How Your Company's Culture can Make or Break Your Business.* Harper Business.

fun. The processes which support innovation are different in each culture too.

Network	Communal
• *unplanned connections* • *diversity* • *slack* • *radical* • *slow implementation*	• *complex* • *long-term* • *innovation all over* • *visionary leadership*
Fragmented	**Mercenary**
• *individuals* • *creative and completers* • *slack through autonomy* • *recruitment is key*	• *planned, measured* • *incremental* • *separated* • *no slack* • *fast implementation*

A point worth noting is that each culture can turn negative, and what this means for innovation in a networked culture is that people talk to each other, not the customer. In the communal culture it means that people preach to the customer about the next innovation. In the fragmented culture it is about serving yourself, not the customer, and in a mercenary culture it would mean focusing on the known competition (and ignoring anyone who comes in from the sidelines).

Critical success factors

So, some critical success factors for kultivating your krazies are:

1. Diversity is an asset, not a problem, so do not homogenise your innovators. One of the things that organisations do more than anything else is to knock the rough edges off people. This kills individuality. If we want our staff to be innovative, we need to cherish their individuality. We need to allow people to be different.
2. Give careful customised development to your innovators (krazies) and avoid the sheepdip approach, as this kills creativity.
3. Recruit people who would rather not work for you. They are the ones that challenge the system and are able to think outside your company box.

4. Use measurable outcomes. Otherwise you may lose creative activity with little impact on the business.

5. Use hot teams. Usually self-selected, they are likely to be passionate and edgy.

6. Do not have a department of innovation. Let innovation loose. If you control it, you will lose it.

The role of market research

'There is a conflict between asking the customer what he wants and wanting to offer something different. Consumers tend to want what they know: if people had been asked whether they want a car they would probably have said they would like faster horses'.

Market research is probably used by most organisations to provide a reality check for the ideas their 'krazies' have come up with. However, while the literature on success and failure in new product development highlights the importance of aligning new products with the needs of consumers, it seems that current market research practices are less than satisfactory.

> 'Market research is not good at telling us what customers really want.'

One reason for the current problems may be that market research is more often than not conducted by an external agency. This means that the information the company receives has been filtered, which can be a problem.

> 'You generally only get a summary of the research but researchers do not necessarily have the knowledge and understanding of the market to interpret the results correctly.'

One car manufacturer, having just finished the prototype of its new small car, commissioned a market research agency to find out what consumers thought about it. When the research report came back, the engineers were surprised to read that consumers were not happy with the engine's performance. It was only a small car and the engine was already quite powerful. But still, give the consumer what the consumer wants. So the engineers re-worked the engine, and the revised model was market-tested again. But still, the results said that consumers wanted more power. This circle was repeated a few times until the engineers threw their hands up in despair and said, 'This cannot be true! Let us speak to the researchers or, even better, let us be present when they conduct their research.' When the engineers were present and could actually observe the consumer and talk to them directly they realised that it was not the *real* power of the engine that was the issue, but the *perceived* power. What consumers were missing was the feeling of being gently

> 'An electronic consumer goods company had invited customers in to find out whether they might like colourful appliances. Everyone seemed enthusiastic. When participants were offered a choice of a coloured or grey radio as a reward they almost all chose the grey one.'

pushed back into the seat when accelerating – something that could be fixed easily, quickly and cheaply by changing the upholstery.

The lesson from this (true) story is that, if you rely on people who do not understand your business and your market, you will not get the answers that help you design a product that consumers will really want to buy. Or as Tim Ambler likes to put it, 'Market research is like a lamp post, it can either illuminate or prop up a drunk.'

During a recent masterclass at the London Business School[3] it was remarked that 65% of market research in one particular car company was undertaken to confirm what was already known rather than to find out what the consumer really wanted. The problem is, people tend to hear what they want to hear and if it does not fit in with their plans they tend to ignore the message. The disconnect between market research and market reality is confirmed by companies which found that even though they had involved consumers in the generation of ideas, and had sought their feedback throughout the development process, consumers failed to purchase their product. There are two reasons for this. Either the product was not really wanted, or the price was too high. This problem seems to be particularly severe in the service industry.

A further problem with most market research practices is that they are not very effective at identifying latent customer needs. But understanding these helps companies come up with radical and novel solutions. One interviewee pointed out, 'Research should help understand

---

[3] '*Creating a market-driven organisation – Staying close to customers and ahead of competitors,*' by George Day and Patrick Barwise, 7–9 March 2001.

consumer aspiration and what stands in the way of achieving it; for example, the microwave. People do not have as much time to prepare meals any more but no one would have suggested nuking food to heat it up!'

The combination of the failure of current market research practices to deliver expected results and the misinterpretation of the results by external research agencies has led companies to reconsider their approach. As one company explained, 'The starting point for innovation is to connect with the customer. This has been a weakness over the past four to five years; we were too removed from the consumers. We are now asking our people to go and talk to consumers where they spend their lives – in bars, on sport fields, in shopping centres – to find out how they actually live. We can already see that where we understand the consumer more, we have greater success.'

Another described their approach as follows: 'We don't try to predict the future; we try to understand consumer ambition and wants. For that we are looking at music and fashion and are in close contact with opinion leaders in these areas. We work with them to build visions. Some of the stuff is based on facts (for example, demographics) other things are speculative. We believe that we shape our future; the future does not just happen. So we look at what we want the future to be, and then work back to understand what we need to do to make it happen.' I really like this approach, and believe it is important that organisations and individuals start to take steps to create their future rather than simply let it happen to them.

A potentially rich source of customer insights ignored by many organisations is the front-line sales staff. These people have direct contact with customers and can observe how products and services are actually used. In order to tap into this source, mechanisms need to be put in place to ensure that the feedback that comes from the front line is as direct and accurate as possible. It is no good asking front-line staff to feed back their insights if anything negative will be held against them or is used to prove that they have not done their job properly. For example, sales staff of one company manufacturing abrasives (sandpaper) would not send rejects back to the factory as it would have reflected badly on their performance. The production team never found out about bad production runs and, as a consequence, could not take measures to address the problem. A reason why many salespeople are not motivated to feed back their insights is that their reward is exclusively based on sales. This may also influence their listening ability: they listen to sell, not to learn. Companies can improve the process by putting systems in place, such as introducing customer visit feedback forms and training their staff accordingly. In addition, it is useful if senior managers visit their customers, as this can provide some revealing insights and help them to stay connected with the coalface.

From concept to implementation

'We are not doing new product development enough – and not structured enough. It is rather driven by personal enthusiasm.'

After idea generation and selection, the next step is the development of the concept through to implementation. Given the importance that most companies attach to the development of new products, it seems surprising that at least 25% of interviewees said their companies had no systematic new product development process in place. A further 25% were doing something about it or had 'sort of' a process and only 50% actually answered this question with a definite yes.

Most companies employ a stage-gate process, involving several sign-offs throughout the design and development of a new product. However, market leaders seem to move from the more rigid stage-gate approach to a more fluid milestone-based process where certain criteria still have to be met but tasks can be undertaken in parallel. The most effective new product development processes are those that are used as guidelines rather than rule books. Moreover, in a negative culture, with no trust and plenty of blame, a formal development process can become the means of covering one's back, rather than a tool for accelerating and monitoring the development of new products.

Companies rarely seem to make an explicit link between innovation, new product development and company strategy. However, those that do find it highly beneficial. The importance of understanding the organisational context in which the product is being introduced is key.

'We are good at innovative thinking but not so good at taking it forward – and I am not even referring to the implementation, but making the innovation stick. Taking things slower would not be the answer, as it is more an issue of trying to do too much. Success means checking up and

> 'The process has great value; it made a link between products and business strategy.'

down the hierarchy so that everyone understands why things are done and how other activities fit in with it.'

As another interviewee put it, 'Innovation needs to be focused.' He also explained why: 'If it is not, there is innovation overload, you will get variability in the quality of work, there will be too many initiatives and no one has an overview. This can lead to confusion and dilution of the brand.'

> 'We have an idea suggestion and what comes through is checked against company strategy and brand.'

Monitoring

Monitoring throughout the product's development and beyond is another aspect generally considered to be important to successful innovation. As one participant pointed out, 'In addition to the standard stages, we place strong emphasis on post-launch monitoring. A new brand – a brand here is considered to be new for the first five years – will be monitored quarterly for all sorts of performance indicators.'

Although from the interviews it seems that less than half of the participating companies track the results of their innovation efforts, some of the most innovative companies find this unnecessary: 'We used to look at the number of projects that drop out of the innovation funnel – but what is the point? Even if people are being told "no" they continue with their project anyway. We have a handful of people who are always breaking the rules.' This attitude towards measuring innovation is reflected in the findings which Tim Ambler reports in his book *Marketing and the Bottom Line*, 'Among those [companies] we talked to, the outstanding innovators do it so naturally that they were amazed by our questions. To them, innovation health is the oxygen in the air: you breathe it, not measure it.'

Taking a Broader Perspective

The importance of considering the complete product portfolio rather than individual projects on a stand-alone basis has already been mentioned in connection with resource planning, but there are other reasons for doing so. Companies need to look at several trade-offs when selecting from potential projects:

- short-term versus long-term;
- size of opportunity versus possibility of success;
- high-risk versus low-risk. Incremental innovations tend to be associated with low risk and radical innovations with high risk. Considering that companies see radical innovation as a path to future growth, many might have to reconsider their attitude towards risky projects. Naturally, a company should aim to find a balance between the two.

In order to do this, companies need to have an overview of the entire product portfolio and place a greater emphasis on coordinating innovation activities across the organisation. Particularly, as one interviewee pointed out, 'There is always the danger of evaluating innovation purely on financial return. If only evaluated commercially, you get lovely, sure projects – but they might not address strategic needs.'

> 'One of the hardest decisions to make is which projects to launch. It is a trade-off between size of opportunity and possibility of success. We use these two criteria to manage our pipeline. We want some savings and quick wins but also some risky and potentially highly rewarding projects. One advantage of doing this out of the centre is the bird's-eye view. Another advantage is cross-funding over a longer time horizon.'

Teamwork

Taking a creative idea and turning it into a product, service or process is a function of innovation. Unlike creativity, which is most frequently an individualistic process, innovation is a team effort whereby a well-balanced, participative group of people produce a plan to sell the creative concept and follow it through to implementation. As such innovation is another form of organisational change and the extensive literature on change is relevant to innovation as well.

Quote from a lecture note by Professor John Hunt,
London Business School (1997)

Teamwork is recognised as a critical ingredient in successful innovation, and Katzenbach & Smith (1993) define a team as 'a small number of people with complementary skills who are committed to a common purpose, performance goals and approach for which they hold themselves mutually accountable.' All companies participating in the interviews use multifunctional teams (three-quarters said they were already in place; the reminder declared they were 'starting to', 'in parts' or 'sort of'). While teamwork is a useful tool for successful innovation, the degree to which teams are employed varies considerably from company to company. One interviewee said, 'We don't really know a different way of working any more. It was introduced because "needs must" and we did not have any specific training. One group got infected and others caught the bug.' While another commented, 'Yes, we occasionally use teams – but they don't work.'

Effective teams have the following benefits:

- Teams can ensure that different viewpoints and perspectives are taken into consideration early on.
- Teams can cut across traditional vertical lines of authority.
- Teams can make better decisions in as much as they consider more points of view than an individual could.
- Teams bring together complementary skills and experiences.
- Teams are flexible and responsive to changes, addressing them with greater speed and accuracy.
- Teams provide a unique social dimension that enhances the economic and administrative aspects of work.
- Teams have more fun.

'How do we come up with genuine innovation? We use cross-country teams, a good mix of genders, people who are experienced and have strong subject knowledge. We also emphasise consumer contact. This is the kind of blend we are trying to create.'

Smith & Reinertsen (1995), in the context of achieving speed in new product development, offer the following guidelines for setting up effective teams:

- A team should have fewer than 10 members.
- Members should volunteer to serve on the team.

- Members should serve on the team for the time of product concept until the product is in production.
- Members should be assigned to the team full-time.
- Members should report solely to the team leader.
- The key functions, including marketing, engineering and manufacturing, should be on the team.
- Members should be located within conversational distance of each other.

The importance of working in teams for innovation was highlighted by Jon Leach, partner in the advertising agency HHCL, in an interview conducted in May 1999.[4] His organisation uses project teams as an organising principle. The teams consist of a core of five to six people from different disciplines who are joined by people from additional functions on a 'when needed' basis. A similar approach was found in dedicated team-users among the interview sample. However, one participant pointed out a potential shortfall: 'We used to involve everyone from the beginning, but found that people were getting bored. The disadvantage of bringing people in 'if and when' can be that it is forgotten to bring them in at all.' Process guidelines and checklists can help avoid such shortfalls.

An example of teamworking best practice, extracted from the article 'A first for small electrics', by Norman C. Remich Jr. (1997) is given in the box overleaf. It mentions key aspects such as cross-functionality, a strong project leader, co-location, frequent communication and mechanisms for ensuring that all relevant parties are heard in the process.

Project leaders

The project leader is probably the most critical factor in any project's success. It is up to him or her to ensure the team runs smoothly and stays on track, as well as to communicate with other key stakeholders within

---

[4] For the full interview please see the Innovation Exchange web site: http://iexchange. london.edu.

'Two teams – cross-functional and cross-cultural – kept the project running smoothly. The cross-functional team consisted of marketing, manufacturing engineering, mechanical design, industrial design, and the team leader (Morrissey). The team was co-located in what Morrissey calls a 'fusion cell', an open environment where team members worked closely on a day-to-day basis. Although not located in the fusion cell, other team members included people from reliability, finance, quality, and market research. The manufacturing team, which was located at Black & Decker's manufacturing facility in Queretaro, Mexico, coordinated efforts at the plant level early in the programme. Team players with a programme leader included people from engineering, fabrication, assembly and quality. "Due to the team atmosphere, I found it easy to get involved in this project," notes Kurt Weiss, application development engineer, GE Plastics. The project got off the ground in March of 1996 for a Design-to-Launch cycle of nine months, which Morrissey describes "as better than average". The iron's commercial launch was made at the International Housewares Show in January in Chicago. The ProFinish hit the stores in July. "It takes about six months to prepare for production and fill the pipeline after the commercial launch," explains Morrissey.'

the organisation. In some companies the latter role is taken on board by a sponsor, generally a senior executive with influence in the organisation. Whether it is the team leader or a senior sponsor, the important message is that the role of communicating between the team and the rest of the organisation (and senior management in particular) needs to be carried out by someone. In the interviews who was seen to be the most appropriate project manager varied from company to company. One interviewee commented, 'The project manager is usually the brand manager or brand leader. We feel it is important that they should own the project, not least because this can stop mind changes which marketing people are usually known for; being in charge makes changes less likely; they have to be focused.'

A different company had recently changed its view on who should lead projects. Whereas before the project would be given to a professional project manager, generally meaning that the originator of the idea would not be involved after handing it over, the company now offered the person who comes up with the idea the opportunity to be involved in the project, commenting, 'In the past, people tended not to be involved in the development of their idea. One reason was that these people do not tend to have the right skills. Now we take a different approach: if someone wants to be involved and does not have the right skills we try to provide them with the right skills through training. We also consider developing a pool of champions who can help people take their idea forward.' This latter approach harnesses the enthusiasm and the often dogged dedication to making an idea happen that only the originator of the idea will have.

One of the biggest challenges faced by participating companies with regard to idea generation and development is how to establish mechanisms that will enable them to identify the really big ideas early on, and how to accelerate their completion. This relates both to choosing ideas in the first place and being able to identify big winners from among the projects that are brought to market: 'One of our products was such a success – but we were not prepared for it and demand far outstripped supply by a factor of about five!'

A note on processes

Although process is a core element in innovation success, when it is badly introduced or poorly executed, it can significantly reduce value.

Problems arise when the company-specific context and requirements are not taken into account and when there is so much detail that the process becomes stifling and an end in itself rather than being the means to an end.

There are three possible culprits when processes go wrong.

1. The literature, which promotes the one 'right' answer. Concepts are often presented in a way that leads the reader to assume that there is only one way of doing something, and if this path is chosen, all will be well for the organisation. Rarely are implications of introducing a new process mentioned, such as the need to provide training, the importance of aligning the new process to specific company needs and ensuring compatibility with existing processes and procedures. An example of a widely heralded concept that, when originally introduced into organisations, did not seem to be able to live up to the promise is teams. Introduced to the management literature in the mid-1980s and

> 'When the new product development process was introduced, my question was: where is the plan for the behavioural aspects? The consultants did not have any advice on attitude or any supporting training.'

more earnestly heralded as a must in the 1990s, most of the literature available focused on the benefits of teamwork, team constellation and team leadership. It seems that in many organisations, employees were informed that from now on they would work in teams, without anything else in the organisation changing. There was no training for teamwork, no change in rewards and remuneration or in reporting structures. As a consequence, employees were facing conflicts between delivering what they were assessed against – their individual performance – and what they were asked to do – contributing to team performance. Another well-known example is the introduction of quality circles. Following the success Japanese companies had with this approach, managers from Western organisations flocked to Japan to find out how to do it. After the first visit they thought, this is easy, and went back to introduce quality circles into their own organisations. They soon realised that it was not quite as easy as it looked, and they had to go back looking several times before they understood what made quality circles really successful. It is not about applying processes, it is about internalising them.

2. The second group of culprits is consultants, particularly those operating with the 'pigeon-drop' approach: flying over an organisation, dropping their wisdom, and leaving it to the people within the organisation to implement. Concepts are often sold into organisations on the back of their success in others. While the claim of past success may be perfectly true, future success is only possible when it is adjusted to the specific company context. Off-the-shelf solutions can turn out to be less than satisfactory and, although cheaper initially, they can become costly in the long run.

3. Companies themselves are, of course, not blameless. Those looking for an easy solution, quick fix or the one best way will only be disappointed.

In order for processes to live up to their full potential, a link between process and company strategy is required. However, one interviewee pointed out, 'It seems that few companies are linking processes and resources to strategy.' Those organisations that make the effort to do so though find it extremely useful: 'Using a structured process [the funnel] helped us to establish the five-year plan – and actually achieve it.' It is also important to accept that processes should not be static. They should evolve and be adjusted to other changes going on in the organisation. Approaching process with this attitude will reduce the pressure of getting it right first time, and allow greater experimentation. It is important to assess which aspects are working well for the organisation and which are not. The former should be retained and the latter improved.

Advantages of effective processes include:

- They enable understanding of the bigger picture and force commitment – it is more difficult to go back on something that has been publicly committed to.
- They help to create a shared understanding and platform from which to start.

Achieving the benefits is not easy, as it requires a careful balancing of the need to provide sufficient information to be helpful and useful but not so much as to be too descriptive and constraining. Another issue is how to disseminate information about the process within the organisation. Most companies would use heavy folders that end up on employees' shelves without ever being

> 'The problem with process is, if you provide too much detail you create information overload. If you have too little detail, people make mistakes and lose perspective.'

looked at. One company suggested taking it a step further, 'We have the process in documents, books and on the intranet but it is still not as widely used as we would like. So we experimented and realised that what would make a difference was individuals who know everything about this process and can act as coaches to the teams until they are comfortable with it.'

Interviewees described the following symptoms of processes going wrong:

- 'We need to stop the business being driven by processes and start being driven by customers.'
- 'In the past we had a process that turned big ideas into small ones.'
- In mergers and acquisitions, companies are often faced with two opposing attitudes towards process: 'A big challenge for us was

how to find a balance between process-driven company A and very informal company B.'

And finally, one interviewee pointed out that: 'Processes are important – but people make it happen.' There are two aspects to this. First, if people do not buy into the processes and understand their value, they become an obstacle rather than a help, and do not deliver their value. Second, it is understood and accepted that direct contact between people makes things happen. While for some time it was believed that IT solutions would sort out problems with information exchange and dispersed teams, organisations have come to realise that face-to-face contact is essential to establish the trust and familiarity that will enable the exchange and sharing of important information.

Approaches to infusing innovation

To find new structures for infusing innovation into the organisation and, where appropriate, help facilitate innovation on a global scale, was one of the major tasks for participating companies. Three approaches could be identified from the interviews:

- the innovation champion (stand-alone);
- the dedicated innovation team (bolt-on);
- the central innovation department with ambassadors (infusion).

Of course, there are hybrids, but the above seem to be the basic forms. Each approach has its merits, and the choice a company makes will generally depend on their specific circumstances. It also seems that it depends on what stage in the innovation journey the company is at.

Innovation champions

The *innovation champion* tends to be a bit of a lone ranger, often tasked with infusing innovation into an organisation single-handedly. Such a position tends to come with a wide remit and lots of freedom but generally little authority. As one champion explained, 'At present I feel I am just adding to people's workload. I can only ask people to do things, not tell them – but then, people are generally very cooperative. We have very good people but they don't [yet] understand the value and role of innovation so it's often hard work.'

The individuals, generally very enthusiastic and highly committed to their course, tend to report to a senior manager, which seems to indicate that it is a top management priority. However, at times it feels as if establishing the position of an innovation champion is a token gesture. One is seen to be doing something but the belief that things will really change is limited.

Also, what happens when the individual leaves or is moved on? It seems that one of two things can happen: either the position disappears, or a team is put in its place. In the former, the organisation goes back to normal – the attempt to infuse innovation has failed. In the latter, management has realised both the value of innovation and that a single person (depending on the size of the organisation of course) cannot by themselves change the attitudes and behaviours of an entire organisation. The InnovationNetwork has this to say on innovation champions:

> The good news . . . individual innovation champions CAN make a difference. In the responses from our readers about centres of innovation and creativity within companies, we heard many examples of individuals who were able to get innovation centres started. The bad news . . . assuring succession of these centres of innovation when the champion leaves is a huge challenge. Polaroid's Creativity Lab lost corporate support and was closed after Suzanne moved on. Lari left Lucent to go out on her own as a consultant when IdeaVerse lost funding. IdeaVerse remains as a strictly voluntary effort to provide facilitators for idea generation sessions. John Tyson recently retired, and people inside the Design Interpretive group responsible for future thinking are concerned that it may be difficult to continue support for their efforts. Laurie at 3M continues to oversee 3M's ILC on top of her 'real job' as a manager in the Health Information Systems division.

However, despite this, if a company is really serious about infusing innovation into their organisation and the innovation champion has authority as well as responsibility, he can make a difference. As one participating company's innovation champion explains, 'I get visible support from the top and everyone knows I am acting on their behalf.' But it should also be pointed out that behind this champion is not one senior manager but an entire group of senior executives: 'Members of the innovation and learning group are all senior people and come from the different divisions, so the initiative is recognised as being high profile – and spans across the entire organisation.'

One last comment on champions: the literature generally highlights the importance of a champion or strong project leader in order for projects – innovative or otherwise – to be successful. This literature tends to refer to new product development and the individual project level, not necessarily to a company-wide initiative. However, looking at the list of desirable attributes for project leaders, taken from *Project Management* by Harvey Maylor (1996) (shown in the box below) this is true for larger projects too – as long as the following two balances are kept: no responsibility without authority, and no authority without accountability.

Harvey Maylor's list of characteristics of successful project leaders:

- A desire not just to satisfy but to delight customers and stakeholders alike.
- Accepting of both challenge and responsibility.
- Being focused on action, rather than procrastination – getting the job done rather than avoiding critical or difficult decisions.
- A desire to make the best use of all resources – minimise waste in all activities.
- Does not lose sight of the light at the end of the tunnel – goal-focused.
- Has personal integrity – people find it very difficult to respect and take the authority of a person who has low integrity.
- Is flexible about the route that must be taken to achieve the stated end goals.
- Has personal goals that are consistent with those of the project organisation – the project team perceives that the project manager and the organisation are going the same way.
- Ability to determine the real needs/desires of the customer; this is done through getting close to the customer via visits and both formal and informal discussions, and asking relevant questions.
- Analytical skills to turn data into information and break down the project into comprehensible component parts.
- Technical skills – the project manager need not be a technical specialist, but must at least be capable of comprehending the work that is being carried out and 'speaking the language' of the people involved.
- Team skills – many battles have been won against poor odds by the ability of individuals to motivate and enthuse a team.
- Ability to delegate effectively – not try to do everything personally.
- Ability to manage your own time – you cannot expect to manage other people unless you can show that you can manage yourself.
- The balancing of stakeholders' perceptions of project progress (otherwise known as being able to 'sell ideas').
- Negotiation skills – ability to resolve potential conflict situations so that all parties can be said to have 'won'.
- Problem-solving/facilitating problem solving.
- Question all assumptions made by stakeholders at all stages of activities.

Dedicated innovation teams

A different approach is the setting up of a separate *innovation team* or *innovation unit*. This tends to be driven by the insight that innovation requires a different culture from the day-to-day business but that establishing an innovation culture may take too long – or a change in the overall company culture does not seem desirable.

> 'The culture in our innovation group is very different from that in the rest of the company, less driven by procedures and processes – and deliberately so.'

In this situation, responsibility for innovation is delegated to the innovation team – it has to be said that the kind of innovation an organisation is looking for when setting up a separate, dedicated innovation team tends to be radical rather than incremental. Incremental and day-to-day

> 'Innovation? People believe it is the innovation team's responsibility.'

tasks – incremental innovation – still happens within the existing business, although people can interpret this as releasing them from any responsibility to think 'innovation'.

The reaction of the rest of the organisation to the establishment of an innovation team is often mixed, at all levels. One participant alluded to the great scepticism they encountered in the main organisation as to whether or not they would have any impact. Another described how differently senior managers reacted to the setting up of the group, reflecting their belief about its potential impact: 'A salesperson (incidentally new to the company) has restructured the group and left space for new categories, to be filled by our team. A different person who has also recently restructured (and who has been with the company for some time) has not done so. The argument was, "I can still fit it (in the unlikely case) if it happens".'

In most cases such a group is set up on the initiative of a very determined individual usually in a senior position, with enough influence to push the project through, usually against the scepticism, if not open opposition, of colleagues. Asked about the buy-in from top management to the concept of the innovation team, one interviewee commented, 'I believe we have 100% buy-in in terms of the positive publicity the setting up of the group creates; however, if it comes to believing that we will be able to produce real results it is probably more 50/50. People need to see results in order to believe.'

A very important consideration when setting up an independent innovation team is what mechanisms need to be developed to bind the group back into the main organisation, and how to ensure that sufficient common ground remains to avoid any resistance when transferring concepts back from the innovation team into the main organisation. Communication, ensuring a mutual understanding of what each part of the organisation can contribute to the whole, and constant exchange between the two parts of the organisation are key in preventing the innovation team from becoming too remote.

The way one company interviewed has structured its innovation team seems to be a very good approach for addressing such issues. The small team is made up of a number of dedicated full-time staff from different functions of the business – not necessarily innovation experts but excited by the idea, open-minded and creative. These are joined by a number of part-time people who spend half of their time in their normal jobs in the main organisation and secondees from the main organisation who spend one to two years with the team. This way, a continuous flow of communication is ensured, which brings with it insights into what is happening in the group. It might even entice other people to join the group.

A challenge to be addressed within such a group was expressed as, 'Not get too process-driven, deliver results – and don't get back into the comfort zone!'

'A variation on this theme is the setting up of a venture unit which acts like a venture capital fund. These units can either focus on external venturing where equity is purchased in external companies, or internal venturing whereby new companies are created internally that tend to be wholly owned. Finally, there are venture incubators where a new company is seeded to be sold off as soon as appropriate.'

Innovation ambassadors

The third approach combines a very senior team or individual (which depends on company size) at the centre, with a team of *innovation ambassadors.*[5] The role of the central team/individual is to coordinate innovation activities across the entire organisation, evaluate and select projects, resource them and monitor their progress, often beyond launch.

The innovation ambassador(s), while being part of the centre, will work alongside local teams and provide them with expertise, a company-wide perspective and company best practice. This means that these people tend to be senior, more often than not with a track record for innovation. This seems to be the approach preferred by multinational innovative companies, as it allows them also to achieve a balance between central and local control.

> 'The (central) innovator is part of the team and works jointly with them. The innovator brings experience, knowledge, a company-wide perspective, and awareness of best practice to the party. The local team provides closeness to the consumer and of course, local insights. That way we get the best of both worlds.'

Also interesting is the difference between the selection criteria used for people on the innovation team and those who become innovation ambassadors. Where characteristics for the first include 'very young', 'fresh perspective', 'not caught up in company traditions', characteristics for the latter are focused more around 'experience and expertise', 'track record', and 'good company knowledge'. But looking at the purpose behind each might help to explain the differences. A separate innovation team tends to be primarily responsible for *generating* ideas whereas the innovation ambassador is brought in to help with the *implementation* of ideas and concepts.

This way of infusing innovation is also different from that of the innovation champion where innovation is seen to be an additional burden. As one interviewee commented, 'The innovation and development department are there to help.' In this scenario, the central innovation function represents an additional resource to local business. And since the innovation ambassador tends to work alongside the local team rather than spreading her wisdom from the lofty heights of headquarters, she tends to become accepted as a part of the team and a welcome extra pair of hands.

---

[5]   It was mentioned that this kind of approach was pioneered by Nestlé.

In the following vignette, Stephen Moon, GlaxoSmithKline and Ben Bryant, London Business School, introduce GalxoSmithKline's thefuturesgroup, which is an example of a dedicated innovation team.

Keeping innovation afloat – innovation as a cycle of tension and tranquillity

Stephen Moon, GlaxoSmithKline & Ben Bryant, London Business School

Charter waters

GlaxoSmithKline (GSK) is a large pharmaceutical business with £18 billion of sales annually, £5 billion profit and just under 8% of the global pharmaceutical market. It spends £4.5 billion on research and development (R&D) every year, of which the Consumer Healthcare division, with its 600 R&D staff, spends £2.7 billion. Consumer Healthcare operates in over-the-counter medication and nutritional healthcare markets.

The Nutritional Healthcare division is a business unit within GSK (£315 million sales). It has three well-established heritage brands: Lucozade, established in 1927, Horlicks, now over 100 years old, and Ribena, introduced during World War II as a health drink. The division has tried to develop new brands and brand extensions several times, but each time has failed to get the products to market, or the product has failed in the market. They have always seen their main competitors as soft drink providers, and hence perceived themselves as a very significant player in the UK beverages industry.

To new horizons

In 1999, the division decided to focus on growing the nutritional healthcare business in the UK, and top management set the goal of £500 million. To achieve this they did not just ask for good ideas but decided on two core strategies. First, using their science and research capability to leverage the three powerful brands, they developed a 'more from the core' strategy. The second was to develop opportunities for step-change innovation and move into new areas, new businesses, new brands and new categories.

After some intense debates at board level on how to achieve our strategic goals, a dedicated innovation team was assembled bringing together 11 high-potential individuals, people who were on their way up in their career, but not yet fully rounded with experience. The team, called thefuturesgroup, reported to the top management through the director of strategy. To make the group as effective as possible, individuals were selected from all the business functions of Nutritional Healthcare, e.g. sales, marketing, technical, supply chain and purchasing. They also looked for diversity in terms of gender, nationality and ethnic background. Locating the team off-site was a major challenge, but it was highly symbolic and reflected the fact that they were trying to achieve something entirely different from what they had done before. Money for the innovation group was ring-fenced – but, even though in comparison with our overall R&D expenditure, its might was not substantial.

A new route to India?

By mid-2002, Nutritional Healthcare had advanced towards its growth targets, but not as rapidly as it might have liked. The following list outlines the strategic outcomes and non-outcomes that have been achieved so far.

Innovation learning
Products developed (but not launched): Several new ideas were developed that were stopped before going to market. Some of these represented new product categories, such as bottled water or soya products, while a third idea involved the development of a health monitor that could be strapped to athletes' bodies, quite outside the boundaries of the organisation's capabilities. The water product was withdrawn because it failed Base 2 marketing, an organisational requirement for all new products, while the health

monitor was withdrawn because it was absorbing large amounts of the budget that had been ring-fenced for all innovation activity. It was not clear how this product would provide returns to the business for the investment required in new and unique capabilities.

Products launched: A new brand of chilled juice was launched when the group had been in existence for about a year. The new product met a lot of the criteria set out when the innovation group was launched; it had a high strategic value and a high margin – and by being able to build on GSK's expertise in vitamins and minerals, it had great potential in healthcare.

New Capabilities: GSK had never had a product that required chilling before – this involved an entirely different supply chain – which may not seem to be a step change, but represented a huge change for the business.

New ways of managing innovation risk: A seeded approach to developing new products was developed using the juice product. The division was only accustomed to doing major national launches, but the complete brand was launched for £70,000 (normally the budget for a launch meeting for a new product).

Beliefs: There was a well-established belief within the division that innovation to develop a new brand was almost impossible. The successful small launch of a new category spawned a change in attitude towards innovation.

The journey

The innovation journey was not straightforward, but was rather a complex series of events which reflected managers and professionals trying to address aspects of uncertainty and coming to agreement about the strategic intent. Much of the consulting advice about 'how to do innovation' is presented to large organisations like GSK as if the road to becoming more innovative can be logically planned with interventions, processes and planning tools. The experience of innovation at GSK suggests that the complex series of events that made up the innovation journey was characterised by patterns of fragmentation and polarisation (which we call *tension*), as well as patterns consensus and certainty (which we call *tranquillity*). We explain these patterns under three broad headings:

1. Strategic intent, leadership and top management communication.
2. Culture and organisational design.
3. Strategic boundaries, capability development, approach to risk.

Strategic intent, leadership and top management communication

The expectation set by top management of the Nutritional Healthcare division was for *step change* innovation. This was focused on the long-term strategy, product and category portfolio of the organisation. Yet, after only 12 months, the organisation was under enormous pressure to deliver innovations quickly, to justify the investment in innovation activities. This created mixed messages about the seriousness of top management's support for innovation. Top management was also under pressure. A bad summer had meant sales forecasts were not being met, and moves were made to curtail the more radical innovation projects in order to meet budget requirements. After 18 months, a consensus emerged among senior management around the types of innovation that would be supported by the business. There would be a strong focus on a radical extension of existing brands, and support for the seeded approach to new categories such as juice and water .

Culture and Organisational Design

The historical model of organisation design for innovation at GSK was one where innovation was managed through cross-functional cooperation between category management (the brands) and R&D. This organisational design was believed to be the root cause of the failure of the organisation to deliver innovations to market.

By creating a new cross-functional team, a strong signal was sent to both category management and R&D that they were not being effective in their role of innovation. Initially the role of the innovation group was distinct from the rest of the organisation's innovation activities – it was focused on long-term, more radical innovations. However, over time, this distinction became fuzzy. The innovation group was unable to hand over its ideas effectively to be implemented (they had created too much differentiation), and as the pressure to deliver quickly emerged, they abandoned the more radical ideas and focused on innovations closer to the existing brands. This created a new set of tensions between thefuturesgroup and category management and R&D, resulting in the polarisation of conversations. After two years, however, the category management group found a way of working more closely with the innovation group, acknowledging that their time 'out of the business' had brought a new perspective to the existing brands, enabling rapid brand prototyping and implementation.

Strategic boundaries, capability, development and approach to risk

The perception of capability and strategic boundaries in Nutritional Healthcare was anchored in the production of non-chilled beverages. While top management emphasised the use of its scientific expertise as part of a pharmaceutical company to develop new innovations, the meaning of science as an innovation enabler was not uniform throughout the division. Some saw 'science' as a way of creating intellectual property through chemical science. Others saw it as making claims about products that would enhance consumer health. Another group saw science as a limitation to true innovation, because it was felt that every innovation had to meet the 'scientific' criteria.

The innovation group attempted to shift the language of the strategic boundaries:

> We then started to get a bit wild because we thought, well,
> beverages and food is all very well but . . . . And we decided to cast

our net a bit wider. If we use 'well-being' as a starting point, where can that take us? What about a device that will tell athletes their hydration level, how much energy remains in their body, their heart rate, blood pressure, and so on. Something that tells élite athletes exactly what is happening in their body. When we realised that this would mean carrying a great big box we said, why not make it digital and automatic? Run by an expert system. Once the idea was born, they decided to start talking to the athletes who quite liked the idea, and when they talked to some of the world's biggest corporations, they were very keen too. Why? Because they saw it as an opportunity to bring together different competencies at a corporate level and start to see whether new opportunities emerged.

As noted earlier, after two years, many of the innovative nutritional and food projects had been put on hold. However, in contrast to this, top management has begun to recognise and articulate that they were competing in the nutritional food market, and not just the beverages market. This broadened the scope of innovation for the rest of the organisation.

Since its inception two years ago, thefuturesgroup has been successful in creating a number of tensions in Nutritional Health-care. These tensions were necessary to shift the mindsets of senior management as well as staff at other levels. Now, many of its radical innovations have been put on hold and the focus has returned to being closer to the existing brands, and an air of tranquility around innovation prevails. There is now less tension about what innovation means.

The future of thefuturesgroup

Thefuturesgroup is currently debating three key challenges for the group:

1. How to make sure the team does not just become another marketing department, an extra overhead with extra complexity and reduced efficiency. But if they get it right and they do more groundbreaking stuff, we can say that we have got 11 people focused on innovation – and not only on Friday afternoon when

   they put the ad campaign to bed and the promotional spend has
   been sorted, but full-time.

2. How to deal with the threats and opportunities that they will
   inevitably face. Typical threats include competition from other
   brands such as Coca-Cola entering newly conquered markets, and
   the current economic uncertainty. Opportunities include redefin-
   ing the business in a way that is completely different from three
   heritage brands, in a way that emphasises a science-driven well-
   being business and keeps building on the conversations we have
   started with various partners from a range of – seemingly –
   complete unrelated industries.

3. Should they extend the group to include other organisations?
   Recently they have been assessing the benefits of going
   completely outside thefuturesgroup, and talking to a number
   of companies and venture capitalists about setting up an inter-
   corporate venture unit with some external investment. Under
   such a set-up, would it be more likely that we would develop
   completely new businesses, things that haven't even been
   invented yet? Would working with two or three large corporations find new, more effective ways of partnering, and
   would it help share the risk? And would it bring in new
   levels of resource or even more high-flying people and external
   cash?

Insights from the two-year journey

Some critical insights on innovation have been gained from the
experience of thefuturesgroup. Innovation is a long-term commitment, even when markets are flat. Inevitably, top managers will be
seduced by the need to secure short-term profits, and this will create
cycles of tension and tranquillity. The gravity of the organisation will
pull innovation back into the mainstream, closer to what the
organisation already knows best, and compete with competitors for
the centre-ground, where it is most comfortable because of the
certainty that known competition creates. This certainty creates
consensus around the organisation, but consensus is also the enemy

of innovation. It will always take strong leadership to pull the organ-isation back into tension, to disrupt strategic intent, to redefine capabilities and to reshape structure and culture. Without this tension, this lack of coherence, this acceptance of uncertainty, innovation will flounder.

Critical success factors

Some critical insights on innovation from the experience of thefuturesgroup include:

1. Innovation is a long-term commitment, even when markets are flat. Whatever you do, do not be seduced by the need to secure short-term profits.
2. Do not allow the gravity of the organisation to pull innovation back into the mainstream. If you allow this to happen, your ability to innovate will be greatly diminished.
3. Build a learning capability into the group, and ensure this is trans-ferred to the rest of the organisation.
4. Be prepared to significantly interrogate the business model and recognise that this might have to change.

Anchor points

- For *idea suggestion schemes* to work, they need to be easy to use, have very clear and well understood guidelines, and offer fast feed-back. Clear selection criteria will help to prevent rejection being taken personally. And remember, people will only offer their ideas if the environment is supportive. It is also useful to bear in mind that recognition is generally more powerful than financial rewards. If the suggestions result in a new development project, the personal involvement of the idea generator can also be a great incentive.
- Provide some focus for *idea generation*: 'We encourage new ideas/ change in defined areas; we call them the six priority challenges for future development, but that does not mean that we are discounting other stuff but ideas linked to the challenges have better chances of

being realised.' And remember, ideas are only as good as the actions taken to implement them.

- For *specific problems*, brainstorming or other idea-generating techniques are more powerful; do not believe that a suggestion scheme will provide the solution to your problems.
- Freedom to *experiment* is a powerful tool for improving concepts and processes. 'We have the habit of experimenting, we never do things the same way twice; we always look at how we have done it last time but then say, what has worked, what has not, let's keep what has worked and try this.'
- *Market research* needs to get under people's skin – asking straightforward questions will give you straightforward answers, not new insights.
- A formalised *new product development process* is a means to an end, not the end itself.
- Rather than looking at individual projects, the company should look at its entire *portfolio* of existing and planned projects. This helps avoid duplication and improves resource management. The portfolio should balance short- and long-term, high- and low-risk, as well as incremental and radical innovation. 'Make sure you coordinate your innovation activities across markets and businesses – even if this means managing a complex matrix.'

We balance our product portfolio at four levels:

1. Between brands/product portfolios – to make sure there is enough innovation in each area.
2. Between developed/non-developed markets, recognising that non-developed markets take longer for pay-back.
3. Between three levels of horizon which equate to different types of innovation: (1) product extension; (2) existing products into new market or changed products into existing markets; (3) more blue sky stuff, not necessarily fitting in at present.
4. Product portfolio against strategy.

- The *successful execution* of innovation projects relies on cross-functional teams as well as strong project leaders.
- *Processes should be aligned* to the company's objectives, and be allowed to evolve over time.
- *Provide training* before asking people to use new processes and tools: 'Every project has project planning now; people are trained at it

with real projects; the training takes two days; it involves behavioural things and tools, and it has a real outcome: a project plan. If something changes during the course of the project, the project plan gets revisited – it becomes a tool rather than "the rule". Implementing the project involves the entire team. There is a formal checklist of who might be needed and when. So even if they are not all part of the core team, they are being informed at the outset of the project if and when they might be needed.'

- There is no one right way of *infusing innovation* into an organisation, it will depend on the company's specific context, including company size, what kind of innovation is sought, and which stage in the innovation journey the organisation is at.

Riding on the crest of the wave – how to stay on top

'To make innovation happen, two things are important: a creative environment and telling people what is going on.'

Even if a company has a clear vision and strategy, with all the processes in place and aligned, innovation still may not happen. Leadership is the key driver of innovation, and culture its main enabler. This chapter will look in more detail at these two aspects, as well as how the physical work environment can contribute to achieving the innovation ambition of an organisation.

The role of leadership

'Leadership should encourage experimentation, turn a blind eye to experimentation and fund it! And of course support failure.'

The quickest way to achieve innovation best practice seems to be: get the right leader(s). Listening to interviewees and observing best practice described in the literature, one has to come to the conclusion that it all hinges on

'I strongly believe that the person at the top is the person with the most influence on company culture.'

the leadership.[1] This is a bold statement, and likely to produced mixed reactions. For example, the InnovationNetwork promotes the idea of grassroots innovation (see box).

---

[1] It should be pointed out that leaders and managers are not the same. As Professor Rob Goffee points out, managers are about managing, about efficiency, and leaders are about 'inspiring others to higher levels of performance.'

One of the most frequent comments made about innovation is that 'it has to start at the top.' We agree with Gary Hamel (*Leading the Revolution*) when he says, 'What utter rubbish.' We agree that it is easier when change is supported by senior management, but the world is filled with examples of change that started at the grassroots. 3M even has a group of 400 activists known as GRIT (Grass Roots Innovation Team). One of the things that often stops us from taking action is the thought that we're the only ones who think change is necessary. That is seldom true. The only problem is that, too often, all of us who see the changes that are needed haven't found each other.

As we have watched successful, and not so successful, innovation initiatives for the past several years, we've noticed some fundamental truths:

- Innovation is a mindset of openness to ideas, all ideas, regardless of the source, plus a masterful ability to implement the best.
- Innovation requires more than a one-time training or motivation event (or even a series of events).
- Innovation is not something that can be delegated to one department or group of people, it's an organisation-wide responsibility.
- Innovation requires a consistent commitment (one that does not change when the champion moves on).

Rather than being a thing, a tool, technique, model or process, innovation is more like a climate, a culture, an environment that supports people in a way that allows them to be smarter than they thought they could be. We especially like Hamel's following statement:

'To institutionalise radical innovation, companies will need to build highly effective electronic markets for ideas, capital and talent. As they do so, it will no longer be the knowledge management function that constitutes the leading edge of corporate IT (information technology), but the innovation marketplace.'

However, it is still up to the leaders to create an environment that allows grassroots teams to emerge. So assuming it were true, all companies would have to do is choose or develop the right leaders, and their organisations would become innovative. The right leader would be able to create the right culture, develop the right strategy and vision, and communicate it throughout the organisation, choose the right processes and procedures, and create a work environment in which innovation can flourish.

Considering the list of characteristics of innovative organisations identified in the 1998 PriceWaterhouseCoopers Innovation Survey, shown in the box, there seems to be a lot of truth in the statement

Characteristics of innovative organisations

The survey of 3000 companies across the world, undertaken in 1998, concluded that the most successful innovative firms were those that had:

1. High management trust.
2. Active flow of ideas.
3. Fewer organisational levels.
4. Effective idea management process.
5. Managers who challenge.
6. Managers who delegate.
7. Managers who involve others.
8. Routine future envisioning.
9. Sources of ideas other than the board.
10. Balanced view of the risk takers.

that it all hinges on the leader, as there is not much on the list that is beyond the influence of a company's leader. One thing comes through quite clearly from interviews and the literature: with the wrong person in charge, innovation is much less likely to happen.

Three questions to address are:

1. What characteristics should a company look for and encourage in its leaders?
2. What does an innovation culture look like?
3. What is it about strategy, vision and process that an organisation attempting to be innovative should be aware of?

The third question has already been addressed in previous chapters, so this chapter will focus on leadership and culture for innovation.

The critical role of leadership for creating an innovative organisation – or any kind of change - has already been highlighted. Unless an initiative is seen to have support from the top it is less likely to be taken seriously. Comments such as 'The executive board are in agreement with the new strategy of interdependence and collaboration but they pay only lip-service to it' indicate that top management is achieving very little. A dif-

> 'Our new CEO is single-handedly changing the culture.'

ferent scenario is painted by another interviewee who commented, when asked whether people would recognise the importance of the innovation initiative, 'Everyone in the organisation recognises it, as there is visible high-level support and we have good troops at the frontline; everyone knows I am acting on their [top management's] behalf.'

The impact of leadership style can be illustrated through more quotes from interviewees:

- 'Leadership here is all about control and cost'
- 'The CEO runs informal lunches to enable people from different departments to meet so people get to know each other and find out what each is doing.'
- 'The present CEO is a receptive manager and encourages people beyond everything, more than anyone else I have known.'

On how to create the right leadership style, and ensure fit between strategic ambition, the desired company culture and leadership style, one participant commented, 'We have a complete leadership programme which is about achieving effective leadership. It goes down to junior management level and has been going for the past four to five years. Its development has involved union members as well as junior and senior management. It lasts one week and we have found that it really has made a difference.'

However, the scale of the leader's influence can cause problems. First, in all but the smallest organisations, there will be more than one leader. An organisation can become very fragmented if each leader pursues his own leadership style or agenda. This problem has been particularly noted in organisations that used to have a strong geographic orientation with significant scope for local decision-making. Many of these organisations are now moving towards a more centralised structure. Understandably, some local leaders are reluctant to give up their power, which means that reaching agreement on common processes and goals can be a tricky and time-consuming process. Gaining buy-in before changes are put in place may be one way to overcome resistance. Careful consideration of how much to centralise is important and, unless a clear rationale can be developed that provides strong arguments for the change, resistance is the most likely outcome. If getting buy-in is not possible, there may also be some value in consciously using this as an opportunity for renewing management layers – and the emphasis here is on *conscious*. As one company explained:

> When I suggested a particular new process to the management group, rather than explaining every detail, I took them carefully through what it meant and why it was important that we should adopt this process. I felt so strongly about it, and that my team should be fully behind it, that I declared that no one would leave the room unless they agreed to it and shook my hand on it. Some people could not shake my hand – and guess who has left the company. It was painful at the time but set a very clear signal through the organisation that we were really serious about it.[2]

---

[2]   The process in question was a new appraisal system which was to be built around personal development plans that were to be developed through discussions. The aim was to build on strengths and reduce the gaps.

A second source of problems is changes in leadership. In US and UK companies, especially, frequent movement of managers is common. Each new leader will have the tendency to want to leave his mark. Hence, every change in leadership is linked to a high degree of uncertainty about direction, culture, values and how he will work with existing senior management. Often initiatives started by a predecessor are stopped and replaced by new ones, project priorities may change, and different people come into favour. Clear and early communication about direction, focus and values can help minimise the negative consequences of uncertainty. A problem relating to frequent movements of managers was also mentioned in connection with accepting failure as part of innovation. One interviewee who stated that their organisation generally accepted failure as an intrinsic part of innovation continued, 'But it can be a bit tricky, as people tend to move fast. So how do you document failure without it seeming that you are pointing the finger at someone who has left?'

Knowing how much change and how much continuity is required is an art which senior management needs to master. Do we want to bring someone in who will change things, or do we need someone who keeps running the ship on our carefully selected course? This is why it may be advisable for a change manager to hand over to someone else once the project has completed.

It is hard to say which is the more difficult, to establish the need for change or create stability, as most of the time a company needs both. The subject of change will be taken up again later in this chapter.

On best practice for leadership and culture for innovation there is quite a bit of literature available – probably more than for the other three key areas for innovation, processes, work environment, and strategy and vision. It is reassuring to note that best practice suggested in the literature conforms to the feedback from participants.

What the 100 UK-based best-practice companies from the 1995 DTI/CBI survey considered to be the most important characteristics of a good leader is shown in Figure 5.1.

Like the top criterion from the 1995 survey, Innovation Exchange members found *inspiring people* to be one of the key abilities of successful innovation leaders. However, it should be pointed out that

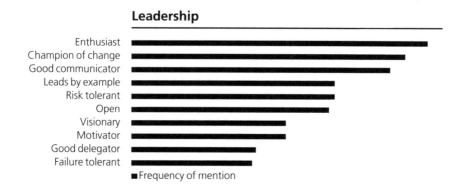

Leadership

Figure 5.1: Characteristics of a good leader

the emphasis lies on 'inspiring by action rather than words'. In terms of what leaders should inspire, experimentation comes first. 'A leader should inspire people to have the courage to experiment', which includes developing mechanisms for terminating projects - rather than allowing them to drag on – and allowing for failure – someone mentioned Hewlett-Packard's famous 'failure parties.'

So what does an inspirational leader do? In their recent *Harvard Business Review* article 'Why should anyone be led by you?' Rob Goffee and Gareth Jones (2000) identified the following four qualities necessary in inspirational leaders:

- They selectively show their weaknesses. By exposing some vulnerability, they reveal their approachability and humanity.
- They rely heavily on intuition to gauge the appropriate timing and course of their actions. Their ability to collect and interpret 'soft' data helps them to know just when and how to act.
- They manage employees with something we call tough empathy. Inspirational leaders empathise passionately – and realistically – with people, and they care intensely about the work employees do.
- They reveal their differences. They capitalise on what's unique about themselves.

Underlying these four qualities is the ability to connect emotionally with employees – something also identified as being crucial by interviewees. However, as one interviewee pointed out, how well the argument for emotional connectedness is accepted may be influenced by the underlying professional culture within an organisation: 'We are disastrous at leadership which is all about connecting with people emotionally; this [accepting the importance of emotional connectedness] is an issue with scientists.'

'It seems that management is trying to get to people through their minds, but I believe strongly that you need to capture peoples' hearts.'

So what can leaders do to remove the barriers to innovation? Rosabeth Moss Kanter, author of *The Change Masters* (1985) suggests the following:

- Encourage a culture of pride – highlight the achievements of the company's own people through visible awards, through applying an innovation from one area to the problems of another, and letting the experienced innovators serve as consultants.
- Enlarge access to the power tools for innovative problem solving. This includes vehicles such as R&D committees for supporting proposals for experiments and innovations.
- Improve lateral communications – bring departments together; encourage cross-fertilisation through exchange of people, mobility across areas; create cross-functional links and perhaps even overlaps; bring together teams of people from different areas who share responsibility for some aspects of the same end product.
- Reduce unnecessary layers of hierarchy – eliminate barriers to resource access; make it possible for people to go directly after what they need; push decisional authority downward; create 'diagonal' slices cutting across the hierarchy to share information, provide quick intelligence about external and internal affairs.
- Increase early access to information about company plans – where possible, reduce secretiveness; avoid surprises; increase security by making future plans known in advance, making it possible, in turn, for those below to make their plans; give people at lower levels a chance to contribute to the shape of change before decisions are made at the top; empower and involve them at an earlier point, such as through task forces and problem-solving groups or through more open-ended, change-oriented assignments, with more room left for the person to define that approach.

However, good intentions and leadership can be disrupted by external events or, as one interviewee put it, 'The leadership agenda can get wrecked by bad decisions [for example from headquarters] and other events beyond the influence of the leadership.' Another commented, 'You can do all the right things but an external event can throw you off track; people get scared and risk-averse.'

But there are certainly some things that leaders should avoid, as a humorous list from Moss Kanter's *The Change Masters* suggests:

Rules for stifling innovation

1. Regard any new idea from below with suspicion because it's new, and because it's from below.
2. Insist that people who need your approval to act first go through several other levels of management to get their signatures.
3. Ask departments or individuals to challenge and criticise each other's proposals (that saves you the job of deciding; you just pick the survivor).
4. Express your criticisms freely and withhold your praise (that keeps people on their toes); let them know they may be fired at any time.
5. Treat identification of problems as a sign of failure to discourage people from letting you know when something in their area isn't working.
6. Control everything carefully; make sure people count anything that can be counted, frequently.
7. Make decisions to reorganise or change policies in secret, and spring them on people unexpectedly (that also keeps people on their toes).
8. Make sure that requests for information are fully justified and make sure that it is not given out to managers freely (you don't want data to fall into the wrong hands).
9. Assign to lower-level managers, in the name of delegation and participation, responsibility for figuring out how to cut back, lay off, or move people around, or otherwise implement threatening decisions you have made, and get them to do it quickly.
10. And above all, never forget that you, the higher-ups, already know everything important about this business.

A final comment on leadership for innovation comes from Tim Ambler (2000) who remarks, 'The main conclusion drawn from the research was that top management should be less directly concerned with innovations. They should agree the menu and then get out of the kitchen.' Meaning, top management needs to prepare the ground and provide the right environment, but then let people get on with it.

Best-practice leadership can be summarised as:

- demonstrate commitment to innovation – in deeds not only words;
- communicate clearly and in a timely fashion;
- create a common purpose;

- be inspirational and involving;
- encourage experimentation and tolerate failure;
- Connect on an emotional level.

Culture

Culture is the soil on which innovation does – or does not – grow. If that is so, then the leader is the gardener who has to prepare the soil and make sure the right fertilisers are put on, so the right kind of innovation can grow. Fertile soil on its own will not make anything grow, but without it there is not even a chance. Or as Tim Ambler (2000) emphasises, 'Culture [and process] are not drivers so much as enablers or, more often, disablers. The right culture [and processes] will not guarantee innovation but when they are wrong, innovation will be blocked.'[3]

Establishing the right culture was one of the biggest concerns of participating companies. The main aspect here is how to establish *one* culture of innovation that is shared by all parts of the organisation. Many companies reported that they had pockets of innovation but were struggling to achieve innovativeness throughout the entire organisation. Reasons for the struggle often lie with the company's history: a lot of participating companies have recently gone through a number of mergers and acquisitions and other major changes, leaving the present leaders to manage and merge a range of different cultures. Below are a number of comments on culture that show the various stages participating companies are at:

- 'After recent mergers and acquisitions, a new culture is still developing.'
- 'There is an old and a new culture.'
- 'Our culture is starting to drift apart as a consequence of our division into business units.'
- 'After having consolidated different cultures after a merger, different – and competing – cultures between divisions are now emerging.'
- 'We are quite a large organisation with various strands of culture.'

---

[3] Brackets added by this author.

- 'In our organisation you would find lots of different cultures between companies but also national cultures.'
- 'We had so many changes over the past two to three years, including some major mergers, there is no culture left, or rather, there is a new culture slowly emerging.'

The fact that there are many cultures within an organisation seems to have become more of an issue, certainly with regard to innovation, since there is an increasing trend towards centralisation, as discussed in Chapter 1. Many organisations have started to centralise as much as possible, including support functions such as human resources, IT and so on. For these central functions, it can be difficult to manage across a variety of different cultures. One interviewee commented, 'Cultural differences will be a problem in bringing the company closer together and when introducing shared processes.' If the company is to think as one, establishing a set of shared values and beliefs – culture – is important. If one part of the organisation accepts failure where another would start a witch hunt, the company will not be able to achieve more than the sum of its parts – probably less. While the introduction of shared processes may be difficult, it might actually help to create some shared ground from which a common culture can grow.

> 'In many companies the leaders of business units used to be king of the castle. What makes companies need to pull together today is the alignment of brands, avoiding duplications, and thereby achieving better efficiencies – but it needs careful management of the kings.'

And there are also some large organisations which, despite their largeness, feel they have a shared culture underlying all their activities: 'Despite the largeness and the multitude of individual companies there seems to be a shared culture, something that bonds the parts together; this is supported and helped by shared processes, a clear focus, and commitment to company strategy and vision.' This comment also highlights that culture and process are – and must be – mutually reinforcing.

Cultural heritage

When trying to introduce an innovation culture it is important to understand where the organisation comes from, and what has influenced it. A company that has its roots in science may need a different internal selling technique to one that has been built by marketers. For example, it was pointed out that scientists tend to see asking for help and collaboration as a weakness – which is a

'Some people are bringing products to market that are 80% right rather than 100% – and by doing that they are able to be much quicker.'

problem when you want to introduce knowledge-sharing and team-working. It was also mentioned several times that another trait of scientists is to expect to get things 100% right, even if it means under-taking another round of experiments. There are of course areas where this is essential, such as medication where human life is at risk, but in most other areas experimentation and bringing products to market that are 95% right will yield greater benefits. Being aware of such cultural heritage might help shape the way that innovation is sold into the organisation.

Preparing the ground for an innovation culture

'In our organisation, if you are passionate about a particular idea you are allowed to pursue it. It is almost as if being passionate is the most important criterion for taking an idea forward. If you fail, the project is closed down and you are moved into a different position. There is no sacking of people for failure. People get fired for being lazy.'

Understanding what motivates people is an important part of the art of infusing innovation into an organisation. However, as one interviewee pointed out, 'In order to put innovation into your culture you need to have hygiene factors in place first.' If people are unhappy with their basic conditions of employment, such as pay or working environment, their willingness to be innovative, cooperative and put their ideas forward will be limited. This is something managers should think more about, given a recent report which emphasised that the number of employees dissatisfied with their working conditions due to long hours and work overload is on the increase, particularly among the better-educated workforce. If there is a war for talent where companies are fighting for the best of the knowledge workers, ensuring staff are content with their working conditions and environment might be one way for a company to differentiate itself from other organisations. But there are other aspects that foster an innovation culture, some of which are explored below.

An important ingredient in the innovation cocktail is *fun*. Interviewees commented, 'There is a tremendous sense of fun, but also real focus on what is important.' Another stated, 'There is a sense of urgency but we are not afraid to inject fun into it - this helps manage stress.'

A *blame-free* culture is always highlighted as being essential for innovation but the freedom to disagree and have constructive conflict are equally important. As one interviewee pointed out, 'Failure? We don't go around pointing fingers, we aim to learn from it. We lost £5 million last year but you have got to take risks. However, somehow there is still a tendency to put failure under a blanket and it is up to our CEO and myself to make sure it stays out in the open. Talking about failure comes from the top, it comes down from HQ – they very much encourage it.' A participant from another company commented on this particular issue too, albeit in a slightly different context: 'In reviews it is essential to share problems. Had you asked people in this organisation a few years ago they would have claimed not to have any problems at all. Now they tend to start the review session by saying, "I have these three problems I need your help with." How did it change? You have to be more explicit about what behaviour you would like to see. They now have to prepare an annual plan for personal development.' So it is not only about having a blame-free culture, it is also about ensuring that it is okay for people to ask for help, which leads to the next point.

> 'We have really strong views and disagreement – but all very friendly; here you find openness rather than bickering behind people's backs.'

Another important characteristic of an innovation culture is *trust*. People will only be happy to experiment and explore, to put their ideas and thoughts forward if they don't fear being ridiculed. Innovation, collaboration and exchange of knowledge will not happen unless people trust each other and feel free to ask for help – without fear of being accused of

> 'There is lots of fear in the organisation, fear of appearing silly and fear about criticising superiors. This is partly because in the past no one was allowed to ask questions; superiors were to be obeyed.'

incompetence.[4] In a company where the atmosphere is described as one of 'high levels of arrogance and very low ability to ask for help' innovation is unlikely to flourish. It should also be noted that trust is not created by net-meetings or telephone conferences. For people to start to trust each other, face-to-face contact is absolutely essential.

Finally, the *ability to listen* – and act upon the information received – is critical. In his research Nigel Nicholson, Professor for Organisational Behaviour at London Business School, has identified a lack of attention to ideas (people may listen but do nothing) as one of three reasons for failing to achieve creativity.[5] Underlying the ability and willingness to listen is *mutual respect*. In his speech during a seminar around this year's findings of the CBI's Innovation Trend Survey,[6] Julian Hildersley of TTPCom commented on their cooperation with Hitachi: 'It was essential that we had been able to establish mutual trust and respect in our cross-company project team. When I asked my Japanese counterpart to do something, he knew I would not ask him unless it was essential for the project. And of course it worked the other way too; when he told me he could not do something I knew it was not lack of will but insurmountable difficulties.'

> 'The top team listens to each other, they have deep respect, though in the end the CEO will make the decision. Our board will also listen to others and ask lots of questions to ensure they understand what is presented to them; they take a deep interest in it.'

Collaboration

Collaboration, such as that between Hitachi and TTPCom, is also an important part of the innovation armoury. Many organisations do not have the resources, or the skills, to execute certain innovation projects by themselves. In this case external collaboration may be the only solution. Hence, alongside internal cooperation (through teams and

---

[4] This is an important point, given the earlier insight that many scientists may consider collaboration to be a sign of weakness.

[5] The other two are fear of criticism or ridicule, and feeling of fatality (nothing will happen).

[6] 28 February 2001 at the TTPCom building, Melbourn Science Park, Melbourn, Royston, Cambridgeshire, UK.

across functions) cooperation with external partners has become increasingly important. Interestingly, one company decided to introduce more collaboration internally because, 'The company is split into separate business units and the [cultural] glue is beginning to unravel. To prevent this from happening, we are trying to become more interactive and collaborative.'

The 2001 CBI innovation Survey found that about 75% of companies surveyed had been involved in external cooperation. A fairly high number of these (48%) had engaged in partnerships with academia. And while partnerships with consultants were almost always described as problematic, the fewest problems were reported in business–academia relationships, despite the commonly-held view that academia may be too slow and unreliable in meeting deadlines. Most collaboration lasted between two and five years, with larger organisations having longer-term relationships than smaller ones. The most common barrier to collaboration was finding the right partner, while reasons for seeking collaboration were:

- access to knowledge outside of own sector;
- opportunities to use someone else's idea(s);
- pressure of competition.

While one company in particular expressed a very positive attitude towards cooperation with suppliers and customers – 'We view our suppliers and customers as partners, which means that we are not screwing them for every penny. We are looking for a win–win situation. If, however, our suppliers are trying to screw us we can and will fight back. We take it seriously when people think they are not being treated fairly' – others were aware that they had not created the best starting positions: 'Our cooperation with customers is limited, and with suppliers it is quite difficult as we have generally screwed them for cost in the past.' Equally counter-productive is the situation described by another interviewee: 'The company negotiates too hard with its suppliers which often causes problems during the contract period, sometimes even going bust. This means in the end we have to pay more than we would have, had we been less aggressive in the first place.' Collaboration only works if a true win–win situation is created.

Constant change

'Pluralism in ideas, among people, within organisations, and across industries is a crucial driver of change, even as that very change significantly alters pluralism.'

Eisenhardt (2000)

Whether it is to collaborate more, or to work more in teams, for most organisations it means that change is an important part of becoming more innovative. Or as Kathleen Eisenhardt (2000), innovation expert at Harvard Business School, points out, 'Change is a crucial driver of innovation.' It is about not accepting that things should be done in a certain way just because it happens to be the way the company has always done things. It involves continuously challenging the way things are done, looking for improvements, finding out how other people are doing it and investigating whether some of their learning could be successfully transferred. What it is not about is change for change's sake.

But there are other issues with change: There can be too much change: 'We had so many significant changes over the past two to three years that there is no culture left, or rather, only slowly is there a new culture emerging. And innovation was not part of the culture 12 months ago.' Or

> 'Change is enforced through changes in contracts, training, briefings etc.'

there can be the problem of changing without defining what is replacing the old, 'Old values, behaviours and processes were abandoned but nothing else was put in their place.' And, finally, it is important to take an holistic approach when wanting to achieve a significant shift in culture – changing systems, procedures, setting new rules for behaviour and so on is all part of the process. Change initiatives can also die due to expecting them to achieve too much: 'If change is suggested in our company, people tend to add on more and more so that in the end it becomes too big and nothing happens.' Change should be orchestrated, explained and supported by training and a thorough communication process.

Managers who are aware that their organisations ought to change but are not sure in which direction they should go also have a problem. Often the solution is to bring in outside people to help with identifying the problem and defining a way forward. However, this can also be used as an excuse not to take any action at all. As one company's situation was described: 'We are in the habit of thinking, we cannot do it ourselves, so let's bring someone in – let's get the consultants in. We love their suggestions and ideas for about four weeks, then we decide we don't like them and throw them out again – and nothing has changed.'

> 'The new CEO should have used the opportunity of his arrival to introduce change. Now everyone has settled back into their normal routine and it will be much more difficult to create an environment for change.'

Assessing the climate or openness for change is an important part in determining a change strategy.[7] External threats or internal changes, such as mergers and acquisitions or changes in leadership, generally help to make people more receptive to change. Very often explicit threats that would open up organisations for change are missing, in which case a threat might have to be generated internally. Depending on the timescale and size of company it may not have to be quite as drastic; for example, one company mentioned that they had used training courses and workshops to address reluctance to change.

While Stephen Denning, quoted in Jeff de Cagna's (2001) article on how to make change happen, believes that 'You get an organisation to change by explaining the reason for the change as clearly as you can, and that people – being rational beings – listen to what you have to say and weigh up the reasons. If your reasons are good and your idea is good, they accept them and they get on with implementing the change.' Jeff de Cagna disagrees, and suggests instead that ideas about change should be stimulated in the minds of the audience. If one can appeal to their own imagery and make the change relevant to their personal context, this is 'far less threatening and can rapidly become part of their own mindset and identity'. This comes back to the need to connect emotionally with people, which was a strong theme in the section on leadership earlier in this chapter. However, to some readers the flow chart below might seem familiar (see Figure 5.2).[8]

---

[7] In their article '*Innovation and marketing: when structure does not follow strategy*' Johne and Davies (1999) provide a case study of a company who has been successful at preparing the ground for an innovation initiative.

[8] The flow chart was kindly sent to me by Mario Gagliardi, student on the MBA Design Management programme at the University of Westminster, London.

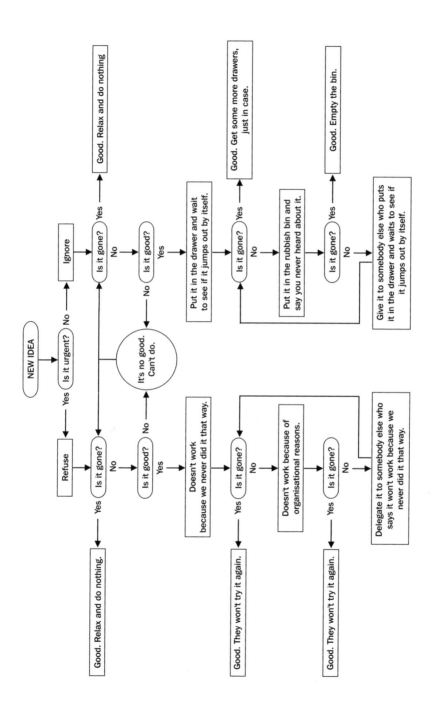

Figure 5.2: A new idea? Great!

In some organisations there is a great willingness to embrace change and, here it is important not to lose that goodwill: 'At present there is so much goodwill and enthusiasm, it needs to be channelled. We need to do something about it otherwise people will get tired and we will have missed a great opportunity.'

To avoid high levels of uncertainty, causing fear and the spreading of rumours, it is important to ensure that people affected by the change are informed early, and that the communication is clear and unambiguous. It is also important that people understand the larger picture and why the changes are so important. It also helps to be aware that the longer the company goes without change, the less experience people will have of changing and the more difficult it will be for them to accept change. 'A lot of the people have worked a long time for the company – they do not know any other place, so it is more difficult for them to accept and embrace change.'

Responsibility for innovation

In many organisations there is an ongoing discussion as to who has responsibility for innovation, an issue that is closely linked to the question of how to structure for innovation, which has already been discussed in the previous chapter. But one characteristic of an innovation culture is that everyone in the organisation feels responsible for achieving the organisation's innovation ambition. Participants reaction to the question 'who in your organisation is considered to be responsible for innovation' varied consider-

> 'We do have a problem: people think, we have a person officially responsible for new product development, so innovation is his job, it has nothing to do with us.'

ably. In one particular organisation the annual employee survey revealed that, '90% of managers felt innovation had nothing to do with them.'

But as well as feeling that innovation is someone else's responsibility, there are also other perceived barriers to innovation, such as people feeling that they cannot do something, and therefore they don't even try. A similar barrier is when people keep asking 'what would my boss think of it? or if people feel they have to spend about half of their time selling the idea internally.

The literature provides many examples of what constitutes a best-practice innovation culture, but it can be best summarised as:

- the freedom to fail;
- learning and challenging environment;
- experimentation and the ability to kill projects early;
- can-do approach;
- results-oriented;
- team culture;
- involving customers and suppliers.

'Best-practice companies are open to ideas from all available sources. Visits to other companies, even those in different sectors, can be a useful stimulus for lateral thinking. Competitors, alongside customers, are seen as a major driver for continuous improvement: "Competition forces innovation. Innovation is driven by the goal of being and staying No 1." '
From 'Winning', a DTI/CBI report, 1995.

In his book *Marketing and the Bottom Line* (2000), Tim Ambler summarises the characteristics of an innovation culture as follows: 'The key enabling factors that emerge for culture are: freedom to fail, autonomy for the innovation team and a willingness to change by the firm as a whole which needs to be balanced by the application of knowledge. These four metrics can be reduced to a balance of two: *freedom to fail* and *responsible knowledge*; that is, an appetite for learning.' This is also the shortest possible list. In his list Ambler also seems to equate 'freedom to fail' with 'freedom to experiment', which is certainly a critical ingredient to successful innovation.

A list of 24 items was used in recent research.[9] Participants were asked to select those items that they most associated with an innovation culture. Table 5.1 shows the five items that were most frequently ranked number one and were ticked most frequently.

Constantly challenging the status quo and constantly learning from others are further characteristics of best-practice organisations. One interviewee commented, 'We are moving much more to a questioning culture. It is no longer, "this is how we have always done it" but instead

---

[9] The findings are based on a study conducted by Alto Design Management between April and November 2000 as a follow-up to an earlier survey with innovative enterprises that preceded the drafting of the new British Standard BS 7000 Part 1: Guide to Managing Innovation. The original survey, conducted in 1998, was commissioned by the British Standards Institution (BSI) and funded by the Department of Trade and Industry (DTI).

Table 5.1: Items most associated with an innovation culture

Ranked number 1 most frequently	Ticked most frequently
1 Clear visions of future used as 'trailers' for future developments.	1 Enterprises are result-oriented, not rigidly regulated; tolerate behaviour outside rules.
2 A can-do approach prevails in adopting a longer-term perspective/planning.	2 Everyone can make improvements; significant decisions not only with elite few.
3 Enterprises are result-oriented, not rigidly regulated; tolerate behaviour outside rules.	3 More direct communication draws out new knowledge and builds intellectual property.
4 Everyone can make improvements; significant decisions not only with the elite few.	4 Keen to acquire knowledge and experience from elsewhere ('borrow with pride').
5 Endeavour to increase overall size of markets and/or create new markets.	5 Constantly check customers' experiences of products/services; rehearse future scenarios.

we are saying, "this is how we have always done it, is there a better way of doing it?"'

So if it is mainly down to leadership to facilitate a culture of innovation, how can this be done? How can a sense of urgency be created that will motivate people out of their complacency and into positive action?

For innovation initiatives to have an impact throughout an organisation, they generally have to be driven by the centre. This can be tricky, particularly in situations where a global organisation has been created through mergers and acquisitions, bringing together a pool of strong existing brands. Here it is particularly important to achieve a balance of local governance and head office guidance to address challenges such as:

- how can we drive initiatives from the centre without running the risk of being rejected by business units?
- how can we create a sense of urgency that will motivate people out of their complacency into positive action?

Finding the fish and aligning the fleet – Making innovation an everyday capability

Jens Maier and Ian Owen, Zurich Financial Services

Good news, bad news: 128 years of experience!

In the first part I will give you a bit of background to our company and then explain the approach we took to infuse innovation into what was a large, traditional organisation. Ian will follow with a description of how he subsequently developed an impressive innovation architecture at his regional level.

Zurich Financial Services is one of those large organisations that are good at what they do – we know what the rules of the game are, and we know the players in the industry. Until now, it had been about being smarter than the competition, and our key executives understood that competing was about using skill sets and capabilities such as target marketing better than the existing competitors. It was all about playing the existing game better.

The company has been around for 128 years and for more than 120 out of these 128 years we have been based on insurance. With its 68 000 employees, in over 300 strategic business units in 65 countries, the company has traditionally applied a highly decentralised operating model.

With such high levels of independence, the question often asked is not only, 'How do we create shareholder value?', but also, 'How can we take advantage of our presence in all those markets?' Of course, it is important to perform in all these markets. However, our shareholders expect that additional value is created from being part of a larger entity, Zurich Financial Services. This is why we needed more that just a leadership programme. We needed an innovation architecture that would enable us to create an entity that provided greater value than the sum of its parts, leveraging our diversity and local market knowledge.

The need to change tack

In the past, being better was sufficient to command a leading position in the industry. But new competitors are entering the market and things are changing. For example, in the UK, many 'non-finance' companies are entering the market such as grocery giant Tesco, clothing and foods retailer Marks & Spencer, the multifaceted Virgin, and Boots the Chemists, to name just a few. We felt that it was time to respond and provide our key executives with tools to exercise 'strategic leadership', allowing the organisation to make the shift from merely playing the game better, to proactively shaping the market of emerging financial services.

Traditionally, Zurich Financial Services would have tackled such a task locally. This time, following a sequence of mergers and acquisitions, the market expectation was to generate extra value from the corporate umbrella. Indeed, many advisors told us, 'Since you have spent so many years having a local focus, you should now turn your attention to the global needs of the organisation.' However, we felt that too strong a swing from local to global focus would cause us to lose touch with local market needs. We wanted to do something very difficult instead, namely making sure that we keep the local touch while at the same time leveraging whatever possible at the global level.

A new course for the Zuricher

To address the challenges we developed a four-step leadership process, LEAD (Leadership Education and Development). Each step involves a workshop, lasting three to four days. The first workshop, which we call 'Activation', focuses on value creation and 'strategies in converging markets' and on 'innovation'. It is very much about creating a shared strategic agenda and, to date, 28 different groups and more than 700 executives have been through this process. But this was not enough. In fact, those who had attended the workshop wanted more than just a classroom exercise. They wanted to do it 'for real'.

In response, we created an innovation workshop with the sole purpose of generating new business concepts and value-creating processes. Over the last two years, the executives have generated 64 new business concepts/processes of which nine are already implemented. A further 15-20% are currently in various stages of development. This is a remarkably high conversion rate.

The third workshop focuses on individual leadership development, providing the executive with an individual toolkit for achieving leadership results. The fourth workshop is focused on performance measurement at the organisational as well as individual level.

Charting unknown waters

The first two workshops provided had a measurable impact: when executives created winning ideas that added to the bottom line, people began to listen. But how did we decide which business concepts to select? Let me briefly introduce the 'innovation landscape', a tool based on different categories of innovation – 10 different categories in our particular case. As well as expected categories such as 'product innovation' or 'core processes', this classification also included 'business model' innovation which might, for example, involve questioning how we get paid. These categories provide a structure around which data can be added from an industry's history, to demonstrate where and when in the past innovations of a certain type had been introduced, creating a pattern – or landscape – that shows peaks and troughs of types of innovation at points in time.

We used the insights into the innovation landscapes for the financial services industry in a number of ways. Clearly, we would not create most value if we focused on the same areas as everyone else. To give you an example from the computer industry: all players are competing on providing ever-higher performing PCs, showing as a peak in the 'performance' category on the computer industry innovation landscape. However, the 'distribution channels' category, at that point in time, would have shown as a trough. Gateway and Dell revolutionised the industry by focusing on the distribution channel, dealing direct with customers and thus changing the business model.

By creating and understanding the innovation landscape for the financial services industry we were able to look at innovating in those areas where we would get the most 'bang for the buck'; i.e. where the effort would be most rewarded and where we could make a real difference. This is very different approach to benchmarking, which essentially ensures that an organisation is doing the same as everyone else, just a bit better. Selecting ideas and concepts based on insights from an innovation landscape removes the randomness and creates the basis for an innovation architecture, allowing us to innovate consecutively and at will.

Once we had identified the initiatives to be taken forward, the next step was to tailor the successful new concept to other markets – and, remember, we were operating in 60+ countries with the traditional view of 'my market is different'. Local protectionism was one of the reasons why the holistic approach – the common experience of more than 700 executives participating in the process, easy understandable decision criteria – was so important. Through this approach, we have achieved a level of involvement and buy-in for 'innovation' we would otherwise not have seen.

However, when looking at the concepts that were not taken forward, we found that many great opportunities had been side-lined because there was no 'natural' home for them. We therefore decided that initiatives launched at the corporate level needed to be supported by a 'local' innovation culture and supporting processes. And this is the point to hand over to my colleague Ian Owen who, having taken part in the corporate LEAD process, has taken the process into our UK operation.

The UK experience

I would like to start by emphasising that the corporate centre has been able to put together a remarkable programme: the first module turned people who started the programme by thinking 'There's no need to innovate - you [from the centre] just do not know how difficult it is', into a group sitting up saying, 'My goodness! If we do not do something we are dead!'

The journey started in November 2000, with a senior management conference at a hotel near Heathrow for the UK's top 200 executives in the general insurance business. We collapsed the first two modules of the leadership programme and innovation workshop. At the end of this some 40 ideas were generated – but generating the ideas was actually very, very easy. The big challenge was, how were we going to take them forward? My appointment to spearhead the innovation projects was a first step – allocating responsibility. As I did not know much about innovation at the time, I felt reminded of the film *A Field of Dreams* where they build a baseball pitch, hoping that people will come to play on it. And it has been a bit like that; people from different parts of the organisation have offered to help, and around this self-selected group we created something we called the *innovation lab*. So at this point in time we had established that innovation was crucial for us to succeed, and we had developed a number of ideas that people felt strongly about. People also started to feel safer about challenging the status quo, which was very important.

However, what we needed to do was to create an environment where it felt safe to fail – not an easy task in an insurance company where people are highly risk-averse and failure is generally followed by the departure of the person responsible! What we wanted to create was not only an environment where people felt safe to fail; we actually wanted people to fail, as we could then learn from our mistakes. Another issue we were aware of is that you can keep generating ideas, and building on ideas, and developing the ideas – without ever achieving anything! So it was about having a passion for results from innovation and not just innovation for innovation's sake. In parallel, we started developing processes that would support innovation – not formal manuals, but guidelines so we could keep track of where we were (see Figure 5.3)

Fairly arbitrarily, we selected 10 of the 40 ideas that had been generated in the senior management workshop. We then contacted the teams who had generated the ideas, in order to select the five which people felt the most passionate about. Once selected, each team was given up to £2500 and four weeks to generate a detailed outline of their idea to present to the innovation panel. At this stage

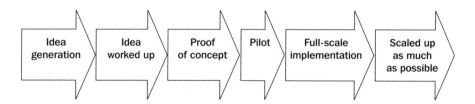

Figure 5.3: The innovation process

we were less concerned about the detailed finances than what the idea would mean for the organisation and what would be required to take it to what we called 'proof of concept'. Zurich Financial Services was willing to invest a quarter of a million pounds on each idea to take it through to pilot stage. Interestingly, the vast majority have required far less funding than that.

Taking the ideas to proof of concept typically took around eight weeks. From there the team moved to a full-blown pilot and implementation.

In order to further foster and embed innovation into the company fabric, we developed a number of supporting concepts and processes, including:

- *Rapid decision environment*. We borrowed General Electric's workout concept. Rather than relying on the senior people, often removed from the day-to-day business, to come up with suggestions about how to drive the organisation forward, you ask the people who are at the coalface. So frontline people would work together over a few days to generate solutions to a given operational or strategic problem. At the end of the few days they would come up with recommendations as to what needed to happen and how they would take it forward to implementation. The results were presented at what we called a town hall meeting with the sponsor (the person who set the problem in the first place) and with relevant subject matter experts present. The purpose of the town hall meeting is to make a decision there and then. The rules of the game are that you cannot say, 'We will think about it.' You cannot just say, 'No'. If 'no' is the answer, you have to state the reasons for the negative response. You can say 'yes', or a qualified 'yes', which normally means some additional work is required before a final decision can be made. So the point is to come to a go/no-go decision where people understand the reasoning behind the decision.
- *Good company*. This concept involves taking a group of people out of the office environment for two or three days, to a hotel or similar venue where they are in an entirely different environ-

ment, which allows them to think outside the box and work up ideas. The use of space, actors, props and sometimes customers is encouraged, as this helps to generate and test the new ideas. Why actors? Actors are very good at creating different environments that people then walk into. The actors get our people to break out of their normal thinking patterns and do crazy things like speaking to mannequins as if they were customers. To give you another example, when people arrived to the last 'good company' session, I was dressed up as a waiter serving the morning coffee. So people immediately got the message that this was something different. At the end of the three-day session, a group of senior people came in to be engaged in conversation around the ideas the group had generated. People learn from this that it is okay to do crazy things, that it is okay to take a risk, and that it is okay to fail as long as we learn from it.

The UK's experience also allowed us to tackle some of the innovations that really ought to have happened anyway. Breaking down the barriers to ownership and commitment helped us to bring in some very simple, yet effective, innovations, including:

- A direct operation for small businesses. The UK has a very large commercial operation that deals with businesses both large and small. The main way of dealing with these customers is through insurance brokers. However, the group does have a substantial direct business dealing directly with individual customers. So w decided to join the dots by taking the products from our com mercial operation and joining them with the marketing an customer service expertise found in our direct operation, resu ing in an ability to offer insurance directly to small businesses.
- Leveraging relationships with house builders. When you b new property, you will often get a National House Bu Certificate which guarantees the build quality of the new h Zurich offers something very similar; in fact, we are so stro this market that the trade often calls the certificate 'a Zur we have a strong relationship with the building industry UK. But we were not exploiting this relationship by

other financial services products related to house purchases, such as home contents insurance or building insurance. How did we realise this? Simply because one person who had been frustrated about this missed opportunity that had not been realised over many, many years, gathered a team together, went to a good company event and took the idea all the way through to implementation.

Before summing up, I would like to share a very interesting insight we gained from our programme. We had three other ideas that have gone through this innovation process in the UK. When these groups came to present to the innovation panel they turned to us and said, very passionately, 'We do not believe this is going to work for the following reasons.' So they were not turned down, but decided themselves that it would not work. That has been very interesting for us as a group, and has given us an opportunity to show that we were serious about celebrating failure. So we said, 'This is brilliant because you guys had the guts to say that you do not believe it will work after all. Now let us see what we can learn from that, and how we can apply the insights to other projects we are doing.' Absolutely brilliant.

Where next?

Having had a number of the original ideas go through the system from concept to implementation, we are now looking at how to generate more ideas. One way we are approaching this is by using our 'Young Tigers'. These are people who have been with the group not much longer than 18 months – the young high-flyers, the sort of people who are considered indispensable to the organisation. We bring them together for a two-day workshop and ask them, if you were our competition, how would you beat Zurich? The ideas they come up with give us great inspiration on how and where to improve our services!

The innovation architecture we have put in place across the organisation will also allow us to start using groups across our business units to address certain customer segments on a global

scale. We do support regional developments, but are keen to leverage benefits and programmes that reach across the entire group. Our industry is converging, changing and morphing all the time, whether we like it or not. The question is, are we *being* merged, morphed and converged, or are we actually *actively* shaping and leading the changes? Our intention is clearly to actively shape our future.

Critical success factors

We believe that the Zurich Financial Services experience of innovation has yielded some important insights for other organisations wishing to shake up their traditional business model.

1. Understand the terrain in which you are operating.
2. Look for external funding. External scrutiny helps to cut through the internal politics, as many opportunities get killed because there is no natural home for them. If you've got outside investors they force the issue and increase the urgency of delivery because they want to get out of the business at some point and see a return on their investment.
3. Incentivise the innovators.
4. Make decisions as rapidly as possible and don't look for excuses why something can't be done. Explore the orthodoxies in your industry and look for ways to change them.
5. Create an architecture around innovation so that you can actually innovate consecutively and not randomly.
6. Celebrate and learn from failures.

The role of the human resource (HR) department

Besides showing how an innovation initiative can be rolled out from the centre to the regions, the Zurich story also shows the important role HR can play. But beyond facilitating training and coaching, and developing programmes that kick-start culture change, HR systems play an important role in establishing and consolidating an organisation's culture:

- HR specialist Edward Lawler III (2000) points out, 'A misaligned pay strategy not only fails to add value, it produces high costs in the compensation area as well as inappropriate and misdirected behaviour.'
- The authors of the report 'Tomorrow's Leaders Today: Career Aspiration and Motivation' declare, 'The HR function is potentially a competitive differentiator – maximise its potential as a contributor to the company's success, particularly for executive development.'[10]

Although reward and remuneration systems encourage and discourage certain behaviours, they can be used to support messages sent from the top. One example where companies have long failed to use reward and remuneration to their best advantage are teams. When teams first came in fashion, many leaders were satisfied to tell their subordinates that henceforth they were expected to work in teams – without any training or changes in any of the other company systems. This often led to conflicting messages: on the one hand the employee was rewarded entirely on her individual performance and achievement of individual goals, while at the same time it was expected that she serve time on teams and contribute to the successful completion of team projects. Often this was made worse by dual reporting lines.

> 'We have hardly any people leaving the company for competitors. If they are leaving it is generally for one of three reasons: to set up their own business; to do something else; or to move into a different industry.'

Another important aspect is training. The 1995 DTI/CBI survey showed that best practice companies in the UK placed a very high emphasis on training (see Figure 5.4). As the report states: 'Training is seen as a key component in achieving empowerment of the individual and in maintaining focus on the customer in order to remain competitive. Not only is "training the epicentre of empowerment", with as much as 10% of employees' time spent on it, but successful companies "use education as a competitive weapon".'

But investment in training is only one component of HR policies in best-practice companies. They generally aim to be good employers all round. This includes:

---

[10] 'Tomorrow's Leaders Today: Career Aspiration and Motivation', is a study by Korn/Ferry International, carried out in collaboration with London Business School, 2001. See www.kornferry.com and www.futurestep.com.

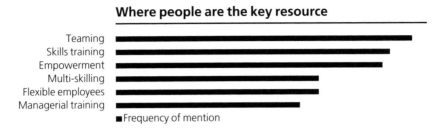

Figure 5.4: Best-practice companies and training

- hiring the best people;
- giving them the best pay package;
- giving them freedom to experiment - and accepting failure;
- seeking diversity;
- having a philosophy of hiring women.

The consequence is low staff turnover, and people leaving to start a different career, rather than moving to a competitor. Companies that frequently use head hunters to fill open positions in their organisations should appreciate this particular benefit of low staff turnover for another reason: finding and winning new people can be a costly business.

Best practice in HR is beautifully summarised by a comment made by one interviewee: 'Our HR processes and activities are all geared up to support our culture. We aim to make sure that the right people are hired, and that they then get the right training. Everyone knows our five principles and we have an induction programme for joiners to ensure they are aligned with and aware of them. People here tend to leave within the first year or stay forever.'

In reward systems there seems to be a trend away from primarily (financial) performance related measures to more skill-based measures. Often personal development plans are based on 360-degree feedback and progress is monitored on a regular basis and in consultation with the individual in question.

> 'We have seen a shift in our bonus, merit and award systems. There is a clear push towards leadership and away from administration.'

Best-practice companies tend to look after their people. Instead of letting good people go because they might get bored with their job or because their job might have disappeared, such companies make an effort to find the right job for their people.

> 'The attitude is to try to keep people and move them about internally rather than lose them. The motto is: try something different if you like.'

A practice that is beneficial to both the employee and the organisation is internal secondments. It offers the employee new insights into a different business area or function, helping with personal development, while the organisation gains through cross-fertilisation between functions or different parts of the business. And it is when different bodies of knowledge are connected that innovation tends to occur. While enabling different bodies of knowledge to connect within an organisation, there is of course also great value to be gained from facilitating the connection of bodies of knowledge between organisations.

Another aspect of looking after people is to offer them a good balance between work and private life. Examples include, no travelling on Sundays or Fridays so employees get a proper weekend at home; another is to provide them with IT that enables them to work from home, such as laptops and ISDN lines. And of course there is also the attitude towards people in economically difficult times. Redundancies can have a significant impact on employee trust, particularly when badly handled. This can have a knock-on effect on a company's innovation culture which depends on having a high level of trust between employer and employee. When trust is eroded, innovation goes right down, and generally takes some time to build up again. This means that people are less willing to come forward with ideas, and share information with others. This is very counter-productive if you are trying to create an innovation culture. Does a company lay off people immediately or do they try to find ways to retain as many as possible? Two very different examples shared by the InnovationNetwork[11] are shown in the box below.

Worst practice includes sacking people as soon as a crisis looms, without realising that attracting these people back might be costly.

---

[11]   InnovationNetwork e-mail, 3 February 2001.

The wrong way

From a reader (the sender's name and the company name have been removed)

I thought you would be interested in these quotes from my former company web site under 'Careers'. Unbelievable!! Incidentally, they axed documentation and the QA department.

> 'Our People, Our Culture At [Xxxxxx].
> Who you are matters just as much as what you do. Our core values – integrity, profitability, people, fun, customers, quality and innovation – are the driving forces behind our corporate culture. We value our employees as individuals and believe that giving each person the opportunity to succeed is key to achieving our overall corporate goals.'
> 'We work hard to attract and retain talented, enthusiastic and productive professionals.'

How timely. I received this the very day I was called into the boardroom at 2:30 pm and told that because of the ongoing 'restructuring' for IPO (initial public offering), my position has been eliminated. I protested that this makes no sense since I am needed to ensure the project the company is banking on is successful. The engineering manager just shrugged his shoulders and said that is the way it is. Then I was told to take a half hour or so to pack my personal belongings.

Working within the hi-tech sector for over 30 years has shown that nothing has changed. What I experienced in 2001 is no different to what happened in the 1990s, or the 1980s, or the 1970s. I have been through this cycle many times. Workers are mere commodities to add when the economy is booming, then to dump as un-needed expenditures when things tighten. In between, we are treated with the same pigslop – 'our employees are our most important asset' and 'innovation is driving our future.' Yeah, right!

Never once in all these years has anyone said, 'Things are turning bad. The last thing we want to do is to terminate employees. So we need your collective brainpower for solutions to this situation.'

The lights may be on in the executive offices. But there is no light on between the temples. Innovation is never driving the company, the stock price is.

The right way

From Virginia Albanese, FedEx Custom Critical

At FedEx Custom Critical (Akron, Ohio) we are doing a lot to combat the 'lay-off'. We have asked all of our team members for cost-saving suggestions and ideas on how we can get through these tough times without a lay-off. To date we have saved a tremendous amount of money and haven't displaced a single worker.

Why? Our people are our greatest asset. We say it and mean it! It takes about six to nine months to get an agent up and running in the customer service area, so turnover is no fun. As I explained to an agent 'about the same time I shook your hand and bid farewell, I would have to welcome a new team member to prepare them for our next peak business season.' It doesn't make any sense. Not to mention the reputation the company gets in the community.
What are we doing?

- Time off without pay has been a big hit. Team members are taking off a day, a week or a month. Some actually just chose to take the time in hours.
- We cancelled the much-loved Christmas party.
- We look for the best travel deals.
- We have come up with new or improved ways to generate business. Our quote call back team is hard at work calling customers back and asking for their business.
- We found a way of changing some of our phone vectoring that would save us quite a bit of money.

These are only a few of the many ways that we are saving money and saving jobs!
In conclusion, I think that our company is doing a wonderful job of containing costs and saving jobs. I am proud to be associated with FedEx Custom Critical, an employer that Walks the Talk!

Another problem with pending redundancies is that at the first rumours, the best people tend to leave rather than the ones who should leave. But how, without risking being sued for unfair dismissal or being seen to be unfair, can one prevent these people from leaving while sacking others at the same time?

With today's changing work environment, HR departments are facing some interesting challenges:

> 'One departing worker in a department that doesn't even hit your radar screen is a networking mentor; one of those people who shares ideas and makes connections that build an invisible, but critical, information network. His or her leaving will rip apart the social fabric connecting hundreds of people.'
> (From Innovation Network e-mail, 2 February 2001)

- How can HR systems be developed that find a balance between individual and team rewards?
- What kind of incentives and rewards structure can be developed to attract the best people in a market where the best people tend to be able to pick and choose?
- What can companies offer people who are not motivated by money or career progression?

Work environment

'You need a working environment that encourages innovation, it needs to stimulate innovation. People should experience new and different things during work, that's why we bring in all kinds of new technology, new products and competitors' products. The aim is to get people to think differently.'

Over recent years, increasing attention has been paid to the physical work environment and its potential contribution to organisational culture and innovation. Ralph Buschow, of architects Buschow & Henley, commented in an interview conducted in April 1999,[12] 'The work environment used to be static. Now it needs to be much more flexible – in fact, it needs to offer both flexibility and continuity. Human beings are very complex, their needs may vary from day to day and this needs to be reflected in the work environment.' He continues, 'Spending

---

[12] The full-length interview can be found on the Innovation Exchange web site (http://iexchange. london.edu), accessible from the editorial page.

money on the work environment makes sense. For most companies, particularly in the service industry, salaries are the largest expenditure. This naturally means that it should be in the interest of an organisation to get the best out of their people – and the best way to achieve that is to make them want to come to work, to make them happy at work. A 1% increase in productivity will pay for all sorts of things!'

'The question is, how do we come up with genuine innovation? The kind of blend we are trying to create combines cross-country teams, a good mix of genders, experienced people, strong subject knowledge and consumer connect. This means that if changes in the work environment are required, they need to be pleasant and inspiring.'

While it would be going too far to say that the work environment can *create* a culture, it can certainly play an important role in *supporting* the kind of culture an organisation thrives to achieve.

A report recently published by International Survey Research entitled 'Tracking Trends in Europe' shows that only 50% of British, Hungarian, French and Italian workers are satisfied with their workplace; this can be

'We use our environment to communicate values and culture.' David Magliano, Marketing Director, Go-Fly, interview, Innovation Exchange interview, May 1999

contrasted with the Swedes, Danes, Norwegians and Dutch who are much more satisfied with all aspects of their work.[13]

Teamwork is one example where the right work environment can be very important. The effectiveness of teams can be greatly improved by co-location, by providing dedicated team space – and many organisations are already doing that. Easier communication between departments can be facilitated through shared spaces such as coffee areas or even photocopying facilities. Where people are given the opportunity to

'In the work environment the kitchen, for example, is a very important element. It used to be in the corner, in the basement – somewhere out of the way. Today we have changed our view on this: the kitchen is a meeting point, people bump into each other, exchange ideas, this is where networking happens – where things generally just happen. Questions which in the old days may have been saved up for the weekly meeting are now discussed in the corridor and in between meetings. Views are collected and decisions made on a much more continuous and spontaneous basis than before.'
Ralph Buschow, architect, interview April 1999

[13]   To find out more, e-mail isr@isrsurveys.co.uk.

bump into each other, ideas get exchanged, new contacts are made and understanding about what 'those people over there' do increases. Open plan offices enhance communication too, but usually only within a particular department.

One Innovation Exchange member company went further. They have no allocated office space for individuals, but practice what they have called ROMPing – which stands for Radical Office Mobility Programme. To quote Jon Leach of the marketing communications agency HHCL,[14] 'No one in the organisation has a fixed working space; people move around but are connected and contactable by mobile phones (with headsets) and e-mail; the office offers different types of environments: quiet zones, meeting rooms, 'standing-up' rooms, group space and so on. To make this structure work we employ three full-time people: an office manager, an IT person and someone with a planning back-ground.[15] While this new way of working is very exciting, the approach we took for implementing it was essential for gaining employees' buy-in and hence its success: rather than imposing the concept on everyone within the organisation, volunteers were asked to come forward to test the first phase of implementation and initially only a small part of the office space was converted.'

If trends towards working from home continue, the work environ-ment will play an even more important role: it has to act as repres-entative of the company's culture, it has to invite employees to come back and spend time there, it has to be inspiring and stimulating. Another reason why the office and the office environment have become more important is that companies seem to be more and more virtual. This means that the office, the physical manifestation of the organisation, becomes the focal point for the organisation's culture. In a way, a virtual organisation needs a much stronger culture than a real organisation. The office can help people to identify with their organisation.

But of course a work environment conducive to communication and exchange alone does not do the trick. If you just change the work environment you may get comments such as 'Our mentality here is still

---

[14] For the full-length interview with Jon Leach, please see Innovation Exchange web site, accessible from the editorial page (http://iexchange.london.edu).

[15] The total number of employees at the time was 160.

in silos, even though the work environment has changed.' Or as Jon Leach emphasised, 'You have got to have an integrated package; it is not just about having a great working environment and hoping that this makes it all happen. The company needs a very clear direction, that's what people are attracted to and that's what they work hard to achieve. The right office environment can help make that happen.'

And finally, each organisation needs to consider its specific issues and requirements. Asked whether there were any rules to use in designing innovative work environments, Ralph Buschow answered, 'You have to look at each organisation's situation individually. You have to understand where they are coming from, what their culture is. You have to consider not only individuals and teams, but also the organisational context. You can't just replicate what you have done on your previous job.'

Anchor points

- Leadership is the one key ingredient that can make or break an innovation culture.
- Culture. Unless the CEO is committed to innovation it will not happen in the business. If CEOs do not support it, it does not happen. Why? Because they simply switch everything off. They also create a culture where nobody actually asks to do anything because they know the CEO will say no. So it never happens.
- Ensure your innovators have the freedom to fail.
- Managing behaviours. Effective innovation means having the right behavioural responses. It might pay to have coaches working with your teams. One best-practice company reported that every single cross-functional team on every project has an external coach who manages the behavioural dimension to innovation because they realise that this does not happen naturally.
- Use your very best people to head the innovation initiative, and treat innovation as a skill in its own right.
- Organise for innovation. You have to be able to execute brilliantly. Most of the things you try fail because they are not executed well, for several reasons.

Endless as the sea – innovation challenges

CHAPTER 6

Innovation paradoxes

'Paradox is the simultaneous existence of two inconsistent states, such as between innovation and efficiency, collaboration and competition, or new and old. Rather than compromising between the two in some sort of Goldilocks fantasy, vibrant organisations, groups, and individuals change by simultaneously holding the two states. This duality of coexisting tensions creates an edge of chaos, not a bland halfway point between one extreme and the other.'

The above quote from a recent article by Harvard Business School's innovation expert Kathleen Eisenhardt (2000) sums up the situation companies are facing today. It is not either or but and: companies have to achieve efficiencies but at the same time continuously produce something new; that is, innovate. Again to improve efficiency but also to achieve wider reach than their own resources would allow, they need to collaborate but at the same time they may be in competition with their partners. They need to renew themselves and innovate but at the same time nurture their existing business and build on what they stand for. Finding ways to balance these contradictions is an essential precondition for becoming not only an innovator but a successful one.

This section introduces a number of such *innovation paradoxes* that have emerged from the interviews in each of the five main areas of investigation: strategy and vision, leadership, culture, process and (physical) work environment.

Strategy and vision

Stretch versus attainability

The challenge for top management is to devise a vision and strategy that is sufficiently challenging to inspire the company's employees and managers but at the same time attainable to prevent frustration and giving up before having even started.

Innovation versus efficiencies

How to balance the quest for innovation, generally associated with the expansion of the product portfolio, with the desire for reducing product lines to achieve greater efficiencies.

Diversity versus megabrands

Again driven by economies of scale and cost efficiencies, companies tend to reduce their brand portfolios to create megabrands. But as with global products, they may not satisfy all tastes and consumer requirements, hence leaving gaps open for competitors to move in.

Global versus local

Economies of scale and cost efficiencies suggest concentrating on the development of global products. However, as discussed earlier, there are not many products that would not benefit from local adaptation – be it in features or simpler things such as colouring or packaging.

Local versus central control

Where should organisation control be placed? It should be central so that all projects can be coordinated, thereby avoiding duplication. But at the same time it should be local because that's where the knowledge of the consumer lies. As one interviewee put it, 'Our company is paradoxical: we have independent business units but at the same time lots of central control.'

Core competencies versus 'out of the box' thinking

There is generally a great emphasis on ensuring that innovation activity is linked to an organisation's core competencies and that strategy and vision set the boundaries within which idea generation and innovation activities can take place. But at the same time companies are looking for radical innovations, things that are outside the box, that can move them to new planes and redefine their business. This was commented on: 'Strange things are going on, things that don't necessarily fit; the boundaries of the organisation are not too tight.'

Openness to innovate versus resource constraints

At times when there is pressure to perform, which innovation may help to achieve, there is generally a reluctance to stick one's head above the parapet and try something new. This also occurs when resources are scarce, particularly for something that is uncertain, as innovation tends to

> 'The other thing is, you cannot turn innovation on and off like that: you have to keep it going through the good and bad times.'

be. On the other hand, when things are going well many organisations are (still) happy to continue with what they have done all along.

Ego versus effective innovation

An interesting observation on how individual interest can influence decisions was made by one interviewee: 'A barrier to innovation can be corporatism. The desire to be big and to preserve bigness is an issue. While spinning off companies might often be a better strategy, CEOs of large corporations might not be too open towards this as their status and remuneration are often attached to size. What is important to individuals and what constitutes success in the wider context, can influence how innovation is treated.'

Leadership

The main paradox for leaders seems to be how to balance *change* and *continuity*. An organisation's leader is key to implementing any kind of change, and making an organisation more innovative requires a change in culture. Hence, leadership is key to implementing an innovation culture. A second argument has been that leaders want to leave their mark, meaning that they seek to change things upon arrival. There is a major tension here: how does one leader establish an innovation culture in a way that is not threatened by his or her departure? Can innovation be ingrained into a culture so that it will survive changes in leadership? The answer may lie with having different types of leaders for situations that require change and those that require stability. In today's fast changing world, will there ever be a time where no change is required? How can organisations identify what needs to stay the same and what needs to change?

Culture

The main paradox in the area of culture – culture here is understood to be manifested through people, their behaviours, values and actions – lies in the need for people to have experience and 'know the way the company does things' but at the same time *not be constrained by their existing knowledge*. Or as phrased by one of the interviewees: 'Innovation is exceptionally difficult to manage. Why? Within innovation there is a dilemma: one is looking for creative ideas, one is looking for people who reject everything and who are not bound by what is there. But at the same time one needs ruthless management who knows and understands what is there'. The problem with this is of course that we are not consciously aware of what we know; certain patterns of behaviour or categorisation of problems happen automatically, conditioned by our past experience.[1]

Process

Too much versus too little detail

One of the dilemmas for any prescribed process is how to define the level of detail with which the process is described. As phrased by an interviewee: 'A problem with process is, if it is too detailed there will be information overload; if there is too little detail people will make mistakes and lose perspective.'

---

[1] This problem has been highlighted by Dorothy Leonard-Barton in her article '*Core capabilities and core rigidities: a paradox in managing new product development*' (1992), *Strategic Management Journal*, 13, 111–125.

True versus perceived differences

How can one assess whether claimed differences in local consumer needs are real or just put forward because of the not-invented-here syndrome? Addressing real differences is likely to be beneficial, and giving in to undercover resistance will delay a fast and efficient rollout of any new product.

Individual versus team rewards

In innovation, there is always a debate as to whether to reward teams or individuals. On the one hand, people are expected to work in teams and share ideas, insights and so on. This would suggest that a team reward is the best solution. On the other hand, it is generally one individual who comes up with the initial idea. Rewarding the team rather than the individual can be very demotivating. To illustrate the point, below is an extract from an interview I conducted with Jon Leach of Howell Henry Caldecott Lury (HHCL), an award-winning marketing communications company, in May 1999.

Rewarding teams or individuals?

BvS: It is often said that an important aspect in encouraging innovation is the recognition and reward systems because very often they are contradictory to what the company say they want.

JL: I don't think that our practice is actually very different from industry practice. We looked into rewarding the team but felt it was quite difficult to define the boundary of the team. Who was part of it and who would be eligible for the award? It seems quite clear that the team who has won the pitch is part of it. But what about the people who have done the research that enabled the first impression and understanding of the task? So whenever we looked at a team-based award we shied away from it but what we have got is a profit share based on length of service not salary. Everyone in each team benefits from success that way.

BvS: But do you avoid strong individually-oriented rewards?

JL: That is a very interesting issue that we as a business have to address. As long as the business is small, there is a feeling of 'we are all in this together against the rest of the world'. As you get beyond 50 or 60 people you no longer have that sort of feeling. In a larger company, people don't feel that they know everyone and don't feel comfortable with the thought of sharing their profit with someone they don't know.

Adding to people's saleability to keep them

If it is true that we are entering a knowledge economy, where the knowledge residing in individuals is key to a company's success, then retaining these people must be a key challenge for organisations. How best to do that might be paradoxical. Rather than trying to bind these people closely to the organisation through contracts or golden hand-cuffs, it might prove more effective to help them develop their sale-ability. In other words, investing in someone's personal development through training and education might stop them from wanting to leave, rather than making it easier for them to leave.

Need to communicate versus information overload

Another critical aspect within organisations is the *distribution of information* and the *level and frequency of communication*. On one hand, people need to be aware of what is happening in the organisation and its positioning and strategic direction. Stories help to build and support culture, and financial information makes people aware of the company's overall situation and pressures. Until recently, printed media was the main form of passing on information; today it is e-mail and the Intranet. Nothing is easier than copying the entire department into an e-mail or putting something up on a company intranet. The problem with sharing information so generously is that people suffer from information overload. For example, there are few ways to identify e-mails that must be read and those that should go straight into the bin. The problem is even bigger with intranets. While people will think, 'I have put my wisdom on to the intranet, I have done my bit to communicate,' there is hardly an intranet site that enables quick and easy access to relevant information. So the question is, how can the level of information that is truly beneficial for the individual be determined, and what medium should be used to do so.

> 'One big concern with the intranet is, people get the attitude, it's on the intranet, why did you not know it? In other words, people feel they do not have to communicate any more.'

Knowledge versus learning

Through learning we acquire knowledge – but often that knowledge then prevents us from learning more and exploring new and different approaches. Once we know how to do something, we stop asking questions as to why and how, and simply repeatedly apply our learned behaviour. While this is useful in routine situations such as driving a car, it is unhelpful for innovation. This is why bringing in non-experts can be extremely useful. They are not aware of, and therefore not constrained by, any knowledge or wisdom in the area and hence can approach the problem with an open mind.

Radical innovation versus quantity

If an innovation has the potential to shift industry standards, how much does it threaten the existing core business? Would managers be willing to sacrifice the present for the future?[2] Another paradox of radically new products – and perhaps the reason for small organisations being more likely to introduce radical innovations – is that many large organisations have minimum production levels. By nature, the market for a radical product will initially be small and take time to grow, which makes it unattractive to large organisations and might result in its withdrawal – particularly with today's increasing focus on megabrands.

Work environment

Designing a work environment that gains all the cost advantages of *hotdesking* without depriving employees of a *sense of belonging* is a big challenge. The trend towards hotdesking and thereby reducing the square metre provided per employee often generates a feeling in employees of being kicked out or not being wanted here. If not managed carefully, it can be counter-productive: employees phoning their colleagues to reserve a space for them, people feeling 'homeless' if there is no space for some personal belongings. In a recent conversation one staff member from a large organisation pointed out, 'We have recently introduced open-plan offices and hotdesking, partly to reduce costs but also to improve communication. This was implemented without the involvement of those who were affected. Quite soon we

---

[2]   An interesting book addressing this dilemma is Clayton Christensen's *The Innovator's Dilemma*, first published in 1997 by Harvard Business School Press.

found that those who could afford to do so started to work from home. Unfortunately, these people were the decision-makers, which of course had a disastrous effect on fast decision-making as well as on the morale of those left in the office.' For hotdesking to work, ways need to be found to counterbalance the negative effects of this strategy. Results also tend to be more positive if innovative office structures are developed for reasons other than cost savings and when people are involved in the decision making and transition process.

Future innovation challenges

A number of future challenges were identified by participants, some of which are truly new while others have occupied management attention for some time. For example, while the need to identify structures for globally operating organisations has arisen relatively recently, as has the quest for new forms of market research to identify latent consumer needs, issues of leadership, motivation and how to achieve change have been on the agenda for decades. However, while best practice leadership and motivation remain an issue of debate, best practice in change is understood much better – at least in theory.[3]

The debate from a workshop held to discuss the findings of the research identified the following themes at macro and micro levels:

Macro Level:

- How can innovation be infused throughout the organisation?
- How can we demonstrate the value of innovation?
- What are the best ways to structure for innovation?
- What type and level of innovation is right for our organisation?
- How can we achieve and maintain one company culture – or is this unnecessary?
- How can we maintain and support levels of innovation in times of economic downturn?

---

[3] For a summary of leadership theory you may want to refer to Goffee and Jones 'Why should anyone be led by you', Harvard Business Review (September–October 2000).

Micro Level:

- How can we identify big ideas early and push them through the system as quickly as possible?
- What processes enable the effective sharing of knowledge?
- How does one actually incentivise innovation, and should it be at the individual or group level?

Final comment

While reading the book, one thing should have become clear: innovation will not work if a fragmented approach is taken. Nor will an 'either or' attitude be successful – to be innovative is to manage paradoxes. Only an holistic approach that aligns strategy and vision, process, leadership style and culture to the innovation ambition has a chance of succeeding. The other key message from the book is that there is no one right way of approaching innovation; each company needs to take its specific context and history into account. And finally, becoming an innovative organisation is a journey. It does not happen overnight and what tools, techniques and processes are right for each company will change over the course of the journey.

On innovation and creativity in general

- *Managing Innovation: Integrating Technological, Market and Organisational Change*, by Joe Tidd, John Bessant and Kevin Pavitt, 2nd edition, Chichester: Wiley, 2001
  BvS comment: This book provides a good introduction to innovation and all kinds of issues around it.
- *?What If! How to Start a Creative Revolution at Work*, by D. Allan, M. Kingdon, K. Murrin and D. Rudkin, Oxford: Capstone, 1999
  BvS comment: The creative company ?What If! share their strategies for improving an organisation's creativity.
- *The Toolbox for the Mind,* by K.D. Denton and Rebecca A. Denton, Milwaukee: Quality Press, 1999
  BvS comment: Full of good ideas and insights on and around innovation and creativity.
- 'Creativity doesn't require isolation: Why product designers bring visitors "backstage"', by Robert I. Sutton and Tom A. Kelly, *California Management Review*, **40**, 75–91, Fall 1997
  BvS comment: In their article the authors argue the benefits to be gained from exposing ideas to a broad range of people – it is about allowing different bodies of knowledge to connect.
- *Creative Management*, by Jane Henry, 2nd edition, London: Sage 2001
  BvS comment: A compendium of articles on creativity and innovation by authors such as Theresa Amabile, Henry Mintzberg, Daniel

Goleman, Michael Kirton, Charles Handy and Rosabeth Moss Kanter. A good starting point and overview.

Leadership

- *'Why should anyone be led by you?'*, by Rob Goffee and Gareth Jones, *Harvard Business Review*, September–October 2000

  BvS comment: The article looks at the qualities displayed by inspirational leaders – see also references for Chapter 5.

- *'Charisma and how to grow it'*, by Jay Conger, in *Management Today*, December 1999, 78–81

  BvS comment: Jay Conger explains that what sets apart charismatic managers from other managers is that they are masters of motivation and superb communicators. By being entrepreneurial and agents of change, these charismatic managers are also often the ones driving innovation. Conger suggests that if you would like to become a charismatic leader, the first thing you have to do is fall in love with what you do. Identifying with your business makes you start to look for unexploited opportunities. Once identified, you need to start developing goals around them, and sell them into the organisation. It is important that the goals are described in ways that will bring others along with you. It is important to show passion in words and deeds, which might mean that you have to do some things that are unconventional, and take calculated risks.

- *'Motivating creativity in organisations: on doing what you love and loving doing what you do'*, by Theresa Amabile, *California Management Review*, **40**, 39–58, 1997

  BvS comment: Many managers believe that financial rewards have highly motivational effects on employees. This article argues that not money but intrinsic motivation - motivation to work on something because it is interesting, exciting, satisfying or personally challenging – is the most important ingredient for stimulating creativity and innovation.

- *'Developing leaders for the global frontier'*, by H.B. Gregersen, A.J. Morrison and J.S. Black, *Sloan Management Review*, **40**, 21–32, 1998

BvS comment: In this article the authors argue that a special breed of leader is needed for global organisations. Building on a three-year study across Europe, North America and Asia, they identify certain qualities that a global leader should have, and propose four strategies for how to develop global leaders.

Culture

Understanding culture

- *'What holds the modern company together?'*, by Rob Goffee and Gareth Jones, *Harvard Business Review*, 133–148, 1996
  BvS comment: In their article Goffee and Jones use two well-established sociological concepts – sociability and solidarity – to explore company culture. They develop a framework that helps organisations to analyse and understand their culture, and assess the suitability for their organisation's ambition.
- *The Character of a Corporation: How your Company's Culture can Make or Break your Business*, by Rob Goffee and Gareth Jones, HarperCollins, 1998
  BvS comment: Building on their earlier *Harvard Business Review* article, they expand and develop their framework. Full of case studies and examples.

Innovation cultures

- *Innovation – Leadership Strategies for the Competitive Edge*, by Thomas Kuczmarski, NTC Business Books, 1996
  BvS comment: This book, equally relevant for the Leadership Section, provides some good insights about how to lead innovation from the top; it contains checklists and questionnaires that will help determine how you or your CEO fare as innovation leaders – Kuczmarski's questionnaire on the Innovation Mindset can also be found on the Innovation Exchange web site.
- *'Building a culture for innovation'*, by A.L. Frohman, *Research Technology Management*, March/April, **41**, 9–12, 1998

BvS comment: In his article, Frohman discusses the principles underlying an innovative team-based culture, namely: (1) Decisions are based on clear goals all the time, (2) People recognise that helping others to be innovative is part of their job, (3) Experimentation is prized and expected from everyone throughout the organisation. Such principles cannot be imposed; leaders must foster the questions and experimentation, and accept the risks and uncertainty inherent in such a climate.

- *Creativity and Innovation for Managers*, by Brian Clegg, Butterworth-Heinemann, 1999
  BvS comment: A useful and easy to read book with lots of helpful stuff, including mechanisms for innovation, training, rewards and remuneration for innovation.
- *Creating the Innovation Culture*, by F. Horbie, Toronto: Wiley, 2001
  BvS comment: Easy to read. Based on the argument that dissent is fundamental to encouraging innovation, outlines strategies to introduce dissent into organisations.

Strategy and Vision

- *All the Right Moves*, by C. Markides, Boston: Harvard Business School Press, 1999
  BvS comment: The book introduces an approach for how to innovate at a strategic level by looking at a company's 'who', 'how', and 'what'.

Strategy development

- *'Strategic staircases: planning the capabilities required for success'*, by Michael Hay and Peter Williamson, *Long Range Planning*, **24** (4), 36–43, 1991
  BvS comment: The authors present a framework that enables managers to break the strategic agenda into bite-sized pieces, it guides the selection of priorities, and provides a powerful device for

communicating strategy throughout the organisation, thereby bridging the gap between strategy and action.

- **'Good strategy: the view from below'**, by Michael Hay and Peter Williamson, *Long Range Planning*, **30**, 651–644, 1997

  BvS comment: In their second article, the authors identify 'the key difficulties associated with prevailing stereotypes of strategy, the sources of much disenchantment with strategy, the qualities that people would look for in a "good" strategy.' They continue, 'We then outline an approach to strategy that will ensure that it passes the quality test defined by the managers and employees who have to implement it.'

- **'Co-evolving: At last, a way to make synergies work'**, by Kathleen M. Eisenhardt and D. Charles Galunic, *Harvard Business Review*, Jan/Feb, **78**, 91–101, 2000

  BvS comment: Building on the insight that capturing cross-business synergies is at the heart of corporate strategy but is often hard to achieve, they identify what differentiates between success and failure, a corporate strategic process they call 'co-evolving'. Co-evolving is based on changing the web of collaborative links – everything from information exchanges to shared assets to multibusiness strategies – among businesses. The authors believe that this results in a shifting web of relationships that exploits fresh opportunities for synergies and drops deteriorating ones.

Change

- **When Giants Learn to Dance**, Rosabeth Moss Kanter, Simon & Schuster, 1989

  BvS comment: In the first part of her book, Rosabeth Moss Kanter sets the scene, establishing the changes in the environment in which companies operate. The second part discusses the required actions, contrasting them with past behaviour and highlighting potential problems, and the third analyses the consequences of those actions on the careers and private lives of the employees.

  Her book is based on research into US companies and focuses primarily on bigger organisations.

- **The Change Masters**, Rosabeth Moss Kanter, Touchstone Books, 1985

BvS comment: As someone commented on www.amazon.co.uk, after you have read this book, you will not need to read any others about how to make successful, positive changes in organisations.

- *The art of continuous change: Linking complexity theory and time-paced evolution in relentlessly shifting organizations'*, by Shona L. Brown and Kathleen M. Eisenhardt, *Administrative Science Quarterly*, March, **42**, 1–34, 1997

  BvS comment: Somewhat on the academic side, but otherwise contains some interesting concepts on how companies achieve continuous change. Organisations that achieve successful multiple-product innovation blends are able to balance structure with responsibilities and priorities with extensive communication, thereby designing freedom to create improvisation within current projects. A second differentiator is that successful firms undertake a variety of low-cost probes into the future, including experimental products, futurists and strategic alliances. Third, successful firms consider both the present and the future through rhythmic, time-spaced transition processes.

Processes

New product development

The new product development process

- *The Complete Idiot's Guide to New Product Development*, by Edwin E. Bobrow, Alpha books, 1997

  BvS comment: Great book with lots of useful stuff, easy and fun to read; contains information on the stage-gate process (pp. 166–174)

- *Choosing a development process that's right for your company*, by Milton D. J. Rosenau, (pp 77–92 in *The PDMA Handbook of New Product Development*, edited by Rosenau, Griffin, Castellion and Anschuetz, Wiley 1996)

  BvS comment: Rosenau provides a useful overview of a generic new product development process and raises some issues and concerns to bear in mind, while tailoring the process to your company's needs. The entire book is useful, though some of the articles are more practitioner-oriented than others.

- ***Product Development Performance***, by K.B. Clark and T. Fujimoto, Boston: Harvard Business School Press, 1991
  BvS comment: The book describes familiar concepts such as the development funnel and other tools for new product development developed by Harvard experts.
- **'Core capabilities and core rigidities: a paradox in managing new product development'**, by Dorothy Leonard-Barton, *Strategic Management Journal*, **13,** 111–125, Summer 1992.
  BvS comment: Alerts readers to the fact that expertise and knowledge can in fact be an obstacle to creativity and innovation.

Idea generation and suggestion schemes

- ***Brainstorming groups in context: effectiveness in a product design firm'***, by R.I. Sutton and A Hargadon, *Administrative Science Quarterly*, **41**, 685–718, 1996
  BvS comment: The article takes a new look at brainstorming, arguing that it is not as inefficient as many believe. A different approach is suggested.
- ***Corporate Creativity: How Innovation and Improvement Actually Happen***, by Alan G. Robinson and Sam Stern, San Francisco; Berrett-Koehler Publishers, 1997
  BvS comment: The authors advocate the view that financial rewards are actually counter-productive. Full of examples and case studies.

Prototypes

- **'Inanimate integrators: a block of wood speaks'**, by Dorothy Leonard-Barton, *Design Management Journal*, 61–67, Summer 1991
  BvS comment: In her article Leonard-Barton describes the power of prototypes in selling an idea and establishing a shared understanding of a concept.
- ***Serious Play – How the World's Best Companies Simulate to Innovate***, by Michael Schrage, Boston: Harvard Business School Press, 2000
  BvS comment: Emphasises the role of prototypes in the innovation process, along with how and when to use them.

Teams

- ***The Wisdom of Teams***, by Jon R. Katzenbach and Douglas K. Smith, Harvard Business School Press, 1993

  BvS comment: This is a very valuable insight into a great variety of aspects surrounding teams. In Part One they address questions such as why teams are useful, why they might be resisted, how to define a team and what its characteristics are. Part Two is concerned with different types of teams, how teams work, what kind of leader they need, what might prevent them from performing well and how to address this. The third part looks at the role of teams in times of major change, in top management, and why they are different, and the role of management.

Collaboration

- ***A Question of Culture? Collaborative Innovation in UK Business***, CBI in cooperation with 3M and the Design Council, February 2001. Contact the Confederation of British Industry, Centre Point, 103 New Oxford Street, London WC1A 1DU

  BvS comment: Provides insights into what differentiates innovative from less innovative organisations, focusing on culture and collaboration.

Human resources

- *'Pay strategy: New thinking for the new millennium'*, Edward E. Lawler III, *Compensation and Benefits Review*, Jan/Feb, **32**, (1), 7–12, 2000

  BvS comment: Emphasises the need to think strategically about pay plans and align it with other changes the business has to address. A misaligned pay strategy not only fails to add value; it produces high costs in the compensation area as well as inappropriate and misdirected behaviour.

- *'Pay can be a change agent'*, by Edward E. Lawler III, *Compensation and Benefits Management*, Summer, **16** (3), 23–26, 2000

  BvS comment: An insightful article; there is some overlap with previous article but on the whole they are complementary.

- *'The real value of variable pay plans'*, *HR Focus*, May, **77**, (5), 3–4, 2000

  BvS comment: Insights into a Towers Perrin Study on 'Compensation effectiveness: is pay delivering its promise?' For a free copy of the full survey, call Towers Perrin's Publications Department at 001 800 525 6741, or e-mail webmaster@towers.com.

- *'Pay design influences company performance'*, by Louisa Wah, *Management Review*, March, **89**, (3), 8, 2000

  BvS comment: Also available at the above telephone number and e-mail address.

- *'Managing new pay program introductions to enhance the competitiveness of multinational corporations (MNCS)'*, by Mary E. Graham and Charlie O. Trevor; *Competitiveness Review*, **10**, (1), 136–154, 2000

  BvS comment: Looks at the importance and influence of cultural differences in designing pay systems in multinational companies (MNCs). A rather long article which can probably be summarised as: multinational companies facing differences in expectations regarding pay systems do well to understand the differences, and if they cannot be addressed and responded to, should ensure the reasons for this are clearly communicated.

- *'Skill-based pay as an organisational innovation'*, by James R. Thompson and Charles W. LeHew, *Review of Public Personnel Administration*, Winter, **20** (1), 20–40, 2000

  BvS comment: Looking at the transfer of skill-based pay from the private to the public sector. Provides a good overview of findings on and around skill-based pay. Based on the review of the literature and of the experiences of three public agencies;

- *Creating a Flexible Workplace*, by Barney Olmsted and Suzanne Smith, AMACOM, 1994

  BvS comment: This book presents alternative work arrangements including flexitime, compressed workweeks, Flexplaces and part-time alternatives such as regular part-time employment, job sharing, phased and partial retirement, voluntary reduced work time programmes, leave time and work sharing. For each option the authors explain its origin, who uses it, where it is appropriate, what its advantages and disadvantages are, whether it might be appropriate for your organisation, how to introduce the concept, and any special considerations for managers and supervisors.

Information technology and knowledge management

- **'The knowledge-creating company'**, by I. Nonaka, *Harvard Business Review*, **69**, 96–104, Nov–Dec 1991
  BvS comment: Classic article on the subject of knowledge creation and management.
- **'Knowledge management and innovation at 3M'**, by Alan Brand, *Journal of Knowledge Management*, **2**, 17–22, 1998
  BvS comment: Another story about the strategies 3M has developed for remaining a highly innovative organisation, in this case the effective management of knowledge. The author points out that while 3M employs a wide range of knowledge management systems, the right environment has to be in place before people will be motivated to input and access such systems, and share their personal insights and experience (tacit knowledge). The article outlines how 3M creates and sustains its innovation and learning culture.
- **'Sharing knowledge through BP's virtual team network'**, *Harvard Business Review*, **75**, 152–153, 1997
  BvS comment: Discusses the use of virtual teamwork at BP, and the measures the CEO John Browne has put in place to excel at learning and engage leaders more deeply in helping to shape the strategy and drive the performance of the business.

Market Research

- **'Where you really need to hear consumers'**, by Ken Miller, *Brandweek*, January 20, **38**. (3), 17, 1997
  BvS comment: The article looks at how successfully innovative companies such as Rubbermaid, Gillette, Black & Decker and 3M identify consumers' needs.
- **'Ignore your customers'**, by Justin Martin, in *Fortune* magazine, 1 May 1995, 83–89

BvS comment: Asking consumers what they want hardly ever results in radical new products. Discusses the design consultancy frogdesign as an example of a company that goes beyond what consumers can imagine today.

- **'Spark innovation through empathic design'**, by Dorothy Leonard and Jeffrey F. Rayport, *Harvard Business Review*, **75**, 102–108, 1997
  BvS comment: States that different approaches to consumer research are needed, and suggests that rather than bring the customers to the company, emphatic design calls for company representatives to watch customers using products and services in the context of their own environments. This can lead to the identification of unexpected uses for products, and can also uncover problems that customers do not mention in surveys. Companies that engage in emphatic design tend to follow the following step process: (1) observation, (2) capturing data, (3) reflection and analysis, (4) brainstorming for solutions, (5) developing prototypes of possible solutions.

Communication

- **Company Image and Reality**, by David Bernstein, Rinehart and Winston, 1986
  BvS comment: A classic on the need and reasons for corporations to communicate with all their constituencies. Bernstein elaborates the fact that a company will have an image, which will be perceived by the outside world in a certain way whether it communicates or not. Hence, it might be of advantage if the image is created, influenced and managed in the way most beneficial to the company. He analyses all aspects of corporate communications, looking at different customer groups, explaining that these groups often overlap and hence the consistency of communication is very important.
- **'New products: harmonious designs come from well-managed and coordinated teams'**, by Denis D. O'Brian, Planned Innovation, **3**, 111–114, 1980
  BvS comment: In this article Denis O'Brian highlights the importance of good interpersonal relationships in teams for the success of projects.

Measurement

- *Marketing and the Bottom Line – The New Metrics of Corporate Wealth*, by Tim Ambler, Pearson Education, 2000

  BvS comment: The entire book is concerned with metrics, albeit primarily from the marketing perspective. The book summarises a 30-month research project into marketing metrics, carried out by London Business School and sponsored by the Marketing Council, the Marketing Society, the Institute of Practitioners in Advertising, the Sales Promotions Consultants Association and London Business School.

Work Environment

- *New Workspace New Culture – Office Design as a Catalyst for Change*, by Gavin Turner and Jeremy Myerson, Gower Publishing, 1998

  BvS comment: The three parts of the book cover the following topics: (1) context and environment of working life, the drivers of change, and the barriers – organisational, psychological and structural – to better working practice, (2) rethinking and adapting traditional structures through the reorganisation of the workplace and the removal of physical barriers to change, (3) six proven workplace layouts: Town Square, Village Neighbourhood, City in Miniature, Space–Time Machine, the Campaign Room and the Club; different scenarios and the benefits of each are explained. Supported by case studies.

- *The New Office*, by Frank Duffy, Conran Octopus, 1997

  BvS comment: The book addresses issues such as the role of the office in supporting and stimulating business performance; lessons to be learned from a century of office design; the response in management thinking to information technology; new directions in the fabric, management and location of the office; the importance of measurement and feedback and their implications for business; and finally an appendix of information sources. The book provides 20 international case studies.

- There are also three interviews on this subject on the Innovation Exchange web site: http://iexchange.london.edu.

  ○ **The office is changing:** interview with Ralph Buschow, partner at architects Buschow & Henley, April 1999.

  ○ **How your office environment can support your culture and strategy:** interview with David Magliano, marketing director of the airline Go Fly, May 1999.

  ○ **How the office environment can support your organisation in achieving its ambition – the case of HHCL:** interview with Jon Leach, partner at HHCL, May 1999.

Paradoxes

- *'Exploring Paradox: Toward a More Comprehensive Guide'*, by Marianne W Lewis, *Academy of Management Review*, **25**, (4), 2000
  BvS comment: The author explains the meaning and value of paradox: it is neither a compromise nor a split between competing tensions, but is rather an awareness of both. While difficult to achieve, the ability to manage paradoxes is essential in business today.

Useful web sites

- **The InnovationNetwork (www.thinksmart.com)**
  BvS comment: The InnovationNetwork offer a wealth of case studies on their web site, plus insights and other information for anyone interested in the subject of innovation. Part of the site is restricted to subscribers. They also used to be publishers of the magazine *FastCompany* **(www.fastcompany.com)** which also has a wealth of stories, case studies and insights on innovation.
- **The Innovation Exchange (http://iexchange.london.edu)**
  BvS comment: The Innovation Exchange web site offers information

about the network's activities, as well as lots of relevant information. Part of the web site is restricted to members only.

- **The Talent Foundation (www.talentfoundation.org)**
  BvS comment: For a couple of interesting research projects relevant to innovation you might want to visit this web site. For example, they investigated what makes an *Adaptive Organisation*, a project supported by experts such as Ari de Geus (author of *The Living Company*), Roger Lewin and David Bodanis. To find out more, contact Kinga Kowalewska, projects coordinator at the Talent Foundation (kinga@talentfoundation.org).

- **The Design Council (www.designcouncil.org.uk)**
  BvS comment: Over the past years it has also published a number of reports and other documents that provide the innovator with useful and practical insights.

- **The Conference Board's web site (www.conference-board.org)**
  BvS comment: Reports and other information can be ordered from the web site.

Other books and articles

- *Hare Brain Tortoise Mind: Why Intelligence Increases when you Think Less*, by G. Claxton, London: Fourth Estate, 1997
  BvS comment: In his book, Claxton elaborates on different ways and speeds of thinking, each with its own role in solving problems.

- *The Living Company*, by A. de Geus, Nicholas Brealey, 1997
  BvS comment: Insights into why some companies have lasted centuries whereas others have perished in decades. If you would like a crisp and short version you migh want to read his article of the same title: 'The living company' published in the *Harvard Business Review,* March–April, 51–59, 1997.

  Management Challenges for the 21st Century, by P. F. Drucker, Butterworth-Heinemann, 1999.
  BvS comment: In his latest book, Drucker talks about future management challenges and practices, suggesting that the biggest challenge is to handle knowledge worker productivity.

- *The Corporate Fool*, by D. Firth and A. Leigh, Oxford: Capstone Press, 1998

BvS comment: I like the concept – and that's what innovation in many companies could do with, a person who is allowed to say anything and keep managers and board on the tight and narrow if they want to stray from the path of innovation (to satisfy short-term needs in lieu of long-term success).

- ***The Elephant and the Flea***, by C. Handy, London: Hutchinson, 2001
  BvS comment: In his latest book, Handy yet again addresses changes to come in our worklives, outlining the mutual need of elephants (large organisations) and fleas (entrepreneurial individuals).

- ***The Dream Society***, by R. Jensen, New York: McGraw-Hill, 1999
  BvS comment: A look into the future, envisionaging a society that is built around stories and community. What I like about this book is that it is much more positive than some of its Anglo-American counterparts, and that it suggests that we shape our future, rather than the future being something that happens to us.

REFERENCES

3M, Hiring innovators, *Research-Technology Management*, **58**, May–June 1997.

Abbott, J., Eurostar one year on, *Modern Railways*, 687–689, Nov. 1995.

Abel, C., Function of tacit knowing in learning to design, *Design Studies*, **2**, 209–214, Oct. 1981.

Abernathy, W.J. and Clark, K.B., Innovation: mapping the winds of creative destruction, *Research Policy*, **14**, 3–22, 1985.

Abernathy, W.J. and Utterback, J.M., Patterns of industrial innovation, *Technology Review*, 154–178, 1978.

Ackoff, R.L. and Vergara, E., Creativity in problem solving and planning: a review, *European Journal of Operational Research*, **7**, 1, May 1981.

Adler, P.S. and Cole, R.E., Designed for learning: a tale of two auto plants, *Sloan Management Review*, 85–94, Spring 1993.

Adler, P.S., Mandelbaum, A., Nguyen, V. and Schwerer, E., Getting the most out of your product development process, *Harvard Business Review*, 124–154, March–April 1996.

Adler, P.S., Riggs, H.E. and Wheelwright, S.C., Product development know-how: trading tactics for strategy, *Sloan Management Review*, 7–17, Fall 1989.

Ali, A., Krapfel, R. Jr., and La Bahn, D., Product innovativeness and entry strategy: impact on cycle time and break-even time, *Journal of Product Innovation Management*, **12**, 54–69, 1995.

Allan, D., Kingdon, M., Murrin, K., and Rudkin, D., *?What If! How to Start a Creative Revolution at Work*, Oxford: Capstone, 1999.

Allen, D., Living the brand, *Design Management Journal*, 35–40, Winter 2000.

Allison, G.T., *Essence of Decision*, Harvard University, US: HarperCollins.

Almassy, S.E., Managing complexity amid a volatile global market, *Electronic Business Buyer*, **19**, 47, April 1993.

Amabile, T.M., A model of creativity and innovation in organisations. In *Research in Organisational Behaviour*, eds Staw, B.M. and Cummings, L.L., Greenwich, CT: JAI Press, 1988 pp. 123–167.

Amabile, T.M., Unlimited genius, *Success*, **43**, 36, Sept. 1996.

Amabile, T.M., How to kill creativity, *Harvard Business Review*, 77–87, Sep–Oct. 1998.

Amabile, T.M., Changes in the work environment for creativity during downsizing, *Academy of Management Journal*, **42**, 630–660, 1999.

Amabile, T.M., Conti, R., Coon, H., Lazenby, J. and Herron, M., Assessing the work environment for creativity, *Academy of Management Journal*, **39**, 1154–1184, Oct. 1996.

Amabile, T.M., Motivating creativity in organisations: on doing what you love and loving doing what you do, *California Management Review*, **40**, 39–58, Fall 1997.

Ambler, T., Sorting through the innovations to find real gold, *Marketing*, **7**, 11 February 1999.

Ambler, T., Innovation metrics, *London Business School, Centre for Marketing*, Working Paper No. 98–903, March 1999.

Ambler, T., *Marketing and the Bottom Line – The New Metrics of Corporate Wealth*, London: Pearson Education, 2000.

Ancona, D.G. and Caldwell, D., Beyond boundary spanning: managing external dependence in product development teams, *Journal of High Technology Management Research*, **1**, 119–135, 1990.

Ancona, D.G. and Caldwell, D., Improving the performance of new product teams, *Research-Technology Management*, **33**, 25–29, March–April 1990.

Anderson, N.R. and West, M.A., Measuring climate for work group innovation: development and validation of the team climate inventory, *Journal of Organizational Behavior*, **19**, 235–258, May 1998.

Andrews, K.Z., Cross–functional teams, *Harvard Business Review*, **73**, 12–13, Nov.–Dec. 1995.

Anonymous, Putting a value on people, *The Economist*, 24 June 1994.

Anonymous, *Winning*, British Department for Trade and Industry (DTI) and the Confederation of British Industry (CBI) 1995.

Anonymous, The outing of outsourcing, *The Economist*, p. 99, 1 Nov. 1995.

Anonymous, Why first may not last, *The Economist*, p. 85, 16 March 1996.

Anonymous, The road from imitation to innovation, *The Economist*, p. 102, 18 May 1996.

Anonymous, A call for innovation, *Trustee*, **49**, 6, July–August 1996.

Anonymous, Outsourcing product development, *Supervision*, **57**, 10–12, October 1996.

Anonymous, Forging a global supply chain, *Electronic Business Today*, **22**, 29, December 1996.

Anonymous, A global ethic: the leadership challenge, *The Canadian Manager*, **21**, 29, Winter, 1996.

Anonymous, Creative Britain: A Design Council report on behalf of the Prime Minister, 31 March 1998.

Anonymous, *The Economist* review: Business strategy: Past, present and future, *The Economist*, **348**, July 1998.

Anonymous, Route to global recognition, *Supply Management*, **3**, 34, 30 July 1998.

Anonymous, Global design styles merge for consumers, *Contractor*, **45**, S3, Nov. 1998.

Anonymous, *A question of culture*, CBI Innovation Survey, February 2001.

Anschuetz, N.F. Evaluating ideas and concepts for new consumer products. In *The PDMA Handbook of New Product Development*, eds Rosenau, M.D.J., Griffin, A., Castellion, G. and Anschuetz, N., New York: Wiley & Sons, 1996, pp. 195–206.

Anthony, M.T., The core team approach to project organisation. In *Setting the PACE in Product Development*, ed. McGrath, M.E., Newton, MA: Butterworth-Heinemann, 1996, pp. 45–65.

Anthony, M.T., Structured product development. In *Setting the PACE in Product Development*, ed. McGrath, M.E., Newton, MA: Butterworth-Heinemann, 1996, pp. 67–83.

Aubert, J.-E., The approach of design and concepts of innovation policy. In *Design and Innovation: Policy and Management*, eds Langdon, R. and Rothwell, R., London: Frances Printer, 1985.

Baker, M.J. and McTavish, R., *Product Policy and Management*, London: Macmilian, 1976.

Baldwin, C.Y., How capital budgeting deters innovation – and what to do about it, *Research Technology Management*, 39–45, Nov.–Dec. 1991.

Ball, M., Brands and people: the GrandMet mix, *Corporate Finance*, **29**, March 1996.

Balmer, J., Increasing sensitivity to corporate branding and identity, Speech given by Professor John Balmer, Director of International Corporate Branding at the 1st Summer Symposium for the ICCIS, 1999.

Barclay, I. and Benson, M.H., Improving the chances of new product success. In *Innovation, Adaptation and growth*, eds Rothwell, R. and Bessant, J., Amsterdam: Elsevier, 1987, pp. 103–112.

Barclay, I. and Benson, M.H., The effective management of new product development, *Leadership and Organisation Development Journal*, **11**, 1–37, 1990.

Barclay, I., The new product development process: Part 2. improving the process of new product development, *R&D Management*, **22**, 307–317, 1992.

Barclay, I., The new product development process: past evidence and future practical application, Part 1, *R & D Management*, **22**, 255–263, 1992.

Barclay, I. and Benson, M., New product development: organisation and current practice, *Leadership Organisation Development Journal*, **11**, 13–23, 1990.

Barclay, I. and Benson, M., New product development: theory into practice, *Leadership Organisation Development Journal*, **11**, 24–30, 1990.

Barclay, I. and Benson, M., Success in new product development: lessons from the past, *Leadership Organisation Development Journal*, **11**, 4–12, 1990.

Barczak, G. and Wilemon, D., Successful new product team leaders, *Industrial Marketing Management*, **21**, 61–68, Feb. 1992.

Barkan, P. and Iansiti, M., Prototyping: a tool for rapid learning in product development, *Concurrent Engineering Research and Applications*, **1**, 125–134, 1993.

Barrett, F.D., Creativity techniques: yesterday, today and tomorrow, *S.A.M. Advanced Management Journal*, **43**, 25, Winter 1978.

Bartlett, C. and Sumatra, G., Managing across borders: new strategic requirements, *Sloan Management Review*, 7–17, Summer 1987.

Bartlett, C. and Sumatra, G., Managing across borders: new organizational responses, *Sloan Management Review*, 43–53, Fall 1987.

Bartlett, C.A. and Goshal, S., From domestic to global: moving up the value curve, *Strategic Leadership Research Programme*, Reference No. SLRP WP59/1999, 1999.

Bartunek, J., Bobko, P. and Venkatramm, N., Toward innovation and diversity in management research methods, *Academy of Management Journal*, **36**, 1362–1373, Dec. 1993.

Batchelor, C., Management: the product's face is the company's fortune, *Financial Times*, 12 Nov. 1991.

Bayne, T., The contribution of new products to organisational success. Presentation notes, Seminar held at London Business School, 29 February 1996.

Baxter, M., *Product Design*, London: Chapmann & Hall, 1995.

Becker, S.W. and Whisler, T.L., The innovative organisation: a selective view of current theory and research, *Journal of Business*, 462–469, 1967.

Beinhocker, E.D., Strategy at the edge of chaos, *McKinsey Quarterly*, **1**, 24–39, 1997.

Beir, H.R., Managing creatives, *Vital Speeches of the Day*, **61**, 501–506, 1 June 1995.

Belbin, M., Design innovation and the team, *Design Management Journal*, 38–42, Summer 1991.

Berner, K.M., Is your prototype yours? *Design News*, **52**, 200, May 1997.

Bernsen, J., The user dimension in the innovation process. In *On Design Leadership*, Anonymous, Helsinki, Finland: UIAH, 1992, 69–73.

Bernstein, D., *Company image and reality*, Eastbourne, UK: Holt, Rinehart and Winston, 1986.

Bidault, F., Despres, C., and Butler, C., *Leveraged innovation – unlocking the innovation potential of strategic supply*, London: Macmillan, 1998.

Birkinshaw, J. and Fey, C.F., Organising for innovation in large firms, *Strategic Leadership Research Programme*, London Business School, Working Paper No. SLRP WP66/1999, 1999.

Birkinshaw, J., Toulan, O. and Arnold, D., How to manage your global customer *Strategic Leadership Research Programme*, London Business School, Working Paper No. SLRP WP57/1999, 1999.

Black, D.H. and Synan, C.D., The learning organisation: the sixth discipline, *Management Accounting*, **75**, 70–72, Nov. 1997.

Blaich, R., Global design, *Journal of Product Innovation Management*, **5**, 296, Dec. 1988.

Blanchard, K., Out with the old and in with the new, *Incentive*, **171**, 59–61, April 1997.

Blau, J.R. and McKinley, W., Ideas, complexity, and innovation, *Administrative Science Quarterly*, **24**, June 1979.

Bobrow, E.E., *The Complete Idiot's Guide to New Product Development*, New York: Alpha books, 1997.

Bohm, D. and Peat, F.D., Science, order and creativity. In *Creative management*, ed. Henry, J., London: Sage Publications in association with the Open University, 1991, pp. 24–33.

Boisot, M.H., Is your firm a creative destroyer? Competitive learning and knowledge flows in the technological strategies of firms, *Research Policy*, **24**, 489–506, 1995.

Bonache, J. and Cervino, J., Global integration without expatriates, *Human Resource Management Journal*, **7**, 89–100, 1997.

Booz Allen Hamilton, *New product development in the 1980s*, New York: Booz, Allen, Hamilton, 1982.

Bouwen, R., De Visch, I. and Steyaert, C. Innovation projects in organisations. In *Organisational Change and Innovation* eds Hosking, D.M. and Anderson, N., London: Routledge, 1992, pp. 123–148.

Brady, T., Tools, management of innovation and complex product systems, Working Paper prepared for CENTRIM/SPRU Project on Complex Product Systems; ESRC Technology Management Initiative 1995.

Brand, A., Knowledge management and innovation at 3M, *Journal of Knowledge Management*, **2**, 17–22, Sept. 1998.

Brinkerhoff, R.O., *Achieving results from training – how to evaluate human resource development to strengthen programs and increase impact*, San Francisco: Jossey-Bass, 1987.

Brinton, J. B. and Elliott, H., Distributors map out global expansion, *Electronic Business Today*, **22**, 18, Feb. 1996.

Brown, J.S. and Duguid, P., Balancing act: How to capture knowledge without killing it, *Harvard Business Review*, **78**, 73–80, May–June 2000.

Brown, S.L. and Eisenhardt, K.M., Product development: past research, present findings and future directions, *Academy of Management Review*, **20**, 343–378, 1995.

Brown, S.L. and Eisenhardt, K.M., The art of continuous change: linking complexity theory and time-paced evolution in relentlessly shifting organisations, *Administrative Science Quarterly*, **42**, 1–34, 1997.

Brown, T., Nurturing a culture of innovation, *Financial Times*, 17 Nov. 1997.

Bruce, M., New product development strategies of suppliers of emerging technologies – a case study of expert systems, *Journal of Marketing Management*, **3**, 313–327, 1988.

Bruce, M. and Biemans, W.G. (eds) *Product development: Meeting the Challenge of the Design–Marketing Interface*, Chichester : John Wiley, 1995.

Bruce, M. and Docherty, C., It's all in the relationship: a comparative study of client–design consultant relationships, *Design Studies*, **14**, 402–422, 1993.

Bruce, M., Leverock, F. and Littler, D. A management framework for collaborative product development. In *Product development: Meeting the Challenge of the Design–Marketing Interface*, eds Bruce, M. and Biemans, W.G., Chichester: John Wiley, 1995.

Bryan, L., Fraser, J., Oppenheim, J. and Rall, W., *Race for the World*, Boston, MA: Harvard Business School Press, 1999.

Buckler, S.A., The spiritual nature of innovation, *Research Technology Management*, **40**, 43, March–April 1997.

Burall, P., Managing Product Creation, London: HMSO, 1991.

Burn, G.R., Quality function deployment. In *Managing Quality*, eds Dale, B.G. and Plunkett, J.J., London: Philip Adam, 1999, pp. 66–88.

Burns, T. and Stalker, G.M., *The Management of Innovation*, Oxford: Oxford University Press, 1996.

Burrows, P., How Texas Instruments attacks the global market, *Electronic Business Buyer*, **17**, 26, 6 May 1991.

Burrows, P., Smith, G. and Brull, S.V., HP pictures the future, *Business Week*, 40–45, 7 July, 1997.

Cabral, D. and Grube, L., Grooming global managers, *Chief Executive*, 69, Sept. 1996.

Caldecote, V., Investment in new product development, *Journal of the Royal Society of Arts*, 684–695, Oct. 1979.

Carson, J.W. and Rickards, T., *Industrial New Product Development*, Farnborough, UK: Gower Press, 1979.

CBI, Probe, promoting business excellence, questionnaire & notes, Manufacturing Division, Confederation of British Industry, London, 1994.

Chase, R., Roth, A. and Voss, C., Service Probe Questionnaire, Confederation of British Industry, London, 1998.

Cheng, Y.-T. and Van de Ven, A.H., Learning the innovation journey: Order out of chaos? *Organization Science*, **7**, 593–614, Nov.–Dec. 1996.

Chesbrough, H.W. and Teece, D.J., When is virtual virtuous? Organizing for innovation, *Harvard Business Review*, 67–73, Jan–Feb 1996.

Child, P., Diedrichs, R., Sanders, F.-H., and Wisniowski, S., The management of complexity, *McKinsey Quarterly*, 52–69, 1991.

Choperena, A.M., Fast cycle time – driver of innovation and quality, *Research-Technology Management*, **39**, 36–40, May–June 1996.

Clapperton, G. (Ed.) *Top UK Companies of the Future*, London: HarperCollins Business, 2001.

Clark, K.B. and Fujimoto T., *Product development and competitiveness*, Working paper: Harvard Business School, 1990.

Clark, K.B. and Fujimoto T., The power of product integrity, *Harvard Business Review*, 107–118, Nov.–Dec. 1990.

Clark, K.B. and Fujimoto, T., Heavyweight product managers, *McKinsey Quarterly*, **1**, 42–60, 1991.

Clark, K.B. and Fujimoto, T., *Product Development Performance*, Boston, MA: Harvard Business School Press, 1991.

Clark, K.B. and Fujimoto, T., Product development and competitiveness, *Journal of the Japanese and International Economies*, **6**, 101–143, 1992.

Clark, K.B. and Wheelwright, S.C., Organizing and leading 'heavyweight' development teams, *California Management Review*, 9–28, Spring 1992.

Clark, P., Managing innovation, *Journal of Management Studies*, **30**, 512–513, May 1993.

Claxton, G., *Hare Brain Tortoise Mind: Why Intelligence Increases when you Think Less*, London: Fourth Estate, 1997.

Claxton, G., *Wiseup: the Challenge of Lifelong Learning*, London: Bloomsbury, 1999

Claxton, G. The innovative mind: becoming smarter by thinking less. In *Creativity, A Cognition*, ed. Henry, J., London: Sage, 2000.

Clegg, B., *Creativity and Innovation for Managers*, Oxford: Butterworth-Heinemann, 1999.

Clegg, B., Hardy, C. and Nord, W.R., *Managing Organisations – Current Issues*, London: Sage Publications, 1999

Clegg, S.R., Ibarra-Calado, E. and Bueno–Rodriquez, L. (eds) *Global Management, Universal Theories and Local Realities*, London: Sage Publications, 1999.

Clipson, C., Innovation by design. In *Managing Innovation*, eds Walker, D. and Henry, J., London: Sage Publications, 1991.

Cocheran, B. and Thompson, G.C., Why new products fail, *Conference Board Record*, 11–18, 1964.

Cohen, M.A., Eliashberg, J. and Ho, T.-H., New product development: the performance and time-to-market tradeoffs, *Management Science*, 173–186, Feb. 1996.

Cohen, S.H. Tools for quantitative market research. In *The PDMA Handbook of New Product Development*, eds Rosenau, M.D.J., Griffin, A. Castellion, G., and Anschuetz, N., New York: John Wiley, 1996, pp. 253–267.

Coleman, J., Slonaker, W. and Wendt, A., True teams or tag teams? *Business Horizon*, **40**, 59–64, 1997.

Collinson, S., Managing product innovation at Sony: the development of the data discman, *Technology Analysis & Strategic Management*, **5**, 285–306, 1993.

Collins, J. and Smith, D. Innovation metrics: a framework to accelerate growth, *Prism,* 1st Quarter, 33–47, 1999.

Conger, J., Charisma and how to grow it, *Management Today*, 78–81, Dec. 1999.

Conger, J.A., The necessary art of persuasion, *Harvard Business Review*, **76**, 84–95, May–June 1998.

Cookson, C., Creativity in reverse, *Across the Board*, **25**, 50–51, Nov. 1988.

Coombs, R., Hull, R. and Peltu, M., Knowledge management practices for innovation: an audit tool for improvement, *CIRC, The University of Manchester*, Working Paper No. 6, June 1998.

Cooper, R.G., How new product strategies impact on performance, *Journal of Product Innovation Management*, **1**, 5–18, 1984.

Cooper, R.G., New product strategies: what distinguishes the top performance, *Journal of Product Innovation Management*, **2**, 151–164, 1984.

Cooper, R.G., *Winning at New Products*, London: Kogan-Page, 1986.

Cooper, R.G., Third-generation new product processes, *Journal of Product Innovation Management*, **11**, 3–14, 1994.

Cooper, R.G., Debunking the myths of new product development, *Research-Technology Management*, 40–50, July–August, 1994.

Cooper, R.G. and Kleinschmidt, E.J., New products: what separates winners from losers? *Journal of Product Innovation Management*, **4**, 169–184, 1987.

Cooper, R.G. and Kleinschmidt, E.J., Success factors in product innovation, *Industrial Marketing Management*, **16**, 215–223, 1987.

Cooper, R.G. and Kleinschmidt, E.J., What makes a new product a winner: success factors at the project level, *R&D Management*, **17**, 175–189, 1987.

Cooper, R.G. and Kleinschmidt, E.J., Resource allocation in the new product process, *Industrial Marketing Management*, **17**, 249–262, 1988.

Cooper, R.G. and Kleinschmidt, E.J., Winning business in product development: the critical success factors, *Research-Technology Management*, **39**, 18–29, July–August, 1996.

Corfield, K.G., Product design, National Economic Development Office, London, 1979.

Cortes-Comerer, N. and Perry, T.S., Organizing the design team – motto for specialists: give some, get some/the designer's designer case study – miniature compact disk players: help from the factory, *IEEE Spectrum*, **24**, 41–46, May 1987.

Coyne, W.E., Building a tradition of innovation, The UK Innovation Lecture, London, 1996.

Craig, A. and Hart, S., Where to now in new product development research, *European Journal of Marketing*, **26**, 1–49, 1992.

Crawford, C.M., New product failure – facts and fallacies, *Research Management*, 9–13, Sept. 1979.

Crawford, C.M., New product failure rates: a reprise, *Research Management*, 30, July–August 1987.

Crawford, C.M., The hidden cost of accelerated product development, *Journal of Product Innovation Management*, **9**, 188–199, 1992.

Crawford, C.M., *New Product Management*, Harlow: Addison–Wesley, 1994.

Cummings, L.L. and Berger Chris, J. Organization structure – how does it influence attitudes and performance? *Organizational Dynamics*, **5**, 34–49, Autumn 1976.

Cuneo, A.Z., Kodak's new vision, *Advertising Age*, **66**, 38, 3 April 1995.

Dalton, D.R., Todor, W.D., Spendolini, M.J., Flielding, G. and Porter, L.W., Organization structure and performance: a critical review, *Academy of Management Review*, **5**, 49–643, Jan. 1980.

Danneels, E. and Kleinschmidt, E., Product innovativeness from the firm's perspective: its dimensions and their impact on project selection and performance, 28th European Marketing Academy Conference, Humbolt Universität zu Berlin, 1999.

Dauphinais, G.W. and Price, C., The CEO as psychologist, *Management Review*, **87**, 10–15, Sept. 1998.

Davidow, W.H. and Malone, M.S., *The Virtual Corporation*, HarperCollins, 1992.

Davis, R.E., From experience: the role of market research in the development of new consumer products, *Journal of Product Innovation Management*, **10**, 309–317, 1993.

Davis, R.E., Market analysis and segmentation issues for new consumer products. In *The PDMA Handbook of New Product Development*, eds Rosenau, M.D.J., Griffin, A., Castellion, G. and Anschuetz, N., New York: John Wiley, 1996, pp. 35–49.

Davis, R.J. and Ueyama, S., Developing customers before products, *McKinsey Quarterly*, **3**, 72–83, 1996.

Davis, S., A vision for the year 2000: Brand asset management, *Journal of Consumer Marketing*, **12**, 65, 1995.

de Bono, E., *Lateral Thinking, A Textbook of Creativity*, Ward Lock Educational, 1970.

de Bono, E., Serious creativity, *Journal for Quality and Participation*, **11**, 1998.

de Brentani, U., Success factors in developing new business services. In *New Product Development, A Reader*, ed. Hart, S., London: Dryden Press, 1996, pp. 401–427.

de Brentani, U. and Kleinschmidt, E., Achieving new product success in highly innovative versus incremental new industrial services, 28th European Marketing Academy Conference, Humbolt Universität zu Berlin, Germany, 1999.

de Cagna, J., Making change happen: Steve Denning tells the story of storytelling, *Information Outlook*, January 2001.

de Geus, A.P., Why some companies live to tell about change, *Journal for Quality and Participation*, **21**, 17–21, July–August 1998.

de Geus, A., The living company, *Harvard Business School*, **75**, 51–59, March–April 1997.

de Kluyver, C.A., Innovation and industrial product life cycle, *California Management Review*, **20**, 21–33, Fall 1977.

de Maio, A., Verganti, R. and Corso, M., A multi–project management framework for new product development, *European Journal of Operational Research*, **78**, 178–191, 1994.

del Prete, D., Winning strategies lead to global marketing success, *Marketing News*, **31**, 1–2, 18 August 1997.

Dearlove, D., Innovation from the chaos, *The Times*, p. 3, 13 August 1998.

Denison, D.R., Hart, S.L. and Kahn, J.A., From chimneys to cross-functional teams: developing and validating a diagnostic model, *Academy of Management Journal*, **39**, 1005–1023, August 1996.

Denton, K.D., and Denton, R.A., *The Toolbox for the Mind*, Milwaukee, WI: Quality Press, 1999.

DeYoung, H.G., Global challenges and promises in the 1990s, *Electronic Business*, **15**, 10, 11 December 1989

Ding, M. and Eliashberg, J., Structuring the new product development pipeline, *Management Science*, **48**, 343–363, March 2002.

DiPalma, K., Local to global: Regionalization – Vendor's views vary, *Pharmaceutical Executive*, **16**, 86, May 1996.

Donlon, J.P., Trotman's global gambit, *Chief Executive*, 48, Sept. 1996.

Donnellon, A., Cross-functional teams in product development: Accommodating the structure to the process, *Journal of Product Innovation Management*, **10**, 377–392, Nov. 1993.

Dougherty, D. and Bowman, E., The effects of organizational downsizing on product innovation, *California Management Review*, **37**, 28–44, Summer 1995.

Dreyfus, H.L. and Dreyfus, S.E., *Mind over Machine – The Power of Human Intuition and Expertise in the Era of the Computer*, New York: Free Press, 1986.

Droz, D., Prototyping: a key to managing product development, *Journal of Business Strategy*, **13**, 34–38, May–June 1992.

Drucker, P., New templates for today's organisations, *Harvard Business Review*, **52**, 45–53, Jan.–Feb. 1974.

Drucker, P. F., The coming of the new organization, *Harvard Business Review*, 56–61, Jan.–Feb. 1988.

Drucker, P.F., *Management Challenges for the 21st Century*, Harper Business, 1999.

Duffy, F., A new world of work, *Qualities of Success*, University of Industrial Arts, Helsinki UIAH, 1993.

Dumaine, B., Payoff from the new management, *Fortune*, **119**, 13 Dec. 1993.

Dumas, A., Creativity in the business context. Managing product development for business turnaround, Working Paper, London Business School, 1994.

Dumas, A., Sakakibara, K. and Watanabe, S., Innovation–creation–innovation: organizational processes for the concept development of a new product in Japan, Working Paper, London Business School, 1992.

Duncan, R., What is the right organisation structure? *Organizational Dynamics*, **7**, 59–80, Winter 1979.

Dunne, P.M., What are really new products? *Journal of Business*, **13**, 20–25, Dec. 1974.

Dutton, G., Enhancing creativity, *Management Review*, **85**, 44–46, Nov. 1996.

Edwards, T., *Innovation and organisational change: developments towards an interactive process perspective*, Aston Business School, Birmingham, UK: Aston Business School, 1999.

Eisenhardt, K.M., Strategy and strategic decision making, *Sloan Management Review*, **40**, 65–72, Spring 1999.

Eisenhardt, K.M., Paradox, spirals, ambivalence: The new language of change and pluralism, *Academy of Management Review*, **25**, 703, Oct. 2000.

Eisenhardt, K.M. and Galunic, D.C., Coevolving: At last, a way to make synergies work, *Harvard Business Review*, **78**, 91–101, Jan.–Feb. 2000.

Eisenhardt, K.M., Kahwaji, J.L. and Bourgeois III, L.J., How management teams can have a good fight, *Harvard Business Review*, **75**, 77–85, July–August 1997.

Ekvall, G., The organisational culture of idea management: a creative climate for the management of ideas, in *Managing Innovation*, eds Walker, D. and Henry, J., London Sage Publications, 1991.

Elliott, A., Design: what prices creativity? *Marketing*, **28**, 47, 12 Feb. 1987.

Eppinger, S.D., Whitney, D.E., Smith, R.P., and Gebala, D.A., A model-based method for organizing tasks in product development, *Research in Engineering Design*, 6, 1–13, 1994.

Espey, J.S., What makes global advertising work? *Chief Executive*, 28, June 1996.

Ettlie, J.E., The impact of inter-organisational manpower flows on the innovation process, *Management Science*, **31**, 1055–1071, Sept. 1985.

Evamy, M., The train that lost its way, *Design*, 16–19, May 1994.

Fairlamb, D., Can anyone get globalization right? *Institutional Investor*, **29**, 40, August 1995.

Farish, M., New product development, the route to improved performance, Design Council, London, 1992.

Faste, R., A visual essay on invention and innovation, *Design Management Journal*, 9–20, Spring 1995.

Faust, W., Cross–functional teams in design: a case study of the thermos thermal electric grill, *Design Management Journal*, 28–33, Fall 1993.

Feitzinger, E. and Lee, H. L., Mass customization at Hewlett–Packard, *Harvard Business Review*, 116–121, Jan.–Feb. 1997.

Fineman, S. and Mangham, I., Datas, meanings and creativity: a preface, *Journal of Management Studies*, **20**, 295–300, 1983.

Firth, D. and Leigh, A., *The Corporate Fool*, Oxford: Capstone, 1998.

Fitzgerald, T.K., Understanding diversity in the workplace: cultural metaphors or metaphors of identity, *Business Horizons*, **40**, 66–70, July–August 1997.

Flanagan, P., The three levels of corporate culture, *Management Review*, **84**, 59, July 1995.

Flynn, J., The biology of business, *Business Week*, 7, 7 July 1997.

Flynn, J. and Bongiorno, L., IKEA's new game plan, *Business Week*, 44–47, 6 October 1997.

Francis, A. and Winstanley, D., Managing new product development: some alternative ways to organise the work of technical specialists, *Journal of Marketing Management*, **4**, 249–360, 1988.

Friedman, T.L., *The Lexus and the Olive Tree*, Anchor Books/Doubleday, 2000.

Frischer, J., Empowering management in new product development units, *Journal of Product Innovation Management*, **10**, 393–401, 1993.

Frohman, A.L., Personal initiative sparks innovation, *Research Technology Management*, **42**, 32–38, May–June 1999.

Frohman, A.L., Building a culture for innovation, *Research-Technology Management*, **41**, 9–12, March/April 1998.

Furnham, A., Reaping the benefits of teamwork, *Financial Times*, 13 May 1993.

Gardiner, P. and Rothwell, R., Tough customers: good design, *Design Studies*, **6**, 7–17, Jan. 1985.

Gary, S., Cultural perspective on the measurement of corporate success, *European Management Journal*, **13**, 269–275, 1995.

Gebhart, J., Leading product development, *Sloan Management Review*, **36**, 103, Spring 1995.

Gilbert, C. and Bower, J.L., Disruptive change – when trying harder is part of the problem, *Harvard Business Review*, 3–8, May 2002.

Gill, B., Nelson, B., and Spring, S. Seven steps to strategic new product development. In *The PDMA Handbook of New Product Development*, eds Rosenau, M.D.J., Griffin, A., Castellion, G. and Anschuetz, N., New York: John Wiley, 1996, pp. 19–34.

Glaser, M., Measuring intuition, *Research Technology Management*, **38**, 43, March–April 1995.

Globe, S., Levy, G.W., and Schwartz, C.M., Key factors and events in the innovation process, *Research Management*, 8–15, July 1973.

Gobeli, D.H. and Brown, D.J., Analysing product innovations, *Research Management*, **30**, 25–31, July–August 1987.

Godfrey, S., Are you creative? *Journal of Knowledge Management*, **2**, 14–15, Sept. 1998.

Goffee, R. and Jones, G., The Character of a Corporation: How your Company's Culture can Make or Break your Business, New York: HarperCollins, 1998.

Goffee, R. and Jones, G., What holds the modern company together? *Harvard Business Review*, 133–148, Nov.–Dec. 1996.

Goffee, R. and Jones, G., Why should anyone be led by you? *Harvard Business Review*, Sep.–Oct. 2000,

Goleman, D., Kaufman, P. and Ray, M., *The Creative Spirit*, New York: Plume, 1992.

Gorb, P., Design and the control of innovation, Handout in MBA class 5.1, 1992, London Business School.

Gregersen, H.B., Morrison, A.J., and Black, J.S., Developing leaders for the global frontier, *Sloan Management Review*, **40**, 21–32, Fall 1998.

Grenier, B., Product evaluation. In *Design Management, A Handbook of Issues and Methods*, ed. Oakley, M., Oxford: Blackwell Reference, 1990.

Griffin, A., Obtaining customer needs for product development. In *The PDMA Handbook of New Product Development*, eds Rosenau, M.D.J., Griffin, A., Castellion, G. and Anschuetz, N., New York: John Wiley, 1996, pp. 153–166.

Gruenwald, G., *New Product Development*, NTC Business Books, 1992.

Guest, R.H., Today's trends for tomorrow's management, *Business Quarterly*, 146–152, Oct. 1982.

Gunz, H., Managing across organisational boundaries. In *Design management, A Handbook of Issues and Methods*, ed. Oakley, M., Oxford: Blackwell Reference, 1990.

Gurteen, D., Knowledge, creativity and innovation, *Journal of Knowledge Management*, **2**, 5–13, Sept. 1998.

Guyson, J. and Woods, W., Why is the world's most profitable company turning itself inside out? *Fortune*, 52–57, 4 Aug. 1997.

Hales, C., Proposals, briefs and specifications. In *Design Management, A Handbook of Issues and Methods*, ed. Oakley, M., Oxford: Blackwell Reference, 1990.

Hamden-Turner, C., *Corporate culture for competitive edge, a user's guide*, London, England: The Economist, 1990.

Hamel, G., Turning your business upside down, *Fortune*, 36–37, 23 June 1997.

Hamel, G. and Prahalad, C.K., *Competing for the Future*, Boston, MA: Harvard Business School Press, 1994.

Handy, C., *The Elephant and the Flea*, London: Hutchinson, 2001.

Hanna, N., Ayers, D.J., Ridnour, R.E. and Gordon, G.L., New product development practices in consumer versus business product organisations, *Journal of Product and Brand Management*, **4**, 33–55, 1995.

Harbert, T., An innovative number, *Electronic Business*, **24**, 83, July 1998.

Hardy, T., Innovation and chaos, *Journal of Business Strategy*, **16**, 7–10, May–June 1995.

Hargadon, A. and Sutton, R.I., Building an innovation factory, *Harvard Business Review*, **78**, 157–166, May–June 2000.

Hargadon, A.B., Firms as knowledge brokers: lessons in pursuing continuous innovation, *California Management Review*, **40**, 209–227, Spring 1998.

Harris, J.R. and McKay, J.C., Pipeline management. In *Setting the PACE in Product Development*, ed. McGrath, M.E., Newton, MA: Butterworth-Heinemann, 1996, pp. 135–146.

Hart, S. and Craig, A., Dimensions of success in new product development. In *Perspectives on Marketing Management*, ed. Baker, M.J., New York: John Wiley, 1993.

Hart, S., Where we have been and where we are going in new product development research. In *Product Development: Meeting the Challenge of the Design–Marketing Interface*, eds Bruce, M. and Biemans, W.G., Chichester: John Wiley, 1995.

Hart, S., *New Product Development, a Reader*, London: Dryden Press, 1996.

Harvey, D., Finding new ways to crack problems, *Chief Executive*, 60, Oct. 1979.

Harwood, A., Global markets require product certification, *Wood Technology*, **124**, 52–53, Oct. 1997.

Hatch, M.J., Organization Theory, Modern Symbolic and Postmodern Perspectives, Oxford: Oxford University Press, 1997.

Hauser, J.R. and Clausing, D., The house of quality, *Harvard Business Review*, 63–73, May–June 1988.

Hayak, F.A., The use of knowledge in society, *American Economic Review*, **35**, 518–530, 1945.

Heany, D.F., Degrees of product innovation, *Journal of Business Strategy*, 3–14, Spring 1983.

Heany, D.F. and Vinson, W.D., A fresh look at new product development, *Journal of Business Strategy*, **5**, 22–31, Fall 1984.

Heap, J., *The Management of Innovation and Design*, London Cassell Education, 1989.

Henderson, R.M. and Clark, K.B., Architectural innovation: the reconfiguration of existing product technologies and the failure of established firms, *Administrative Science Quarterly*, **35**, 9–30, 1990.

Hendrikse, G., Organizational choice and product differentiation, *Managerial and Decision Economics*, **12**, 361–366, Oct. 1991.

Henke, J.W., Krachenberg, A.R. and Lyons, T.F., Cross–functional teams: good concept, poor implementation! *Journal of Product Innovation Management*, **10**, 216–229, 1993.

Henry, J., *Creative management*, 2nd edition London: Sage, 2001.

Henry, J., (ed.) *Creativity and Perception in Management*, London: Sage Publishing, 2001

Henry, J., Making sense of creativity. In *Creative Management*, ed. Henry, J., London: Sage, 1991, pp. 3–11.

Henry, J. and Walker, D., *Managing Innovation*, London: Sage, 1991.

Hershock, R.J., Cowman, C.D. and Peters, D., From experience: action teams that work, *Journal of Product Innovation Management*, **11**, 95–104, 1994.

Hickman, C.R. and Silva, M.A., Creating Excellence – Managing Corporate Culture, Strategy and Change in the New Age, London: George Allen & Unwin, 1984.

Hill, C.W.L., Strategies for exploiting technological innovations – when and when not to licence, *Organization Science*, **3**, 428–441, 1992.

Hirshberg, J., The Creative Priority – Putting Innovation to Work in your Business, London: Penguin, 1998.

Hobday, M., Product complexity, innovation and industrial organisation, *Research Policy*, **26**, 689–710, 1998.

Hoecklin, L., Managing Cultural Differences: Strategies for Competitiveness, London: Addison–Wesley, 1994.

Hohner, G., Integrating product and process designs, *Quality Progress*, **26**, 55–61, May 1993.

Holahan, P.J. and Markham, S.K., Factors affecting multifunctional team effectiveness. In *The PDMA Handbook of New Product Development*, eds Rosenau, M.D.J., Griffin, A., Castellion, G. and Anschuetz, N., New York: John Wiley, 1996, pp. 119–135.

Holt, K., *Innovation: A Challenge to the Engineer*, Amsterdam: Elsevier, 1987.

Holt, K., Product Innovation Management: A Workbook for Management in Industry, Cambridge: Cambridge University Press, 1988.

Hopkins, D.S. and Bailey, E.L., New product pressures, *Conference Board Record*, 16–24, June 1971.

Hopkins, D.S., New product winners and losers, *Research Management*, 12–17, May 1981.

Horbie, F., *Creating the Innovation Culture*, Toronto: John Wiley, 2001.

Hughes, G.D. and Chafin, D.C., Turning new product development into a continuous learning process, *Journal of Product Innovation Management*, **13**, 89–104, 1996.

Hultink, E.J. and Robben, H.S.J., Measuring product development success and failure. In *The PDMA Handbook of New Product Development*, eds Rosenau, M.D.J., Griffin, A., Castellion, G. and Anschuetz, N., New York: John Wiley, 1996, pp. 455–461.

Hunt, R.E. and Adams, D.C., Entrepreneurial behavioral profiles and company performance: A cross-cultural comparison, *International Journal of Commerce and Management*, 8, 33–49, 1998.

Hurley, R.F., Group culture and its effects on innovative productivity, *Journal of Engineering and Technology Management*, **12**, 57–75, July 1995.

Hutchings, A. and Knox, S.T., Creating products customers demand, *Communications of the ACM*, **38**, 72–80, May 1995.

Inkpen, A.C., Creating knowledge through collaboration, *California Management Review*, **39**, 80–105, 1996.

InnovationNetwork: see http://www.thinksmart.com.

Iwamura, A. and Jog, V.M., Innovators, organization structure and management of the innovation process in the securities industry, *Journal of Product Innovation Management*, 8, 104–116, June 1991.

Jackson, S.C., How to think and act globally, *Small Business Forum*, **14**, 71, Fall 1996.

Jackson, S.E., The consequences of diversity in multi-disciplinary work teams. In *Handbook of Work Group Psychology*, ed. West, M.A., Chichester: John Wiley, 1996, pp. 53–76.

Jancsurack, J., Change now or die, *Appliance Manufacturer*, **44**, 7 June 1996.

Janzen, F., *The Age of Innovation*, London: Prentice-Hall, 2000.

Jelinek, M. and Schoonhoven, C.B., *The Innovation Marathon*, San Francisco: Jossey-Bass, 1990.

Jelinek, M. and Schoonhoven, C.B. Strong culture and its consequences. In *Managing Innovation*, eds Walker, D. and Henry, J., London: Sage Publications, 1991.

Jensen, R., *The Dream Society*, New York: McGraw-Hill, 1999.

Johne, A. and Snelson, P., Marketing's role in successful product development, *Journal of Marketing Management*, **3**, 256–268, 1988.

Johne, A., Successful market innovation, *European Journal of Innovation Management*, **2**, 6–11, 1999.

Johne, A. and Davies, R., Innovation and marketing: when structure does not follow strategy, 28th European Marketing Academy Conference, Humbolt Universität zu Berlin, Germany, 1999.

Johne, A. and Snelson, P., *Successful Product Development*, Basil Blackwell, 1990.

Johne, F.A. and Snelson, P.A., Success factors in product innovation: a selective review of the literature, *Journal of Product Innovation Management*, **5**, 114–128, 1988.

Johnston, D.J., Responding to global change, *Organisation for Economic Cooperation and Development. The OECD Observer*, 4, June–July 1998.

Jones, T., *New Product Development, An Introduction to a Multifunctional Process*, Oxford: Butterworth-Heinemann, 1997.

Karatani, K., Kohso, S. and Speaks, M., *Architecture as Metaphor*, MIT Press, 1995.

Karger, D., *The New Product*, New York: Industrial Press, 1960.

Kasarda, J.D. and Rondinelli, D.A., Innovative infrastructure for agile manufacturers, *Sloan Management Review*, **39**, 73–82, Winter 1998.

Katzenbach, J.R. and Smith, D.K., Why teams matter, *McKinsey Quarterly*, **3**, 3–27, 1992.

Katzenbach, J.R. and Smith, D.K., *The Wisdom of Teams*, Boston, MA: Harvard Business School Press, 1993.

Kay, H., The acquirers of knowledge, *Director*, 32–40, May 1994.

Kekale, T. and Kekale, J., A mismatch of cultures: A pitfall of implementing a total quality approach, *The International Journal of Quality and Reliability Management*, **12**, 210, 1995.

Kellaqway, L., Colour code for the workplace, *Financial Times*, 15, 26 March 1997.

Kennedy, C., ABB: The dancing giant, *Director*, **52**, 113.

Kiely, T., The idea makers, *Technology Review*, 32–40, Jan. 1993.

Kiernan, M.J., Get innovative or get dead, *Business Quarterly*, **61**. 51–58, Autumn 1996.

Kim, W.C. and Maugorge, T., Fair process: managing the knowledge economy, *Harvard Business Review*, **75**, 65–75, July–August 1997.

Kimberly, J.R., Managerial innovation. In *Handbook of Organisational Design: Adapting Organisations to their Environments*, eds Nystrom, P.C. and Starbuck, W.H., Oxford: Oxford University Press, 1981, pp. 84–104.

King, N. and West, M.A., Experiences of innovation at work, *Journal of Managerial Psychology*, **2**, 6, 1987.

Kinsey Goman, C., Adapting to Change: Making It Work for You, Crisp Publications, 1993.

Kirton, M.J., The way people approach problems, *Planned Innovation*, **3**, 51–54, 1980.

Klein, N., *No Logo,* London: Flamingo, 2001.

Klimoski, R.J. and Karol, B.L., The impact of trust on creative problem solving groups, *Journal of Applied Psychology*, **61**, 630, Oct. 1976.

Kline, S.J., Innovation is not a linear process, *Research Management*, July–August 1985.

Klompmaker, J.E., Hughes, G.D., and Haley, R.I., Test marketing in new product development, *Harvard Business Review*, 128–138, May–June 1976.

Koberstein, W., Local to global: how regionalization changes the industry, *Pharmaceutical Executive*, **16**, 50, May 1996.

Kogut, B., What makes a company global? *Harvard Business Review*, **77**, 165–170, Jan.–Feb. 1999.

Kroeber, A.L. and Kluckhohn, F., Culture: a critical review of concepts and definitions, *Peabody Museum Papers*, **47**, 181, 1952.

Krubasik, E., Customise your product development, *Harvard Business Review*, Nov.–Dec. 1988.

Kuczmarski, T., Inspiring and implementing the innovation mindset, *Planning Review*, **22**, 37, Sep.–Oct. 1994.

Kuczmarski, T., Innovation – Leadership Strategies for the Competitive Edge, Chicago: NTC Business Books, 1996.

Kuczmarski, T., The ten traits of an innovation mindset, *Journal for Quality and Participation*, **21**, 44–46, Nov.–Dec. 1998.

Kuczmarski, T., Tools@work: The CEO innovation mindset test, *Journal for Quality and Participation*, **21**, 48–49, Nov.–Dec. 1998.

Kuczmarski, T.D., *Managing New Products*, London: Prentice Hall, 1988.

Kuczmarski, T.D., Five hallmarks of innovators, *Research & Development*, **32**, 155, May 1990.

Kuczmarski, T.D., Creating an innovative mindset, *Management Review*, **85**, 47, 1996.

Kuczmarski, T.D., and Shapiro, T., Measuring your return on innovation, *Marketing News*, **31**. H10, 9 June 1997.

Lampikoski, K. and Emden, J.B., Igniting Innovation – Inspiring Organisations by Managing Creativity, Chichester: John Wiley, 1996.

Landa, R., Thinking Creatively – New Ways to Unlock your Visual Imagination, Cincinnati, OH: North Light Books, 1998.

Landry, J.T., A future perfect: the essentials of globalization, *Harvard Business Review*, **78**, May–June 2000.

Lawler III, E.E., Total quality management and employee involvement: are they compatible? *Academy of Management Executive*, **8**, 68–76, 1994.

Lawler III, E.E., Pay strategy: New thinking for the new millennium, *Compensation and Benefits Review*, **32**, 7–12, Jan.–Feb. 2000.

Lee, W.G., Going global, *Executive Excellence*, **13**, 15, May 1996.

Leighton, L., How culture clashes can ambush the unwary buyer going abroad, *Mergers & Acquisitions*, 26–29, March–April 1993.

Leonard, D. and Rayport, J.F., Spark innovation through empathic design, *Harvard Business Review*, **75**, 102–108, Nov.–Dec. 1997.

Leonard, D. and Strauss, S., Putting our company's whole brain to work, *Harvard Business Review*, **75**, 111–121, July–August 1997.

Leonard-Barton, D., Managerial influence in the implementation of new technology, *Management Science*, **34**, 1252–1265, Oct. 1988.

Leonard-Barton, D., Inanimate integrators: a block of wood speaks, *Design Management Journal*, 61–67, Summer 1991.

Leonard-Barton, D., Core capabilities and core rigidities: a paradox in managing new product development, *Strategic Management Journal*, **13**, 111–125, Summer 1992.

Leonard-Barton, D., The factory as a learning laboratory, *Sloan Management Review*, 23–38, Fall 1992.

Leonard-Barton, D., *Wellsprings of Knowledge*, Boston: Harvard Business School Press, 1995.

Leonard-Barton, D., Bowen, H.K., Clark, K.B., Holloway, C.A. and Wheelwright, S.C., How to integrate work and deepen expertise, *Harvard Business Review*, **72**, 121–130, Sep.–Oct 1994.

Lester, D.H., Critical success factors for new product development, *Research Technology Management*, **41**, 36, Jan.–Feb. 1998.

Lester, R.K., Piore, M.J., and Malek, K.M., Interpretive management: what general managers can learn from design, *Harvard Business Review*, 86–96, March–April 1998.

Lewin, R., *Life at the Edge of Chaos*, Collier Books, 1992.

Lewis, R., From chaos to complexity, *Executive Development*, **7**, 16–17, 1994.

Lewis, R.D., *When cultures collide: managing successfully across cultures*, London: Nicholas Brealey Publishing, 1996.

Light, P.C., *Sustaining Innovation – Creating Nonprofit and Government Organisations that Innovate Naturally*, San Francisco: Jossey-Bass, 1998.

Lilly, P., Innovation: competition and culture. A speech to an invited audience at the University of Warwick, 21 May 1991.

Link, P.L., Keys to new product success and failure, *Industrial Marketing Management*, **16**, 109–118, 1987.

Little A.D., *Total Product Management*, DIT, 1991.

Littler, D., *Marketing and Product Development*, Oxford: Philips Allan Publishers, 1984.

Lockamy, A.I. and Khurana, A., Quality function deployment: total quality management for new product design, *International Journal of Quality and Reliability Management*, **12**, 73–84, 1995.

Lodge, G.C., Global leadership, *Executive Excellence*, **13**, 5, May 1996.

Loeb, M., Ten commandments for managing creative people, *Fortune*, **131**, 135, 16 Jan. 1995.

Lonsdale, R.T., Noel, N.M., and Stasch, S.F., Classification of sources of new product ideas. In *The PDMA Handbook of New Product Development*, eds Rosenau, M.D.J., Griffin, A., Castellion, G. and Anschuetz, N., New York: John Wiley, 1996, pp. 179–194.

Lorenz, A., How cultural revolution put GM ahead, *The Sunday Times*, 27 Nov. 1994.

Lorenz, C., How Ford broke the Detroit model. In *Design Management: A Handbook of Issues and Methods*, ed. Oakley, M., Oxford: Blackwell Reference, 1990.

Lorenz, C., Management: teamwork is tricky, *Financial Times*, 1 Oct. 1990.

Lorenz, C., Management: here, there and everywhere – the lives of 3M's managers have been transformed by a Europe-wide reorganisation, *Financial Times*, 11, 10 Nov. 1993.

Lorenz, C., Management: facing up to responsibility, *Financial Times*, 11, 15 Dec. 1993.

Louchez, A.F. and McIntyre, J.R., The globalization of telcos: A normative view, *International Executive*, **38**, 731, Nov.–Dec. 1996.

Lowry-Miller, K., The cost of change at Hoechst, *Business Week*, 14–15, 1 Sep. 1997.

Lundqvist, M. A., Organizing for cross-functional learning in product development. In *Technological Innovation and Global Challenges, eds* Bennett, D. and Steward, F., 5–7 July 1995.

Lundvall, B.A. User–producer relationships, National systems of innovation and internalisation. In *National Systems of Innovation: Towards a Theory of Innovation and Interactive Learning*, ed. Lundvall, B.A., London: Printer Publishers, 1992, pp. 45–67.

Luthans, F., Conversation with Edgar H. Schein, *Organizational Dynamics*, **17**, 60, Spring 1989.

Lynn, G.S., New product team learning: Developing and profiting from your knowledge capital, *California Management Review*, **40**, 74–93, Summer 1998.

Mabert, V.A., Muth, J.F., and Scemenner, R.W., Collapsing new product development times: six case studies, *Journal of Product Innovation Management*, **9**, 200–212, 1992.

Machlis, S., Rapid prototyping weeds out bad designs early, *Design News*, 70–74, 8 July 1996.

MacVicar, J., How to manage creative people, *Management Quarterly*, **29**, 30–33, Fall 1988.

Madell, R., Local to global: face-to-face with regionalization, *Pharmaceutical Executive*, **16**, 58, May 1996.

Magretta, J., Growth through global sustainability: An interview with Monsanto's CEO, Robert B. Shapiro, *Harvard Business Review*, **75**, 78–88, Jan.–Feb. 1997.

Mahajan, V. and Wind, J., New product models: practice, shortcomings and desired improvements, *Journal of Product Innovation Management*, **9**, 128–139, 1992.

Maidique, M.A. and Zirger, B.J., A study of success and failure in product innovation: the case of the US electronics industry, *IEEE Transaction on Engineering Management*, **31**, 192–203, 1984.

Maidique, M.A. and Zirger, B.J., The new product learning cycle, *Research Policy*, **14**, 299–313, Dec. 1985.

Maira, A.N. and Curtice, R.M., From process management to complexity management, *Prism*, 12–23, 1995.

Majaro, S., The what and how of creativity, *Marketing*, 79, Oct. 1978.

Majchrzak, A. and Wang, O., Breaking the functional mindset in process organisations, *Harvard Business Review*, **74**, 93–99, Sep.–Oct. 1996.

Manimala, M.J., Entrepreneurial innovation: beyond Schumpeter, *Creativity and Innovation Management*, **1**, 46–55, 1992.

Marken, G.A., Nurturing creativity in a productivity society, *Public Relations Quarterly*, **36**, 31–32, Winter 1991–1992.

Markides, C., *All the Right Moves*, Boston: Harvard Business School Press, 1999.

Martin, J., Ignore your customers, *Fortune*, 83–89, 1 May 1995.

Maurice, M., The Social Bases of Industrial Innovation and Product Development, Cambridge, MA: MIT Press, 1986.

Maylor, H., *Project Management*, London: Pitman Publishing, 1996.

Mazur, L., Brands break down borders, *Marketing*, 28, 9 Dec. 1993.

McAleer, N. The roots of inspiration. In *Creative Management*, ed. Henry, J., London: Sage Publications, 1991, pp. 12–15.

McDonough III, E.F., Faster new product development: investigating the effects of technology and characteristics of the project leader and team, *Journal of Product Innovation Management*, **10**, 241–250, 1993.

McDonough III, E.F. and Barczak, G., Speeding up new product development: effects of leadership style and source of technology, *Journal of Product Innovation Management*, **8**, 203–211, 1991.

McGivern, J. and Thompson, J., Focusing on 'fiction' as management text, *Training and Management Development Methods*, **9**, 301, 1995.

McGrath, M.E., *Setting the PACE in Product Development*, Newton, MA: Butterworth-Heinemann, 1996.

McGregory, P., The role of integrator in multi-disciplinary product development team *Arttu!*, **1**, 8, 1993.

McIntyre, J.M. and Peck, M.A., Managing and measuring for customer loyalty: A yin and yang perspective, *Direct Marketing*, **61**, 48–52, Oct. 1998.

McPherson, J., The wonderful world of creative problem-solving, *International Management*, **39**, 110, Sep. 1984.

McWilliam G. and Dumas, A., Using metaphors in new brand design. Centre for Marketing Working Paper No. 95–401; London Business School, September 1995.

Meeks, J., A global scourge, *Harvard International Review*, **20**, 32–35, Fall 1998.

Menke, M.M., Improving R&D decisions and execution, *Research-Technology Management*, **37**, 25–32, Sep. 1994.

Merchant, D. and Roberts, D., Data management enables global design teams, *Electronic Engineering Times*, 94, 21 June 1999.

Merrick, N., Theatrical treatment, *People Management*, **4**, 44–46, 22 Jan. 1998.

Mestel, R., It's child's play, *New Scientist*, 24–27, 13 April 1996.

Meyer, C., *Fast Cycle Time: How to Align Purpose, Strategy and Structure for Speed*, New York: Free Press, 1993.

Meyer, C., How the right measures help teams excel, *Harvard Business Review*, **72**, 95–103, May–June 1994.

Meyer, C., *Relentless Growth – How Silicon Valley Innovation Strategies can work in your Business*, New York: Free Press, 1998.

Meyer, C. and Purser, R.E., Six steps to becoming a fast cycle-time competitor, *Research-Technology Management*, **36**, 41, Sep.–Oct. 1993.

Michalko, M., *Cracking Creativity*, Berkeley, CA: Ten Speed Press, 2001.

Michelli, D., Turning workers into rebels, London Business School *Alumni News*, 8–10, Autumn 1996.

Miles, M., Getting bright ideas from your team (Part 1), *Computer Decisions*, **15**, 192–195, Feb. 1983.

Miller, D. and Friesen, P., Archetypes of strategy formulation, *Management Science*, 921–933, 1978.

Miller, K., Where you really need to hear consumers, *Brandweek*, **38**, 17, 20 Jan. 1997.

Millson, M.R., Raj, S.P. and Wilemon, D., A survey of major approaches for accelerating new product development, *Journal of Product Innovation Management*, **9**, 44–52, 1992.

Millson, M.R., Raj, S.P. and Wilemon, D., Strategic partnering for developing products, *Research-Technology Management*, 41–49, 1996.

Mintzberg, H. Planning on the left side and managing on the right. In *Creative Management*, ed. Henry, J., London: Sage Publishing, 1991, pp. 58–71.

Mitchell, A., P&G's new horizons, *Campaign*, 34–35, 20 March 1998.

Mitchell, R., Masters of innovation: how 3M keeps its new products coming *Business Week*, 58–63, 10 April 1989.

Mitroff, I., Organization as if people mattered *Executive Excellence*, **11**, 14, July 1994.

Moody, S., The role of industrial design in technological innovation, *Design Studies*, **1**, 329–339, Oct. 1980.

Morita, A., Selling to the world: the Sony Walkman story. In *Managing Innovation*, eds Walker, D. and Henry, J., London: Sage Publications, 1991.

Morita, A., S ≠ T, T ≠ I, The UK Innovation Lecture, London, 1992.

Morris, F., Deschamps, J.P., Floyd, C. and Marlow, G., Innovation: the key process for business growth, *Prism*, first quarter 1997.

Moss Kanter, R., *The Change Masters*, Touchstone Books, reprint edition, January 1985.

Moss Kanter, R., *When Giants Learn to Dance*, Simon & Schuster, 1989.

Muffatto, M., The global challenge of Honda product development, in *Technological Innovation and Global Challenges,* eds Bennett, D. and Steward, F., 5–7 July 1995, Aston.

Myers, S. and Marquis, D., Successful industrial innovations; a study of factors underlying innovation in selected firms, Institute of Public Administration, Washington DC, National Science Foundation Report No. NSF 69 17, 1969.

Myerson, J., *IDEO Masters of Innovation,* London: Laurence King Publishing, 2001.

Nadler, L. and Nadler, Z., *Achieving Results from Training – How to Evaluate Human Resource Development to Strengthen Programs and Increase Impact,* San Francisco: Jossey-Bass, 1987.

Naisbitt, J., Global paradox, *Executive Excellence,* **13**, 3, May 1996.

Neely, A. and Hii, J., Innovation and business performance: a literature review, Judge Institute of Management Studies, University of Cambridge, England. Commissioned by the Government Office for the Eastern Region, 1997.

Neely, A. and Hii, J., The innovative capacity of firms, University of Cambridge, England, Centre for Business Performance, Judge Institute of Management Studies, 1998.

Nemeth, C.J., Managing innovation: when less is more, *California Management Review,* **40**, 59–74, 1997.

Nicholson, N., Organisational innovation in context: culture, interpretation and application. In *Innovation and Creativity at Work,* ed. West, M.A.J.L., Chichester: John Wiley, 1990.

Nobel, R. and Birkinshaw, J., Innovation in multinational corporations: Control and communication patterns in international R&D operations, *Strategic Management Journal,* **19**, 479–496, May 1998.

Nolan, V., The Innovator's Handbook – The skills of Innovative Management, London: Sphere Books, 1987.

Nonaka, I., The knowledge-creating company, *Harvard Business Review,* **69**, 96–1044, Nov.–Dec. 1991.

Nonaka, I. and Kennedy, M., Towards a new theory of innovation management: a case study comparing Canon, Inc. and Apple Computer Inc., *Journal of Engineering and Technology Management,* **8**, 67–83, June 1991.

Nonaka, I. and Yamanouchi, T., Managing innovation as a self–renewing process, *Journal of Business Venturing,* **4**, 299–315, Sep. 1989.

Nooteboom, B., Innovation, learning and industrial organisation, *Cambridge Journal of Economics,* **23**, 127–159, March 1999.

Norman, A.L. and Shimer, D.W., Risk, uncertainty and complexity, *Journal of Economic Dynamics and Control,* **18**, 231–249, 1994.

Norman, D.A., *The Psychology of Everyday Things,* Basic Books, 1988.

Nussbaum, B., Hot products – smart design is the common thread, *Business Week,* 54–57, 7 June 1993.

Nussbaum, B., Winners, the best product designs of the year, *Business Week,* 44–47, 5 June 1994.

O'Conner, P., From experience: implementing a stage-gate process: a multi-company perspective, *Journal of Product Innovation Management,* **11**, 183–200, 1994.

O'Hare & Company, *The NPD Crisis, New Product Development Strategies Approaches and Performance,* London, 1989.

Oakley, M., *Managing Product Design,* London: Weidenfeld and Nicolson, 1984.

Olshavsky, R.W. and Spreng, R.A., An exploratory study of the innovation evaluation process, *Journal of Product Innovation Management,* **13**, 512–529, 1996.

Oram, M., Product innovation ... a comparative perspective. Presentation to the NPD Seminar at London Business School, London, 15 February 1996.

Papanek, V., *Design for the Real World,* Thames and Hudson, 1991.

Patterson, F., *Innovation Potential Indicator,* Oxford Psychologists Press.

Peak, D., and Frame, M., *Chaos Under Control: The Art and Science of Complexity,* New York: W.H. Freeman and Company, 1994.

Peat, F.D., *The Blackwinged Night: Creativity in Nature and Mind,* Cambridge, MA: Perseus Publishing, 2000.

Pearson, A.W., Managing innovation: an uncertainty reduction process. In *Managing Innovation,* eds Walker, D. and Henry, J., London: Sage Publications, 1991.

Peet, W.J. and Hladik, K.J., Organizing for global product development, *Electronic Business Buyer*, **15**, 62, 6 March 1989.

Pennings, J.M. and Buitendam, A., *New Technologies as Organizational Innovation*, Ballinger Publishers, 1987.

Perry, T.S., Designing a culture for creativity, *Research Technology Management*, 14–16, March–April 1995.

Peters, T., A world turned upside down, *Academy of Management Executive*, **1**, 233–243, August 1987.

Peters, T., Brave leadership, *Executive Excellence*, **13**, 5–6, Jan. 1996.

Peters, T. and Waterman, R.H., *In Search of Excellence*, New York: Harper & Row, 1982.

Petroski, H., Designed to fail, *American Scientist*, **85**, 412–416, Sep. 1997.

Pierce, J.L. and Delbecq, A.L., Organisation structure, individual attitudes and innovation, *Academy of Management Review*, **2**, 27–37, Jan. 1977.

Pilditch, J., What makes a winning company? In *Managing Innovation*, eds Walker, D. and Henry, J., Sage Publications, 1987.

Pilditch, J., *Winning Ways*, Mercury Business Books, 1989.

Pinker, S., *How the Mind Works*, London: Penguin, 1997.

Pinto, J.K. and Kharbanda, O.P., How to fail in project management (without really trying), *Business Horizon*, 45–53, July–August 1996.

Piore, M.J., Lester, R.K., Kofman, F.M. and Malek, K.M., The organization of product development, *Industrial and Corporate Change*, **3**, 405–434, 1994.

Polanyi, M., *The Tacit Dimension*, Gloucester, MA: Peter Smith, 1983.

Polley, D. and Van de Ven, A.H., Learning by discovery during innovation development, *International Journal of Technology Management*, **11**, 871–882, 1996.

Poole, M.S. and Van de Ven, A.H., Using paradox to build management and theories, *Academy of Management Review*, **14**, 562–578, Oct. 1989.

Potter, S. and Roy, R., Innovation: design environment and strategy. Teaching material T302, the Open University, Milton Keynes, UK 1996.

Power, C., Flops, too many new products fail – here's why – and how to do better, *Business Week*, 16 August 1993.

Prokesch, S.E., Unleashing the power of learning: an interview with British Petroleum's John Browne, *Harvard Business Review*, **75**, 146–168, Sep.–Oct. 1997.

Pugh, S., *Creating Innovative Products using Total Design*, Reading, MA: Addison–Wesley, 1996.

Pugh, S.D., Hickson, D.J., Hinings, C.R., and Turner, C., Dimensions of organizational structure, *Administrative Science Quarterly*, 65–105, 1968.

Purser, R.E., Pasmore, W.A., and Tenkasi, R.V., The influence of deliberations on learning in new product development teams, *Journal of Engineering and Technology Management*, **9**, 1–28, 1992.

Quintas, P., Programmed innovation? Trajectories of change in software development, *Information Technology and People*, **7**, 25–47, 1994.

Quintas, P., Lefrere, P. and Jones, G., Knowledge management: a strategic agenda, *Long Range Planning*, **30**, 385–391, 1997.

Rafii, F. and Perkins, S., Cross-functional integration: moving beyond physical co–location, *Design Management Journal*, 62–68, Summer 1995.

Rayner, B.C.P., A new global economic order to come of age in the 1990s, *Electronic Business*, **15**, 16, 11 Dec. 1989.

Remich Jr., N.C., A first for small electrics, *Appliance Manufacturer*, **45**, 83–84, Aug. 1997.

Rettig, M., Prototyping for tiny fingers, *Communications of the ACM*, **37**, 21–27, April 1994.

Richards, L.A., A key to creating winning products, *National Underwriter*, **98**, 33, 14 Nov. 1994.

Richardson, L., Global rebels, *Harvard International Review*, **20**, 52–56, Fall 1998.

Ridderstråle, J. and Nordström, K., *Funky Business*, London: Person Education, 2000.

Robb, W.L., Don't change the engineers – change the process, *Research-Technology Management*, **35**, 8–9, March–April 1992.

Robinson, A.G. and Stern, S., *Corporate Creativity: How Innovation and Improvement Actually Happen,* San Francisco: Berrett-koehler Publishers, 1998

Rodrik, D., Has globalization gone too far? *California Management Review*, **39**, 29–53, Spring 1997.

Rosenau, M.D.J., Leading product development: the senior manager's guide to creating and shaping the enterprise, *Journal of Product Innovation Management*, **12**, 361–363, Sep. 1995.

Rosenau, M.D.J., Griffin, A., Castellion, G. and Anschuetz, N., *The PDMA Handbook of New Product Development*, New York: John Wiley, 1996.

Rosenfeld, R. and Servo, J.C., Facilitating innovation in large organisations. In: *Managing Innovation*, eds. Walker, D. and Henry, J., London: Sage Publications, 1991.

Ross-Ashby, W., *An Introduction to Cybernetics*, London: Chapman & Hall, 1964.

Rothwell, R. and Robertson, A.B., The role of communications in technological innovation, *Research Policy*, **2**, 204–225, 1973.

Rothwell, R. and Whiston, T.G., Design, innovation and corporate integration, *R&D Management*, **20**, 193–201, 1990.

Rotschild, E.E., *Product Development Management*, T. Wilson Publishing Company, 1987.

Roy, R. and Riedel-Johann, C.K.H., The role of design and innovation in competitive product development, proceedings of the conference *Contextual Design – Design in Contexts,* held in Stockholm, Sweden, 23–25 April 1997.

Rubinstein, A.H., Charkrabarti, A.K., OKeefe, R.D., Souder, W.E. and Young, H.C., Factors influencing innovation success at the project level, *Research Management*, 15–20, May 1976.

Rueckert, R.W., Cross-functional interactions in product development and their impact on project performance, *Design Management Journal*, 50–54, Summer 1995.

Rugman, A., *The End of Globalization*, London: Random House Business Books, 2000.

Rugman, A. and Hodgetts, R. The end of global strategy, *European Management Journal*, **19**, 333–334, August 2001.

Russ, G.S., Organizational culture and leadership, *Personnel Psychology*, **46**, 919, Winter 1993.

Sackmann, S.A., Culture and subcultures: an analysis of organizational knowledge, *Administrative Science Quarterly*, **37**, 140–161, March 1992.

Sahal, D., *Patterns of Technological Innovation*, Reading, MA: Addison-Wesley, 1981.

Sakakibara, K., Dumas, A. and Watanabe, S., The new product trajectory: the Japanese context of product innovation. Working Paper Centre for Design Management, London Business School, June 1993.

Sanchez, R., Strategic flexibility in product competition, *Strategic Management Journal*, **16**, 135–159, 1995.

Sanchez, R. and Sudharshan, D., Real-time market research, *Marketing Intelligence and Planning*, **11**, 29–38, 1993.

Santora, J.C. and Sarros, J.C., Bob Mansfield on what it takes to be a global leader, *Practising Manager*, **17**, 8 Oct. 1996.

Saren, M.A., A classification and review of the intra-firm innovation process, *R&D Management*, **14**, 11–24, 1984.

Schein, E.H., What you need to know about organizational culture, *Training and Development Journal*, **40**, 30, Jan. 1986.

Schein, E.H., *Organisational Culture and Leadership*, San Francisco: Jossey-Bass, 1992.

Schein, E.H., Culture: The missing concept in organization studies, *Administrative Science Quarterly*, **41**, 229, June 1996.

Schein, E.H., Three cultures of management: The key to organizational learning, *Sloan Management Review*, **38**, 9, Fall 1996.

Schlender, B., Peter Drucker takes the long view, *Fortune*, 94–100, 28 Sep. 1998.

Schrage, M., The culture(s) of prototyping, *Design Management Journal*, 55–65, Winter 1993.

Schrage, M., *Serious Play – How the World's Best Companies Simulate to Innovate*, Boston, MA: Harvard Business School Press, 2000.

Schumacher, T.R., Building team vision with scenario planning, Portland International Conference on the Management of Engineering Technology (PICMET), 27–31 July 1997.

Seltzer, K. and Bentley, T., *The Creative Age*, London: Demos, 1999.

Shapira, A., Laufer, A. and Shenhar, A.J., Anatomy of decision making in project planning teams, *International Journal of Project Management*, **12**, 172–182, Aug. 1994.

Sharma, A., Central dilemmas of managing innovation in large firms, *California Management Review*, **41**, 146–164, Spring 1999.

Shenhar, A.J. and Shulman, Y., Adapting your product development style: the key to project success, presented at 3rd International Product Development Conference, Insead, Fontainebleau, France, 14–16 April 1996.

Smith, M., Innovation and the great ABM trade-off, *Management Accounting*, **76**, 24–26, Jan. 1998.

Smith, P.G. and Reinertsen, D.G., *Developing Products in Half the Time*, New York: Van Nostrand Reinhold, 1995.

Souder, W.E., *Managing New Product Innovations*, MA: Lexington, 1987.

Souder, W.E., Managing relations between R&D and marketing in new product development projects, *Journal of Product Innovation Management*, **5**, 6–19, 1988.

Sowrey, T., *The Generation of Ideas for New Products*, London: Kogan-Page, 1987.

Stagg, C., Saunders, J. and Wong, V., A study of success and failure literature in new product development, University of Loughborough, Loughborough, UK, 15 July 1996.

Stalk, G.J., Time and innovation, *Canadian Business Review*, **20**, 15–18, Autumn 1993.

Sternberg, R.J. and Wagner, R.K., Tacit knowledge: an unspoken key to managerial success, *Creativity and Innovation Management*, **1**, 5–13, March 1992.

Stevens, G.A. and Burley, J., 3,000 raw ideas = 1 commercial success, *Research-Technology Management*, 16–27, May–June 1997.

Stevens, T., Creative genius, *Industrial Week*, **243**, 17–18, 7 April 1994.

Stewart, T.A., Why dumb things happen to smart companies, *Fortune*, 72–73, 23 June 1997.

Stewart, T.A., A satisfied customer isn't enough, *Fortune*, 70–71, 21 July 1997.

Story, V., Smith, G. and Saker, J., Developing appropriate measures of success and failure in new product development: a contingency approach, 28th European Marketing Academy Conference, Humbolt University of Berlin, Germany, 1999.

Subramaniam, M., Rosenthal, S.R., and Hatten, K.J., Global new product development processes: preliminary findings and research propositions, *Journal of Management Studies*, **35**, 773, 1998.

Sutton, R.I. and Hargadon, A., Brainstorming groups in context: effectiveness in a product design firm, *Administrative Science Quarterly*, **41**, 685–718, Dec. 1996.

Sutton, R.I. and Kelly, T.A., Creativity doesn't require isolation: Why product designers bring visitors 'backstage', *California Management Review*, **40**, 75–91, Fall 1997.

Swamidass, P.M. and Aldridge, M.D., Ten rules for timely task completion in cross functional teams, *Research-Technology Management*, **39**, 12–13, July–August 1996.

Syrett, M. and Lammiman, J., The art of conjuring ideas, *Director*, April 1997.

Takeuchi, H. and Nonaka, I., The new product development game, *Harvard Business Review*, 137–146, Jan.–Feb. 1986.

Taylor, H.L., Developing creative ability *Mark II*, **19**, 4, Jan.–Feb. 1978, Scarborough.

Tellis, G.J. and Golder, P.N., First to market, first to fail? Real causes of enduring market leadership, *Sloan Management Review*, 65–75, Winter 1996.

Temple, P. and von Stamm, B., *Design and ISO 9000*, Preliminary report to the Design Council, 1996.

Thomas, M., In search of culture: holy grail or gravy train? (Part 1) *Personnel Management*, **17**, 24, Sep. 1985.

Thomke, S. and Reinertsen, D., Agile product development: Managing development flexibility in uncertain environments, *California Management Review*, **41**, 8–30, Fall 1998.

Thomke, S. and Nimgade, A., *IDEO Product Development*, Boston, MA: Harvard Business School, 2000.

Tidd, J., Development of novel products through intraorganizational and interorganizational networks: the case of home automation, *Journal of Product Innovation Management*, **12**, 307–322, Sep. 1995.

Tidd, J., Bessant, J. and Pavitt, K., *Managing Innovation Integrating Technological, Market and Organisational Change*, 2nd edition, Chichester: John Wiley, 2001.

Tiersten, S., Setting up global telecom networks that work, *Electronic Business*, **15**, 98, 1 May 1989.

Tomes, A., Amstrong, P., and Clark, M., User groups in the NPD process. Working paper, Sheffield Management School, 1996.

Tomkins, R., Wanted. team spirit, *Financial Times*, 16 June 1994.

Tushman, M.L. and Nelson, R.R., Introduction: technology, organisations, and innovation, *Administrative Science Quarterly*, **35**, 1–8, 1990.

Tushman, M.L. and O'Reilley III, C.A., *Winning Through Innovation: A practical Guide to Leading Organizational Change and Renewal*, Boston, MA: Harvard Business School Press, 2002.

Twiss, B.C., (ed.) *Managing Technological Innovation:* 2nd edition, Longman, 1980.

Ulijn, J., O'Hair, D., Weggeman, M., Ledlow, G. and Thomas, H., Innovation, corporate strategy and cultural context, *Journal of Business Communication*, **37** (3), 293–316, 2000.

Utterback, J.M., The process of technological innovation within the firm, *Academy of Management Journal*, 75–88, March 1971.

Utterback, J.M., Mastering the Dynamics of Innovation: How Companies can Seize Opportunities in the Face of Technological Change, Harvard Business School Press, 1994.

Van de Ven, A., Angle, H. and Poole, M., *Research on the Management of Innovation*, New York: Harper and Row, 1989.

Van de Ven, A., Central problems in the management of innovation, *Management Science*, **32**, 590–607, May 1986.

Van de Ven, A.H., Problem solving, planning, and innovation part I. test of the program planning model, *Human Relations*, **33**, 711–740, Oct. 1980.

Van de Ven, A.H., Problem solving, planning, and innovation. part II. speculations for theory and practice, *Human Relations*, **33**, 757–770, Nov. 1980.

Van de Ven, A.H. and Poole, M.S., Explaining development and change in organizations, *Academy of Management Review*, **20**, 510–540, July 1995.

Van Nest, D.G., *Developing Global New Products*, UMI Research Press, 1985.

Venkatraman, N. and Henderson, J.C., Real strategies for virtual organizing, *Sloan Management Review*, **40**, 33–48, Fall 1998.

Vishwanath, V. and Mark, J., Your brand's best strategy, *Harvard Business Review*, 123–129, May–June 1997.

von Braun, C.-F., The acceleration trap, *Sloan Management Review*, 49–57, Fall 1990.

von Stamm, B., Interview with Jon Leach, Conducted for the Innovation Exchange, London Business School, 1999.

von Stamm, B., Interview with Ralph Buschow, Conducted for the Innovation Exchange, London Business School, 1999.

von Stamm, B., Innovation is about the one great idea and creativity is for off-the-wall people. True or false? Talk given at the DBA Design Debate, London, 29 Nov. 1999.

Voss, C., Coughlan, P. and Chiesa, V., *Innovation – Your Move, Self-assessment Guide and Workbook*, London: DTI, 1993.

Wagstyl, S., Innovation zealots a cut above the rest, *Financial Times*, p. 8, 22 April 1996.

West, M., Creativity and innovation at work, *Psychologist*, **13**, 460–464, 2000.

West, M.A. and Farr, J.L., *Innovation and Creativity at Work – Psychological and Organizational Strategies*, Chichester: John Wiley, 1996.

Whitfield, P.R., *Creativity in Industry*, Harmondsworth: Penguin, 1975.

Whiting, R., Drawing the road map for product development, *Electronic Business*, 60–61, 17 June 1991.

Whiting, R., In search of the perfect product, *Electronic Business*, 70–74, 17 June 1991.

Whitney, D., *Corporate New Ventures at Procter & Gamble*, Boston, MA: Harvard Business School Press, 1997.

Williams, A.J. and Souder, W.E., Involving purchasing in product development, *Industrial Marketing Management*, **19**, 315–319, 1990.

Wilson, B., Managing the product innovation process. In *Design Management, A Handbook of Issues and Methods*, ed. Oakley, M., Oxford: Blackwell Reference, 1990.

Wilson, S., Tranfield, D., Parry, I., Smith, S. and Foster, M., Developing your team-based organisation: where legacy meets strategic design, British Academy of Management Conference, 8–10 September, London, 1997.

Wind, J. and Mahajan, V., Issues and opportunities in new product development: an introduction to the special issue, *Journal of Marketing Research*, **34**, 1–12, Feb. 1997.

Wind, Y. and Mahajan, V., New product development process: a perspective for re-examination, *Journal of Product Innovation Management*, **5**, 304–310, 1988.

Wood, B.D. The globalization question, *Europe*, **402**, 12–14, Dec. 2000/Jan. 2001.

Worthington, J., *Reinventing the Workplace*, Oxford: Architectural Press and Butterworth-Heinemann, 1997.

Zobel, J., Unilever's butter-beater: innovation for global diversity, *Harvard Business School Case Study*, March 1998.